# Debates in Design and T Education

Design and technology is a relatively new subject compared to more traditional subjects, and during its brief existence, it has garnered widespread debate in schools. This book aims to explore some of these debates and challenges the reader with new perspectives about the subject by presenting and questioning arguments about the purpose, content and place of design and technology in the school curriculum. It will encourage the reader to critically reflect on their own beliefs and practices to reach informed judgements and perspectives that will affect how they teach and think about design and technology.

Exploring the major issues that design and technology teachers encounter in their professional lives as well as introducing new topics they may never have considered before, this comprehensive second edition has been fully updated with 16 chapters focusing on emerging and enduring debates:

- How do we do race in design and technology?
- What's so special about design and technology anyway?
- What is design cognition in design and technology classrooms?
- What is the potential of feedback in the creative processes of a design and technology classroom?
- Does food fit in design and technology?
- What is the role of making in design and technology?

With its combination of expert opinion and fresh insight, *Debates in Design and Technology Education* is the ideal companion for any student or practising teacher engaged in initial training, continuing professional development or master's-level study.

**Alison Hardy** is an associate professor, writer, researcher, and podcaster. Alison's work centres on design and technology education. She has edited *Learning to Teach Design and Technology* and *Redesigning D&T*. You can find out more about Alison on her website – dralisonhardy.com – or on Twitter – @hardy_alison.

# Debates in Subject Teaching
Series edited by Susan Capel, Jon Davison and James Arthur

Each title in the Debates in Subject Teaching series presents high-quality material, specially commissioned to stimulate teachers engaged in initial teacher education, continuing professional development and Master's level study to think more deeply about their practice, and link research and evidence to what they have observed in schools. By providing up-to-date, comprehensive coverage the books in the series support teachers in reaching their own informed judgements, enabling them to discuss and argue their point of view with deeper theoretical knowledge and understanding.

Debates in Physical Education, 2nd edition
*Edited by Susan Capel and Richard Blair*

Debates in English Teaching, 2nd edition
*Edited by Jon Davison and Caroline Daly*

Debates in Mathematics Education, 2nd edition
*Edited by Gwen Ineson and Hilary Povey*

Debates in Primary Education
*Edited by Virginia Bower*

Debates in Art and Design Education, 2nd edition
*Edited by Nicholas Addison and Lesley Burgess*

Debates in Second Language Education, 1st edition
*Edited by Ernesto Macaro and Robert Woore*

Debates in Science Education, 2nd edition
*Edited by Justin Dillon and Mike Watts*

Debates in Design and Technology Education, 2nd edition
*Edited by Alison Hardy*

For more information about this series, please visit: https://www.routledge.com/Debates-in-Subject-Teaching/book-series/DIST

# Debates in Design and Technology Education

Second Edition

Edited by Alison Hardy

LONDON AND NEW YORK

Cover image: © Andrew Holt / Getty Images

Second edition published 2023
by Routledge
4 Park Square, Milton Park, Abingdon, Oxon, OX14 4RN

and by Routledge
605 Third Avenue, New York, NY 10158

*Routledge is an imprint of the Taylor & Francis Group, an informa business*

© 2023 selection and editorial matter, Alison Hardy; individual chapters, the contributors

The right of Alison Hardy to be identified as the author of the editorial material, and of the authors for their individual chapters, has been asserted in accordance with sections 77 and 78 of the Copyright, Designs and Patents Act 1988.

All rights reserved. No part of this book may be reprinted or reproduced or utilised in any form or by any electronic, mechanical, or other means, now known or hereafter invented, including photocopying and recording, or in any information storage or retrieval system, without permission in writing from the publishers.

*Trademark notice*: Product or corporate names may be trademarks or registered trademarks, and are used only for identification and explanation without intent to infringe.

First edition published by Routledge 2013

*British Library Cataloguing-in-Publication Data*
A catalogue record for this book is available from the British Library

*Library of Congress Cataloging-in-Publication Data*
Names: Hardy, Alison, editor.
Title: Debates in design and technology education / edited by Alison Hardy.
Other titles: Debates in design and technology education (2023)
Description: Second edition. | Milton Park, Abingdon, Oxon ; New York, NY : Routledge, 2023. | Earlier edition: Debates in design and technology education / edited by Gwyneth Owen-Jackson. 2013. This second edition contains all new essays. | Includes bibliographical references and index.
Identifiers: LCCN 2022026006 (print) | LCCN 2022026007 (ebook) | ISBN 9780367763718 (hbk) | ISBN 9780367763732 (pbk) | ISBN 9781003166689 (ebk)
Subjects: LCSH: Industrial arts--Study and teaching. | Technology--Study and teaching. | Design--Study and teaching. | Curriculum planning--Great Britain.
Classification: LCC T65 .D362 2023 (print) | LCC T65 (ebook) | DDC 607.1--dc23/eng/20221006
LC record available at https://lccn.loc.gov/2022026006
LC ebook record available at https://lccn.loc.gov/2022026007

ISBN: 978-0-367-76371-8 (hbk)
ISBN: 978-0-367-76373-2 (pbk)
ISBN: 978-1-003-16668-9 (ebk)

DOI: 10.4324/9781003166689

Typeset in ITC Galliard
by SPi Technologies India Pvt Ltd (Straive)

# Contents

*Acknowledgements* vii
*List of contributors* viii
*Introduction to the series* xii

**Introduction** 1
ALISON HARDY

## PART I
## Political and international debates about design and technology 7

1 Government policies and design and technology education 9
  DANIEL WAKEFIELD AND ALISON HARDY

2 International perspectives on technology education 26
  FRANK BANKS AND P. JOHN WILLIAMS

3 How do we do race in design and technology? 45
  BHAVNA PRAJAPAT, ROSE SINCLAIR, AND ALISON HARDY

## PART II
## Debates about design and technology 63

4 Why did design and technology education fail, and what might replace it? 65
  DAVID SPENDLOVE

5 What's so special about design and technology anyway? 77
  MATT MCLAIN

6 Does food fit in design and technology? 98
  SUZANNE LAWSON AND SUSAN WOOD-GRIFFITHS

## 7 Role of making in D&T 111
MIKE MARTIN

## 8 Entrepreneurship in technology education 120
ADRI DU TOIT

## 9 Gendering the curriculum 134
ULRIKA SULTAN

## 10 Managing curriculum change 149
SARAH DAVIES

# PART III
# Teaching design and technology 163

## 11 Influence of teachers' perceptions of subject knowledge on pedagogical approaches 165
DAWNE IRVING-BELL

## 12 Transition between primary and secondary school 178
CATHY GROWNEY

## 13 Teaching for technological justice: embracing indigenous designs 194
MISHACK GUMBO

## 14 Design cognition in design and technology classrooms 209
NICOLAAS BLOM

## 15 A hybrid design sketching approach that can drive critical thinking in design and technology 221
YAONE RAPITSENYANE, RICHIE MOALOSI, AND THATAYAONE MOSEPEDI

## 16 Exploring the potential of feedback within the creative processes of a design and technology classroom 238
ALICE SCHUT

## Endpiece 252
ALISON HARDY

## Index 255

# Acknowledgements

First, I would like to thank Gwyneth Owen-Jackson, editor of the first edition of this book. This second edition builds on the debates from the first, which Gwyneth brought together.

Next, thank you to all those colleagues who contributed to the previous version, some of whom have updated their chapters in this edition and others who shared the issues related to the research they have done since the first edition. Thanks also to the new contributors who enthusiastically agreed to share their research experiences in the book. Chapters have been written during a global pandemic, which has affected all the contributors in different ways, and I am grateful to all for giving your time and energies to your writing and our debates whilst so much was going on around you. I am humbled by your dedication to design and technology (D&T) and empowered by your contributions to this book.

Thank you to the series editor, Susan Capel, who entrusted me with editing this book and for their pertinent and useful feedback at key points during the process.

Colleagues at Routledge recognised the challenges contributors and I have faced writing during a global pandemic. Once again, I have benefitted from Annamarie Kino's publishing expertise and understanding of D&T, and Will Bailey and Ashley Johnstone's editorial guidance.

Acknowledgement is given to colleagues who have contributed through their conversations outside the pages of this book. I regularly talk with others on my podcast and these conversations have influenced the book's shape. In some chapters, contributors have drawn on their research studies – thank you to their research participants for stepping forward to be interviewed, surveyed or observed. Research and new thinking about D&T only happen because others volunteer to take part in research studies.

In Chapter 2, Frank Banks and P John Williams have collated descriptions of the curriculum content from over ten different countries. Thank you to the colleagues in each of those countries for providing these summaries.

Finally, this book is dedicated to my mum – my champion.

# Contributors

**Frank Banks** is an emeritus professor of teacher education at The Open University, UK. There he authored the first distance learning initial teacher education course in design and technology. A former schoolteacher, he has taught science, technology, 'engineering science' and mathematics in high schools in England and in Wales.

**Nicolaas Blom** is a technology education lecturer at the University of Limerick. He completed his PhD in 2019, which involved the study of secondary students' design cognition in integrated STEM environments. Nicolaas teaches courses on engineering, technology and graphics subject pedagogics and design and communication graphics.

**Sarah Davies** has more than 20 years of teaching experience, having moved into education from industry, and at Nottingham Trent University has responsibility for work across a range of teacher education programs. Her research includes subject change and teachers, electronic textiles and initial teacher education.

**Adri Du Toit** develops curricula and trains teachers for a complex world via Technology and Consumer Studies education at the North-West University, South Africa. She continually explores and develops ways in which school-level learners' entrepreneurship education can be fostered and has published widely in this field.

**Cathy Growney's** career in design and technology began after four years of employment in carpentry, joinery and wood machining. Initially, she worked in the secondary sector; subsequently, research led her to working in primary and tertiary education as well in England and overseas. Her main areas of interest are transition, development education, values, sustainability and craftivism.

**Mishack T. Gumbo** is a National Research Foundation C1–rated researcher and a professor of indigenous technology knowledge systems in the Department of Science and Technology Education at the University of South Africa. He serves on numerous academic structures and committees locally and internationally. His research interests are indigenisation/

Africanisation/decolonisation of the technology education curriculum, technology teachers' professional development, distance education and e-learning.

**Alison Hardy** is a writer, researcher, lecturer and podcaster. Alison's work centres on design and technology education. She has edited *Learning to Teach Design and Technology* and contributed to *Mentoring Design and Technology Teachers and Design Epistemology and Curriculum Planning*. You can find out more about Alison on her website – dralisonhardy.com – or on Twitter – @hardy_alison

**Dawne Irving-Bell** is a reader and senior learning and teaching fellow at Edge Hill University, a principal fellow of the Higher Education Academy, a CATE2020 Award winner and a recipient of a national award recognising her outstanding contribution to teacher education. With a passion for visual thinking and technology education, she established the National Teaching Repository and edits the *Journal of Social-Media for Learning*.

**Suzanne Lawson** is a principal lecturer at the University of Worcester. She taught design and technology for 14 years before working in initial teacher education at two different universities. Research interests include food education, pupils' perceptions of food technology and mentoring in teacher education and textiles technology.

**Mike Martin** is a Senior Lecturer in Teacher Education at Liverpool John Moores University. Mike has been involved in Design and Technology for 30 years as a teacher, teacher educator across primary, secondary and masters level programmes. Mike has a keen interest in values, sustainability and increasingly the philosophy of technology.

**Matt McLain** is an experienced teacher educator working in higher education, having previously taught design and technology in two Merseyside secondary schools. Matt has had the privilege and opportunity to shape the National Curriculum, the General Certificate of Secondary Education and A Level for design and technology. He has been an active member of the Design and Technology Association throughout his career. His other professional and research interests include subject knowledge development and the philosophy of technology.

**Richie Moalosi** is a professor of industrial design in the Department of Industrial Design and Technology, University of Botswana. His specialisation and research interest areas include design and culture, design education, sustainable design, social innovation, additive manufacturing and post-graduate students' supervision.

**Thatayaone Mosepedi** is a product design lecturer in the Department of Industrial Design and Technology, University of Botswana. He has taught design and technology at secondary schools. His research interests include design management, design education and additive manufacturing. He has also published research works, both locally and internationally.

**Bhavna Prajapat** is a senior lecturer for education and teaches undergraduate, postgraduate and master's-level courses. Bhavna is involved with training teachers for early years, primary and secondary design and technology education. Bhavna leads the secondary education and professional studies programme as well as supports teacher apprentice and school direct programmes. Her research interests are in learning and teaching.

**Yaone Rapitsenyane** is a lecturer of sustainable design in the Department of Industrial Design and Technology, University of Botswana. His research interests include sustainable business models, design education and product design. He has been involved in various research projects and has published research papers and contributed book chapters.

**Alice Schut** works as a lecturer and researcher at The Hague University of Applied Sciences. Her PhD research, at the Science Communication & Education group of the Delft University of Technology, focused on developing and testing peer feedback interventions to encourage pupils' creative thinking while designing and mitigating design fixation.

**Rose Sinclair** is a lecturer at Goldsmiths, University of London. She has led on initiatives related to new textiles technology. More recently, she has gained a national profile for her work evolving from her research based on the development of Dorcas Clubs, textile networks used by Caribbean women on arrival in the UK in the 1950s and 1960s. In 2022, Sinclair was the co-curator of 'Colour Is Mine', a posthumous exhibition of the Trinidad-born British designer and artist Althea McNish.

**David Spendlove** is a professor of education at the University of Manchester having previously had a successful career in secondary education in a wide range of schools. Since moving into higher education, David has been involved with policy and practice and publishing in a variety of areas, including teaching and learning, teacher education, technology education and creative and design education.

**Ulrika Sultan** is a former teacher turned researcher. Her research focus is on girls' interests in technology. Her commitment to the subject has led her to different engagements such as writing textbooks, collaborating with the industry and being a subject expert for a Swedish TV show for young children about technology.

**Daniel Wakefield** is currently the head of design and technology at Birkenhead High School Academy girls' school. He is particularly interested in the development of the subject, classroom practice and leadership of design and technology within schools.

**P. John Williams** is a professor of education and the director of graduate research in the School of Education at Curtin University in Perth, Western Australia, where he teaches and supervises research students in STEM and technology education. He is a long-standing member of eight professional associations, the series editor of the Springer Contemporary Issues in Technology Education, is on the editorial board of six professional journals and has authored or contributed to more than 250 publications.

**Susan Wood-Griffiths** led the Post-Graduate Certificate in Education Secondary Design and Technology programme at the University of Worcester from 2007 until 2018. Before moving into higher education, she taught for 21 years in the UK and overseas. She is now retired but continues to take an interest in developments in design and technology.

# Introduction to the series

This book, *Debates in Design and Technology Education*, is one of a series of books entitled Debates in Subject Teaching, many of which are now in their second and third editions. The series has been designed to engage with a wide range of debates related to subject teaching. Unquestionably, debates vary among the subjects, but may include, for example, issues that are related to:

- the definition, purpose and aims of the subject;
- the curriculum and content of the subject;
- subject pedagogy;
- the development of the subject and its future in the twenty-first century;
- the relationship between the subject and broader educational aims and objectives in society, and the philosophy and sociology of education.

The outcome of these debates might, for example, support the justification for the subject; be addressed in the classroom through the teaching of the subject and/or impact on initial teacher education and continuing professional development (CPD) in the subject.

Likewise, debates change within subjects over time. Consequently, each book presents key debates that subject teachers should understand, reflect on and engage in at the time it was written (and subsequent editions of the book are likely to include debates about different issues, as well as revisiting some enduring debates in the subject). Chapters have been designed to highlight major questions, and to consider the evidence from research and practice in order to find possible answers. Some subject books or chapters offer at least one solution or a view of the ways forward, whereas others provide alternative views and leave readers to identify their own solution or view of the ways forward. It is anticipated that readers will want to pursue the issues raised; hence, chapters include questions for further debate and suggestions for further reading. Debates covered in the series provide the basis for discussion in university subject seminars and meetings between professionals in school departmental meetings and in the context of CPD courses. The topics are also appropriate for consideration in assignments or classroom-based research. The books have been written for all those with a professional interest in the subject, including student teachers learning to teach the subject in secondary schools; newly qualified teachers; teachers undertaking study at Master's level; teachers with a subject coordination or leadership role and those preparing for such responsibility; as well as school-based mentors, university tutors and advisers of the aforementioned groups.

Because of the range of issues covered, each subject book is an edited collection. Editors have commissioned new writing from experts on particular issues for debate, which, collectively, represent many different perspectives on a subject and the teaching of the subject. Readers should not expect a book in this series to: cover all aspects of a debate, cover the entire range of debates in a subject, offer a completely unified view of the subject/teaching of the subject, deal with each debate discretely. Part of what each book in this series offers to readers is the opportunity to explore the interrelationships between positions in debates and, indeed, among the debates themselves, by identifying the overlapping concerns and competing arguments that are woven through the text. Many initiatives in subject teaching continue to originate from central government, and, as a result, teachers have decreasing control of subject content, pedagogy and assessment strategies. It is strongly felt that for teaching to remain properly a vocation and a profession, teachers must be invited to be part of a creative and critical dialogue about subject teaching, and should be encouraged to reflect, criticise, problem-solve and innovate. This series is intended to provide teachers with a stimulus for democratic involvement in the development of the discourse of subject teaching.

Susan Capel, Jon Davison and James Arthur
March 2019

# Introduction

*Alison Hardy*

White (2011) states that design and technology (D&T) is a relatively new subject compared to 'traditional subjects'; Williams (1961, p. 130) concurs that some subjects are more established: 'the quadrivium of music, arithmetic, geometry, and astronomy goes back to at least the fifth century'. These positions are often used as the basis for why D&T is not seen as part of a core curriculum. However, Archer (2005) is of the view that design education is an essential component of education, part of a three-part education: humanities, science, and design. Unfortunately, we are seeing this position and the place of D&T as being threatened in schools, some of the reasons for this are debated in this book.

Although arguments are made for D&T's place in the curriculum, because it is still a young subject, D&T does not have a long tradition on which to draw for its identity and its pedagogy. That is not to say that it has no history, in England or in other countries. There are antecedents to D&T; in the mid-sixteenth century, schools were established to provide apprenticeships in trades and crafts, and in the early nineteenth century, girls were taught spinning, sewing and how to cook (Gillard 2011). D&T, however, is not the same as these. Fortunately, a new generation of researchers is coming through in D&T and bringing new debates derived from their research. Some who contributed different debates in the first edition are presenting their research here, including Sarah Davies, Dawne Irving-Bell, and Mike Martin. New contributors have been invited to write chapters using their research to prompt the readers to think in different ways about important topics, such as the following:

- Matt McLain, Chapter 11 'So what's so special about design and technology anyway?'
- Niekie Blom, Chapter 13 'Design cognition in design and technology classrooms'
- Alice Schut, Chapter 15 'Exploring the potential of feedback in the creative processes of a D&T classroom'

In response to the important call to ensure that #BlackLivesMatter, this second edition seeks to stimulate debate and suggest resolutions to our

DOI: 10.4324/9781003166689-1

observation in Chapter 3 that 'much of [the] design discourse across the secondary curriculum is taught through the lens of a global North discourse'. This edition also includes contributors from different international locations, presenting issues and debates that may, at first sight, not seem relevant to the UK classroom:

- In Chapter 12, Professor Mishack Gumbo explores the potential of teaching about indigenous designs.
- Chapter 14's contributors are from Botswana, drawing on their research conducted in their country to debate topics relevant to design and technology in the UK.

The book is divided into three sections:

(1) Political and international debates about design and technology.
These three chapters set the scene with a macro perspective on design and technology, such as government policies and an international perspective.
(2) Debates about design and technology
Debates in this section centre on the nature and perceptions of the subject.
(3) Debates about teaching design and technology
This final section is about classroom debates, what is taught and how it is taught.

## Political and international debates

In Chapter 1, Daniel Wakefield and Alison Hardy provide the history of D&T in the UK curriculum as this is where the subject, as we currently know it, began. Although some aspects of D&T, mainly the practical elements of 'making', had been on the curriculum for some time, and craft, design, and technology preceded it and contributed much to the development of D&T, it was the UK National Curriculum of 1988 that conceived and introduced the subject as we now know it. Chapter 1 charts the development of D&T from its inception through to the present day, highlighting the source of some of the current and ongoing discussions.

The introduction of D&T in the UK was influential in many other countries. They all had their own traditions on which to draw, the Sloyd tradition of Sweden and the indigenous technologies of African countries such as South Africa and Botswana, but many of these have developed in surprisingly similar ways. In Chapter 2, Frank Banks and P. John Williams, drawing on the experiences of their network of colleagues across the world, look at the curricula of D&T, or technology, considering recent developments, present classroom experiences, and the likely future of school technology. The contrasting cases of Australia, Bangladesh, Belgium, Brazil, China, Israel, Malawi, Taiwan, and the US are explored.

The final chapter in the first section breaks new ground in debating the issues around race by including contributors of colour who, drawing on their experiences as teachers, parents, and subject leads, share their thoughts on the question, How do we do race in D&T? The contributors provide honest perspectives on what is a challenging and complex issue. Bhavna Prajapat, Rose Sinclair, and I discuss the challenges of language, global inclusion in representation in design, and how people are represented in the subject and, thanks to Marlene Wylie, share a way forward.

## Debates about design and technology

In Part II, contributors discuss some of the broader issues about the nature of the subject.

According to David Spendlove, few subjects in the history of education have experienced, in the way that design and technology has, such a rapid rise followed by a dramatic implosion in popularity. In Chapter 5, Spendlove discusses the complex and multifaceted reasons for this rapid rise and fall, categorising them into three themes: first, political disregard, educational change, and school structures; second, issues related to teacher supply and development; and, finally, the impact of government initiatives. Although Spendlove could have chosen to end the chapter with a summary of the dire state of D&T; instead, he suggests a way forward: design and/or technology 2.0. What this redesigned D&T might look like is another debate to take place outside this book involving the whole design and technology community.

Matt McLain has written previously about design and technology's signature pedagogies (McLain 2018) – pedagogies that are fundamental to the subject. McLain questions in Chapter 5 what the subject is for and how it is taught in a technologically advanced and evolving world. He debates the problematic terms of designing, making and evaluating, suggesting alternatives – ideating, realizing, and critiquing. Building on this, he proposes that the four-fold model of designing and making activities supplemented by mainly designing, mainly making and exploring technology and society (based on work by Trebell [2009] and trialled at Nottingham Trent University as part of its teacher training programme) provides a broad and balanced design and technology curriculum.

Chapters 6 and 7 focus on the content of D&T. In Chapter 6, Suzanne Lawson and Susan Wood-Griffiths ask: Does food fit in design and technology? Some argue that D&T is not where food studies should be in the English school curriculum; others argue that it is. This chapter debates food in the English D&T curriculum, food and health, vocational education, and changes in food education. In Chapter 7, Mike Martin debates the role of making. He presents different roles making has in the design and technology curriculum; these include skills, knowledge, design, and well-being. Martin argues that it is working with natural and human-made materials that allows us to keep our connection with the world and avoid any further disconnection from it.

One ongoing debate about D&T education is how it, and even whether it should, directly prepare pupils for specific careers. Adri Du Toit, from South Africa, focuses on one aspect of preparing pupils for the world of work: entrepreneurship education. She evaluates two issues: should entrepreneurship be included in technology education – if at all – and, if it should, then how can it be embedded in technology education effectively? Du Toit goes beyond focusing on how television programmes showcasing entrepreneurship (e.g., The Apprentice and Dragon's Den) can be mimicked in technology education and instead analyses to what extent entrepreneurship education can be successfully included in technology subjects.

Ulrika Sultan, from Sweden, debates how gender is demonstrated and expressed in the aims, objectives and subject content of design and technology education. In Chapter 8, Sultan moves beyond previous discussions about why fewer girls than boys study design and technology, focusing on how the subject is gendered by teachers viewing certain content as more suitable for girls and other content more suitable for boys.

By now you might be feeling overwhelmed by the debates and issues that have and could affect your teaching; as a response to this, Sarah Davies concludes the section with some thoughts from practising teachers in England about how they have managed curriculum change. Using examples from her research, Davies organises the issues that can drive curriculum changes into three categories: natural events, policy reform, and voluntary reasons. Then she debates how these categories can be managed.

## Debates about teaching D&T

This final section is about classroom debates, what is taught and how it is taught. Starting with the teacher and their confidence, Dawne Irving-Bell debates the effect teachers' perceptions of their subject knowledge have on the pedagogical approaches they use in their classrooms. In Chapter 11, Irving-Bell argues this is of particular importance to design and technology because of the challenges facing the subject, such as curriculum marginalisation and difficulties in the recruitment and retention of specialist teachers (two issues discussed by Spendlove in Chapter 4). Combining these two issues with the limited opportunities for continued professional development, she debates the potential consequences on teacher efficacy.

Cathy Growney, in Chapter 12, examines pupils' experience of D&T as they move from primary to secondary school. For many pupils, this is a time of both excitement and anxiety, but in D&T there seems to be disruption in their learning. Growney looks at the historical context in England and aims to clarify the differences in primary and secondary characteristics and disentangle the concerns associated with design and technology transition. Using teachers' voices from five secondary schools and six primary schools, she discusses strategies employed by primary and secondary schools to improve continuity in learning.

The question, *Why are indigenous technological designs always taking a backstage?* is an important constituent of the discussions which confront design and technology; in this book, Mishack Gumbo's opening question in Chapter 13 relates to Chapter 3 when tokenistic approaches are used in an attempt to include representation from other cultures. Gumbo suggests it is a question motivated by the Western dominance in the conceptualisation of the subject. Using examples, he debates how Heek's model of pro-indigenous (design for indigenous peoples), para-indigenous (design with indigenous peoples), and per-indigenous (design by indigenous peoples) design is used and how it can be used in schools.

It is well-known that learning and thinking in design and technology result from the interaction between mind, body, and environment. However, according to Nicolaas Blom, current theories of cognition are limited in describing how design thinking emerges because of these interactions. In Chapter 14, Blom debates the effects of these limitations and explores other theories that could be better placed to support teachers to think differently about the way in which internal and external resources could support thought and action during design projects.

Yaone Rapitsenyane, Richie Moalosi and Thatayaone Mosepedi, from the University of Botswana, believe that design sketching holistically supports critical thinking and creativity, important competencies of the 21st century. In their chapter, they debate the future-scape of design sketching in the context of hybrid sketching, highlighting the benefits of manual and digital sketching in D&T education. At a time when digital skills seem to be prioritised over hand skills, when pupils may have little opportunity to develop their sketching, this chapter reminds readers why there are benefits to both retaining a place in the design and technology curriculum.

Books and professional development about feedback practices tend to focus on assessment and be general in nature, the final chapter in the book focuses on a key aspect of feedback in design and technology: design feedback. Alice Schut, from The Netherlands, writes in Chapter 16 about the issues with providing and receiving effective design feedback. This is a practical chapter, drawing on analysis from her research, which provides some new ways for teachers to think about their teaching.

The Endpiece summarises the discussions in the book and tries to look forward to what future debates and discussions will ensue. It must be noted that the debates and discussions presented here represent only a selection of those that could have been included. It is acknowledged that some have been missed, for example around the place of 'design' in D&T; is design a general skill or is it different in the different areas of D&T? The place of values in D&T is not fully explored; neither are the issues around the teaching about sustainability within D&T. It is not because these debates are not important, but constraints on space meant that choices had to be made. It is hoped that debate on these other important issues will continue alongside the debates presented here.

Debate is healthy, it indicates an interest and a passion for the subject and can contribute to moving the subject forward. In contrast, it can also lead to fragmentation and polarisation. Both have been evident in D&T over the last 30 years. This book aims to present some of the main issues in the subject, many of which have resonance in countries across the world, in the hope that students and teachers of the subject will continue to show interest and passion, continue to debate and continue to develop the subject.

## References

Archer, B. (2005). The three Rs. In B. Archer, K. Baynes & P. Roberts (Eds.), *A framework for design and design education* (pp. 8–15). Design and Technology Association.

Gillard, D. (2011). Education in England: a brief history, www.educationengland.org.uk/history (accessed 8 March 2012).

McLain, M. (2018). Emerging perspectives on the demonstration as a signature pedagogy in design and technology education. *International Journal of Technology and Design Education, 28*(4), 985–1000. doi:10.1007/s10798-017-9425-0

Trebell, D. (2009). Studying classroom interaction during a design-without-make assignment. *Design and Technology Education: An International Journal, 14*(3).

White, J. (2011). *The invention of the secondary curriculum [electronic resource]*. Palgrave Macmillan.

Williams, R. (1961). *The long revolution*. London: Chatto & Windus.

Part I
# Political and international debates about design and technology

# 1 Government policies and design and technology education

*Daniel Wakefield and Alison Hardy*

## Introduction

Education historians will point out many significant developments, policies and legislation that have shaped the English education system. However, the 1988 Educational Reform Act, and specifically the introduction of the National Curriculum for England and Wales, had a major impact on what and how pupils are taught. The 1988 Act introduced design & technology (D&T) into the National Curriculum and this chapter considers the development of the subject in the UK since then. It considers the influences of the government, the Department for Education (DfE), the Design and Technology Working Group, the National Curriculum Council, and the Expert Panel, along with teachers and the wider D&T community, in shaping the curriculum and influencing the perception of D&T and the impact that this has had on the subject.

To explore the extent to which the National Curriculum has influenced the subject as it is today, we need to consider the following:

- Where it all began
- The introduction of the National Curriculum
- National Curriculum developments

## Where it all began

A review of the history of (design and) technology in the UK reveals that controversy and division have been present throughout. Early education in Britain, as in many other countries, was provided by the church and was an academic preparation for the upper classes. Trade and craft skills were learnt through apprenticeship, and it was not until the mid-sixteenth century that these became a formal part of the education system (Gillard 2011). The Industrial Revolution in Britain, which took place between 1750 and 1850, led to massive social and political change, which included the expansion of basic education to those who had previously not had access. During the Industrial Revolution, major design, industrial, and manufacturing advancements made Britain a leading industrial nation, but, by the end of the nineteenth century, this was no longer the case and Britain lagged behind many

DOI: 10.4324/9781003166689-3

of its competitors. This could be attributed partly to the lack of attention to technical education for its young people, during the same period, countries across Europe had been investing both in industry and education.

Although there is evidence of technological activities in school before 1902, it was at this point when 'manual work' was introduced to English state schools, and many of our issues with design and technology education may be traced back to this era. For example, woodwork was a mandatory subject for boys while 'housewifery' was the option for girls (Mulberg 1992). The development of manual work on the curriculum in England, and to the same extent the American elementary system, had a utilitarian approach 'as a pre-vocational training for the rapidly growing ranks of manual and domestic workers' (Eggleston 1976, p. 5).

In the early twentieth century, manufacturing, industry and domestic life were very different from those of today. Highly skilled craftsmen and well-trained, resourceful housewives were the ideals of the day. Industry and the factory workshop were predominantly the domain of the male, so exposing boys to industrial practices and techniques at school allowed them to develop skills and attitudes for the workplace. Little emphasis was placed on the challenge of new design:

> The things boys made solved no problems. There was no challenge to think either why or how. Shape, size, construction, materials, tools, processes were all taken for granted, and as a result much of the educational value of the work was lost. There was little connection between the crafts and the technical drawing intended to be the language of expression.
>
> (Kingsland 1969, p. 11)

The Spens Report of 1938 introduced the idea of 'technical' schools alongside grammar schools, and this was enacted in the 1944 Education Act, which introduced into Britain the 'tripartite' system of education. This provided grammar schools for academic pupils, technical schools to teach mechanical and engineering skills and secondary modern schools for the academically less able. For some reason, the technical schools, which would beave been the ideal place for technology education, failed to properly establish themselves, and a great opportunity was missed to make technical education a viable alternative for pupils.

Over the course of the twentieth century, through various acts of parliament, the government became increasingly involved in educational provision, leading to the 1988 Education Act, which introduced the first National Curriculum in the UK.

## Introduction of the National Curriculum

Educational developments do not occur in a vacuum, they are part of the political and social context of the time. Table 1.1 provides an outline of some

Table 1.1 Developments in politics and curriculum since 1990

| Year | Event |
| --- | --- |
| 1987 | Foundation for the National Curriculum outlined by the Conservative government |
| 1988 | Design and Technology Working Group Interim Report published |
| 1989 | Final report by working group presented to DES |
| 1990 | First Technology Orders published |
| 1991 | Non-statutory guidance and INSET (In-Service Training) material published to support Orders |
| 1993 | Full National Curriculum review for all subjects (lead by Sir Ron Dearing) and redeployment of subject working groups |
| 1994 | Statutory Technology at Key Stage 4 ended<br>National Curriculum Review (The Dearing Report) published<br>Design and Technology identified as a subject in its own right |
| 1995 | New Orders implemented at Key Stage 1, 2 and 3 |
| 1996 | New Orders implemented at Key Stage 4, starting with Year 10 |
| 1997 | New Orders implemented at Key Stage 4, Year 11<br>Labour Party victory at General Election (May)<br>Excellence in Schools white paper published |
| 1998 | National Literacy Strategy introduced |
| 1999 | Full National Curriculum review in England<br>All subject descriptions published for the first time<br>National Numeracy Strategy introduced |
| 2000 | New National Curriculum launched<br>Launch of Specials Schools<br>Learning Skills Act allowed City Technology Colleges to become City Academies |
| 2004 | Five Year Strategy for Children and Learners allowing all schools to become specialists and expanding academy schools<br>14–19 Curriculum and Qualifications Reform report published suggesting changes to traditional qualifications |
| 2005 | Labour win third term in office |
| 2006 | Cambridge Primary review launched |
| 2007 | QCA (Qualifications and Curriculum Authority) consultation over new curriculum for Key Stages 3 and 4 |
| 2008 | Diploma qualification launched (in particular engineering, manufacturing and construction) |
| 2009 | Cambridge Primary Review and the Rose Report published |
| 2010 | Coalition government between Conservative Party and the Liberal Democrats |
| 2011 | Call for evidence towards National Curriculum review (first teaching 2014)<br>Introduction of the English Baccalaureate (EBacc) |
| 2012 | Expert panel to review evidence and recommend subjects for the curriculum and propose Programmes of Study (POSs) to ministers |
| 2013 | Draft National Curriculum and PoSs released for consultation |
| 2014 | Implementation of National Curriculum 2014 |
| 2015 | Examination reform for General Certificate of Secondary Education (GCSE) and A Level subjects |
| 2017 | Start of new GCSE and A Level exams |

of the key events that have shaped today's curriculum. To analyse the changes in government thinking and legislation regarding D&T, it is important to appreciate some of the wider curriculum developments that have taken place and the context in which these occurred.

In 1976 the then prime minister, James Callaghan, made a speech at Ruskin College in which he said, among other things, that consideration should be given to a basic curriculum to be agreed on for all pupils. This led to a series of discussions and documents and in 1987 the secretary of state for education, Kenneth Baker, launched foundations for a National Curriculum, meaning that, for the first time in England and Wales, all pupils would be taught (broadly) the same skills and knowledge in 11 subject areas and would be assessed by the same criteria.

The Department of Education and Science (DES) commissioned subject-specific working groups to produce a series of recommendations for subject content, programmes of study, and assessment criteria (attainment targets; Penfold 1988; Norman 1990).

## *The Design and Technology Working Group*

The D&T Working Group, led by Lady Parkes, included those with backgrounds in CDT (craft, design and technology), home economics, vocational studies, science, economics, business studies and information technology (Harris and Wilson 2003). Terms of reference were issued to the group by the DES, which outlined its duties, principally to develop clear objectives, curriculum content and attainment targets.

The terms of reference make interesting reading; point 6 under the heading of 'approach' identified a number of areas for the working group to focus on. They were encouraged to think of the subject as an opportunity for pupils to design and make useful objects. A list of suggested materials was identified, and the need to develop pupils' experiences of craft and the world of work was also suggested. The terms highlighted not only the implicit link between design and technology and information technology but also links with mathematics, science, and several other subjects. However, there was a suggestion that technology did not need to become a discrete subject of its own and that many of its skills and knowledge bases could be identified, even located, within other areas of the curriculum. This brings into question immediately what the position of technology in the curriculum would be.

Initially, the task of the Working Group was to develop the curriculum for pupils aged 11 to 16, with the responsibility for the primary technology curriculum resting with the Science Working Group (McCormick 2002). This was an early signal to science as a senior partner to technology (Penfold 1988). Science was to be a core subject within the curriculum and initial discussion had suggested aspects of technology education could be taught within the science curriculum. However, following an interim report from the Science Working Group, the responsibility for the technology at the primary level was transferred to the D&T Working Group. Again, it is worth questioning the position of design and technology in the National Curriculum – was it to be the supportive senior party for the rapidly growing information technology department? Or the junior partner to science?

The working group produced a set of proposals that included a rationale of why the subject should be taught. This suggested that design and technology should allow pupils to meet the needs of the twenty-first century and engage in design, investigation, and appraisal activities to acquire knowledge. Practical experiences were identified as the main process by which to develop understanding, but there was little emphasis on developing products. The Working Group also proposed five attainment targets:

AT1 Explore and investigate contexts for design and technology capabilities
AT2 Formulate proposals and choose a design for development
AT3 Develop the design and plan for the making of an artefact or system
AT4 Make artefacts and systems
AT5 Appraise the process, outcomes and effects of design and technological activities.

Questions can be asked about how the initial DES terms of reference were influential in shaping the design and technology proposals. Although a structure was needed for the working group, the terms of reference suggested material areas and approaches that were traditional and heavily influenced by CDT. By the same token, there was a drive towards it becoming a more open-ended subject, a subject with roots in many others and with its own unique features.

Technology was seen as a new, interdisciplinary subject, a fusion of CDT and home economics with close links to science and mathematics (Eggleston 1996), which led to initial concerns over the practical element of the subjects. Nearly 10 years earlier (1981), the DES had written that CDT and home economics 'make a particular contribution to the acquisition of physical and practical skills which are [an] essential complement of the pupil's intellectual and personal development' (DES 1981, p. 7).

Already, it is possible to see the potential for a clash of identity – Is D&T to remain a discrete subject? Will it become a 'science and technology' curriculum? Or will the traditional making skills continue, with some designing for modernity? Does this make the position of technology in the curriculum any clearer? So, from the outset, there were concerns within the technology community over the appropriateness of 'technology' as a subject, the proposed content, and its place in the curriculum.

## *National Curriculum Council*

The National Curriculum Council (NCC) was established by the Education Reform Act 1988 to review the work of the subject working groups and produce final consultation documents. The working groups had included experts and practitioners from within the subject, but the NCC was less independent from the government and, on its face value, had little connection with the subject areas (McCormick 2002).

Following a short period of consultation, the technology report was published and met with mixed reactions. Much of the 'new' subject content was already present in CDT and home economics, but it also drew on elements from art and business studies (Norman 1990). One aspect that caused some consternation in the teaching profession was the apparent loss of CDT and home economics from the school curriculum as separate subjects. Other subjects had seemingly survived, but there was a perception that 'technology' was a new subject rather than a development from existing ones. Although this may seem to be a matter of semantics for some, for others, it was a major change for the subject (Paechter 1995).

One noticeable difference between the proposals from the working group, and the final report was the reduction in the number of attainment targets, from five to four:

AT1 Identify needs and opportunities
AT2 Produce a design proposal and develop it into a realistic design
AT3 Planning and making
AT4 Evaluating the processes, product and effects of their activities and those of others

This reduction combined 3 of the previous attainment targets (formulate and select; develop and plan; make) into two (design and develop; plan and make). The revision down may have been an attempt to further distil as the terms of reference identify that students should be able, by the end of compulsory study, to design and make artefacts and be familiar with the design process, taking into consideration social, cultural and environmental factors which influence design. By reducing the attainment targets, the aims of the curriculum, crucially for teachers, the method of assessment became clearer, and in doing so, the objectives of the subject were further underpinned.

With the implementation of the National Curriculum in 1990, schools in England and Wales become the first in the world to offer technology as a compulsory subject from the ages of 5 to 16 (Kimbell and Perry 2001). However, the implementation and sustainability of the subject were no easy feat.

Technology was described as a subject that would incorporate and expand on work currently being undertaken in art, business studies, CDT, home economics and information technology. It would require a coordinated approach among those departments and teachers to help pupils develop their understanding of the 'significance of technology to the economy and life' (NCC 1991, p. 1).

It had also been recognised that in technology 'the capability to investigate, design, make and appraise' was as important as the 'acquisition of knowledge' (DES/WO 1989, p. 1). The first National Curriculum for technology was, however, packed with information and long lists of content for designing and making. The sheer volume of information and content, and the need to work with teachers from other departments, meant that it was not easy for teachers to understand or implement these curriculum requirements:

> Besides the complexity of the proposals, one of the major problems was the difficulty in interpreting what some of the statements meant. They had been deliberately kept at a level of generality to try and avoid prescription but, even with examples, this meant that the various statements were somewhat abstract or vague.
>
> (McCormick 2002, p. 37)

Although the terms of reference to the D&T Working Group had contained references to specific materials and components, the long list of content in the programme of study did not (Eggleston 1996). On one hand, this was helpful, as it gave teachers the opportunity to use whichever materials and teaching methods that they felt equipped to use. On the other hand, it added to the confusion and a lack of clarity about what was needed and led some teachers to continue much as they had done, rebranding existing projects and work as 'technology'.

Some departments attempted to shoehorn existing practice into the Programmes of Study in an attempt to comply, others amended their practice to reduce practical work and spend longer designing and developing ideas. This, however, as Rutland (2009) identified 'to design and plan on paper is not the complete process'. Concerns were raised over the increased knowledge and theoretical base that pupils were required to cover, for example in electronics, pneumatics, or food science. This was addressed by the NCC in 1991, which stressed that practical work was a core competency within the subject:

> D&T capability empowers people to operate effectively, creatively and confidently in the made world and the Order for Technology assumes that practical engagement by pupils in the processes of D&T is fundamental to an education with this aim.
>
> (NCC 1991, p. 3)

The uncertainty felt by teachers was exacerbated by the fact they found it difficult to access guidance documents and support that had been promised; post-introduction meetings at which professionals could discuss and clarify their understanding of the requirements were not readily available (Benson 2000).

Debate continued not only about the content of the subject, and the methods by which pupils were exposed to it but also about the purpose of the subject. Mulberg (1992) identified that the traditional view of pupils' making was no longer to be accepted, that the subject had to look beyond the manufacturing of a product and focus on how both design and technology can respond to a need and improve or enhance individuals, groups, or society.

The purpose of D&T was no longer to produce a skilled, manual workforce but to educate more rounded citizens able to draw on a set of skills for both life and work:

> Although it will provide a sound and extremely useful foundation for professional training, Design and Technology Education for 5 to 16 is not intended to make every child a professional designer or technician any more than mathematics or science are intended as groundings for future professionals in those fields.
>
> (Eggleston 1990, p. 37)

As the National Curriculum began to establish itself in schools, it brought a growing optimism that design and technology would benefit from an improved status:

> One of the most exciting aspects of the National Curriculum is the higher profile given to design and technology; the 1990s could be the time when this subject area and its relationship to our culture receives the wider recognition it deserves. A lot of enthusiasm will be needed to exploit the full potential of the opportunity whilst the initiative remains fresh.
>
> (Norman 1990, p. 96)

During its first year of implementation of the National Curriculum, the NCC reviewed its impact and received both positive and critical feedback. As a result of this, they developed a series of non-statutory guidance documents to help schools with issues such as curriculum structure, the role of the subject leaders and developing schemes of work with some exemplar materials. The idea of producing a national scheme of work (particularly for primary schools) was considered, but it was decided that this would be too prescriptive (Benson 2000) and instead teachers should be allowed to develop their own schemes and projects. Significantly, one of the objectives of the guidance for technology was to clarify the nature of the subject, something the working group had earlier suggested, and which later proved to be needed.

## National Curriculum developments

In 1991, the NCC publication *Aspects of National Curriculum design & technology* set out to further explain what the 'new' aspects of the subject were and what its educational contributions were:

> Firstly, never before has an attempt been made to teach D&T to all children through 11 years of compulsory schooling. To engage the

interests and sustain the motivations of all pupils, it would not be enough to simply extend the provision of existing precursors . . . the requirement is for something broader and more generally relevant in terms of outcomes, contexts and operation and kinds of knowledge and skills involved. . . .

Secondly, D&T differs from other subjects in the National Curriculum in that it does not have an established tradition of teaching and learning. . . . Such traditions are not forged overnight, however, and one of the tasks associated with the implementation of D&T in the National Curriculum is the creation of a subject culture with which teachers can identify.

Thirdly, the departure is new in that there has obviously been little research into pupils' understanding and learning in D&T . . . it would be invalid to make inference from past performance in, say, CDT and home economics.

(NCC 1991, pp. 2–3)

This statement emphasises the broader approach, links to other subjects and the development of non-traditional projects that could be achieved. Crucially, however, it made the point that continuing to teach CDT and home economics projects was not appropriate; more relevant knowledge and skills needed to be developed. Cross-curricular themes, including economic and industrial understanding, were also to be developed. The NCC was also keen to emphasise the importance of teaching values, ensuring that pupils considered aesthetic, moral, environmental and spiritual issues.

For technology, however, curriculum implementation still faced uphill struggles. Teachers had still not received the support and training needed to change their practice, and uncertainty about the nature of the subject and its place in the school curriculum persisted. There was intense debate and lobbying about the technology curriculum from two particular groups, educationalists, and industrialists, particularly the Engineering Council, supported by the Design Council (Wright 2008). The Engineering Council, which had been represented on the D&T Working Group, was 'alarmed' by the way in which technology was evolving, and it commissioned research into the teaching of technology (Smithers and Robinson 1992). This report reinforced the teachers' lack of clarity about what was required and concluded that the subject was not clearly defined and 'lacks identity' (Smithers and Robinson 1992, p. 13).

The NCC had been monitoring the implementation of the National Curriculum and its report, together with others, led to a revision of the technology curriculum in 1992. They reduced the number of attainment targets from four to two, a recommendation from Smithers and Robinson; these were 'designing' and 'making'. However, designing was made up of two strands and making of three, so the streamlining was not as evident as it would first appear. Curriculum content was under five headings and much reduced from the original version:

1. construction materials and components
2. food
3. control systems and energy
4. structures
5. business and industrial practices.

This curriculum did not last long, however, as in 1993 there was a review of the whole National Curriculum. Although Offices for Standards in Education (OfSTED) reported improvements to teaching (McGimpsey, 2011) problems within the subjects continued and such was the discussion over technology, in 1994, the government announced that it was no longer a statutory requirement on the curriculum. Unwilling to lose ground and knowing that it would return in one form or another later, some continued to teach technology as prescribed by the National Curriculum.

The National Curriculum review of 1993 became known as the Dearing Report, after its author. As a result of this report, working groups were re-established, this time for design and technology, not merely technology. Recommendations were published in 1994 and implemented in 1995. This new curriculum brought greater clarity to the subject (McCormick 2002; Breckon 2009) and was met with relief and acceptance by teachers. The links to business studies, industry and enterprise and the relationship to other subjects were made clearer, pupils would 'apply skills, knowledge and understanding from the programmes of study of other subjects, where appropriate, including art, mathematics and science' (DfE/WO 1995, p. 2). Industrial practices were required only at the examination level, not in lower secondary schools, which many teachers welcomed and information technology was no longer subsumed within technology but became a curriculum subject in its own right.

The revised content also made it clear that pupils were to be encouraged to design and make products, which had been in the terms of reference but not the original curriculum: 'Pupils should be taught to develop their design & technology capabilities through combining their *Design* and *Making skills with Knowledge and understanding* in order to design and make products' (DfE/WO 1995, p. 6).

While these revisions were welcomed by many, there was some concern that food became an option rather than a compulsory part of the curriculum, highlighting again the difficult relationship that has always existed. For many, however, the identity of the subject became clearer and its place on the curriculum more assured.

## Developments beyond 2000

Following the five years of stability recommended by the Dearing Report the curriculum remained largely unchanged until September 2000. In 1999, there was a further whole curriculum review, and a new D&T curriculum was published (QCA 1999). The subject content had one main heading 'Skills, Knowledge and Understanding' and was set out under headings to reflect the design-and-make process:

- developing, planning, and communicating ideas
- working with tools, equipment, materials, and components to produce quality products
- evaluating processes and products
- applying knowledge and understanding

Food technology teachers were pleased to see that the revised curriculum encouraged the study of food. There was a strengthening of technology within the subject through CAD/CAM (Computer Aided Design/ Computer Aided Manufacture) and the requirement for pupils to learn about new technologies and new materials, including smart and modern materials. It further identified that pupils should learn through focused practical tasks and product analysis, as well as design and make activities.

Product analysis tasks involved students exploring how a product is designed with a focus on manufacturing techniques, functionality or the interaction between the user and the product. Whereas focused practical tasks allowed students to try out and develop practical skills manufacturing techniques with little designing element. Both approaches to teaching would allow students to develop knowledge and skill which could be used when developing more sophisticated outcomes during the design-and-make activities.

The attainment targets were reduced again, this time to a single one 'designing and making'. This brought significant change within the subject and left Kimbell (1999, p. 3) feeling that the new orders, although offering several benefits, were 'less designerly, less entrepreneurial, less challenging . . . and conversely it was more straightforward, more limited and more safe'.

The curriculum was reviewed again in 2007, and all the subjects were required to present their content under the same headings:

- Key concepts – for D&T, these were identified as design and making, cultural understating, creativity, and critical evaluation. These are to be seen as the pillars around which the subject is built.
- Key processes – which lists the essential skills and processes that pupils need to learn, including generating, modelling, and communicating ideas, responding to briefs, applying knowledge of materials and ingredients designing and making, considering the work of other designers, to plan for manufacture, evaluate the most appropriate tools and equipment for manufacture, solve technical problems and reflect critically on their work to develop their ideas further.
- Range and content – which specifies the knowledge to be covered, under the headings design, food, resistant materials and textiles, systems and control.

There was also a list of 'curriculum opportunities' that described some of the learning experiences pupils should have, including analysis of products, focused practical tasks, design-and-make assignments, working individually and in a team, working with designers and manufacturers and using information and communication technology (ICT) to develop, manipulate and evaluate design work and data. There was also reference to the importance of making links between D&T and other areas of the curriculum. The prescribed content was much reduced, but 'Explanatory Notes' were produced alongside the text to make clear what was required. In the content, food was pitted against textiles in that pupils' study should include 'at least one of food or textiles' (QCA 2007, p. 55), although no rationale was given for this option.

## 2011 – onwards: towards a 'world-class curriculum' for all

In February 2011, the then new secretary of state for education Michael Gove outlined the need to develop a curriculum that was reflective of the modern world and prepared students for the future (Department for Education and Gove 2011). The review was set in the backdrop of a political ideology which was seen as a more traditional approach to education with knowledge and facts playing central positions (Hardy 2017), this was a significant shift from the 2007 National Curriculum (Qualifications and Curriculum Authority). An expert panel of educationalists were appointed and tasked with the following:

- replace the current substandard curriculum with one based on the best school systems in the world, providing a world-class resource for teachers and children
- consider what subjects should be compulsory at what age
- consider what children should be taught in the main subjects at what age

(Department for Education and Gove 2011)

Following consultation with teachers, school leaders, stakeholders and the public and a 'call of evidence', the expert panel reported a series of recommendations. One of these was that should D&T be removed from the National Curriculum and instead be part of a Basic Curriculum, where the subject's aims and content would be determined locally. Stephanie Atkinson (2017, p. 13) explains that this recommendation stemmed from the panel having been 'not entirely persuaded by claims that D&T had what they termed 'sufficient disciplinary coherence' (DfE 2011, p. 24). The panel defined disciplinary knowledge as 'a distinct way of investigating, knowing and making sense with a particular foci, procedures and theories' (DfE 2011, p. 24). Furthermore, there was a clear view that D&T was not an academic subject, nor one relevant or suitable for all children as part of a general education:

> It was mentioned [by people who responded to the call of evidence] that D&T should be a compulsory subject because not all pupils had the ability to excel in the academic subjects, and if it was removed some pupils would be forced to spend more time on subjects they did not enjoy.
>
> (DfE, 2011, p. 31)

Not only was the place and purpose of D&T being questioned, but it was also unclear where or how food technology and food as a material fitted in these new proposals. The call for evidence findings highlighted a 'key strength of the current National Curriculum was the provision of practical cooking lessons for all pupils, particularly at Key stage 3' (DfE 2011, p. 10), even though 'practical cooking' was not actually part of the 2007 National Curriculum. (For a more detailed discussion about the place of food in D&T, see Chapter 7, 'Does Food Fit in Design and Technology?')

When the draft National Curriculum was released, Programmes of Study for the subject were created for Key Stages (KSs) 1, 2 and 3 with the first consultation papers published in February 2013. (Note: these three KSs are labels for lower primary, upper primary and lower secondary, respectively.). As with previous National Curriculum frameworks, the new Programmes of Study had distinct headings. The subject content was defined as design, make, evaluate, and technical knowledge.

Considering the high value given to knowledge by the government, it was surprising to read that the D&T curriculum should 'develop sophisticated practical skills and carry out diagnostic, repair and maintenance tasks in a range of contexts' (DfE 2013a, p. 160). This was interpreted by some as a 'make do and mend' curriculum which was also accompanied by horticulture and construction as potential areas of study (DfE 2013a). Making skills remained a priority of the curriculum with students encouraged to use 'complex tools, equipment, machinery, and techniques skilfully to develop well-conceived and well-executed practical solutions' (DfE 2013a, p. 160). Food also played a significant role within the Programmes of Study not only as an emerging area of design and technology (food design) but also through the teaching of diet and nutrition to develop students' love of cooking and build their 'repertoire of savoury meals' (Department of Education 2013a, p. 160).

The expert panel report and the ensuing draft National Curriculum, published in February 2013 (Department of Education 2013a), demonstrated a perception that the value and purpose of D&T was for pupils to learn practical and life skills plus to prepare them for employment in the manufacturing and industry. Hardy's (2017) analysis showed that these perceptions did not align with the values held by those within the D&T community, which could have been the reason for the vehement reaction from this community (Design and Technology Association 2011; Hardy 2013).

## 2013 National Curriculum

In April 2013 the Royal Academy of Engineers, with the Design and Technology Association and Education for Engineering (E4E), brought together D&T stakeholders from schools, national organisations, and higher education to 'to begin the process of re-drafting the Programme of Study for Design and Technology as part of the National Curriculum Review'. Following this meeting, a new D&T National Curriculum was written and subsequently approved by Michael Gove (then secretary of state for education) and with Liz Truss (then parliamentary under secretary of state for education):

> [W]e have revised the draft programmes of study for design and technology to ensure that they sufficiently reflect our aspirations that it should be a rigorous and forward-looking subject that will set children on a path to be the next generation of designers and engineers.
> (Department for Education and Gove 2013, The updated National Curriculum)

This approved D&T National Curriculum (Department of Education 2013b) was published in July 2013 with cooking and nutrition included as a sub-section of the D&T curriculum. Whilst the D&T content was reduced, new topics were added including an iterative design approach and biomimicry and that D&T design activities should take place within domestic and industrial contexts. Another development in the final publication was the separation of the content into four distinct areas:

- Design – cultures, solving design problems, develop specifications, range of approaches and specific design skills (including digital) and mathematical modelling
- Make – use of specialist tools and equipment precisely and the use of CAD
- Evaluate – focus on the work of past and present designers, new and emerging technology, evaluation in its traditional sense against the criteria and with clients, and the links to society and the environment
- Technical knowledge – properties of materials, mechanical systems, electrical and electronic systems

## Conclusion

This chapter has explored some of the key moments in the development of design and technology in the school curriculum in England. This has been by no means a smooth and comfortable journey, with tensions from the very start (McCormick 1990). The challenges of marrying different disciplinary areas have proved a significant one and attempt to find commonality for a holistic approach to the subject could be generated. The vision and purpose of the curriculum have, over the years, also generated much discourse (Hardy 2016, 2018; Bell et al. 2017).

At each of stage, there have been attempts to clarify the aims and objectives of the subject. However, along the way, there have been miscommunications, unexpected additions or subtractions of both content or material area, and a struggle to align the subject within, or alongside, 'complementary' subject areas. None more so than internally within the subject around the difficult relationship between the teaching of food and the ideals of the broader subject of D&T.

Yet, throughout these difficult times, a set of core values have remained:

- *Knowledge and understanding* of materials, their properties and uses
- *Designing* and working with clients/users/target groups to explore and generate solutions
- *Making* by using a range of tools and equipment via a range of different material areas
- *Evaluation* and reflection on pupils' own work and the work of others

The curriculum today still reflects these key elements that were identified in 1988 with the original attainment targets. So, despite the lack of clarity and poorly communicated aims in the first version of the National Curriculum, a core set of objectives remain. It could now be argued that the individual school has full jurisdiction over how it implements the National Curriculum and can fit the elements of the subject to the expertise, resourcing and internal, or contextual, view of the school. This does create a debate to the purpose of having a standardised, 'national' curriculum and the experiences and understanding of a student at one school being very different to that at another school. Whilst the latest iteration of the D&T National Curriculum has provided detailed the content to be taught, what progression looks like in the D&T subject, and its signature pedagogies has been sidelined in policy documents, leaving teachers, and those who support them, with little guidance on planning a coherent D&T curriculum. These are two areas that need further debate.

## Questions

1 What do you perceive the role of D&T to be within the wider National Curriculum?
2 How does your vision for the subject marry those outlined in the National Curriculum?
3 Have policymakers gone far enough to develop the subject into a forward-thinking, world-class subject equipping pupils for a modern world?

# References

Atkinson, S. (2017) 'So what went wrong and why?' in Eddie Norman, K.B. (ed.), *Design epistemology and curriculum planning*. Loughborough: Loughborough Design Press, pp. 13–17.

Bell, D., Wooff, D., McLain, M. and Morison-Love, D. (2017) 'Analysing design and technology as an educational construct: an investigation into its curriculum position and pedagogical identity', *The Curriculum Journal*, 28(4), pp. 539–558.

Benson, C. (2000) 'Ensuring successful curriculum development in primary design and technology', in Eggleston, J. (ed), *Teaching and learning design and technology: a guide to recent research and its application* (pp. 1–14). London: Continuum.

Breckon, A.M. (2009) 'National Curriculum review 2000', *Journal of Design and Technology Education*, 3(2), pp. 101–103.

Department for Education (2011) *The Framework for the National Curriculum. A report by the expert panel for the National Curriculum review*. London: Department for Education.

Department of Education (2013a) *The National Curriculum in England Framework document (February 2013)*. London: Department of Education.

Department of Education (2013b) *The National Curriculum in England Framework document (July 2013)*. London: Department of Education.

Department for Education and Gove, M. (2011) *National curriculum review launched* [online]. Available at: https://www.gov.uk/government/news/national-curriculum-review-launched (Accessed 21 March 2022).

Department for Education and Gove, M. (2013) *Written statement to Parliament – Education reform: schools* [online]. Available at: https://www.gov.uk/government/speeches/education-reform-schools (Accessed 21 March 2022).

DES (1981) *The school curriculum 1981*. London: HMSO.

DES/WO (1989) *Proposals of the Secretary of State for Education and Science and the Secretary of State for Wales: design and technology for ages 5 to 16*. London: HMSO.

Design and Technology Association (2011) *Report by the expert panel for the National Curriculum review (DfE, December 2011)* [online]. Design and Technology Association. Available at: http://bit.ly/14GHAZv (Accessed 24 July 2013).

DfE/WO (1995) *Design and technology in the National Curriculum*. London: HMSO.

Eggleston, J. (1976) *Developments in design education*. London: Open Books.

Eggleston, J. (1990) *Delivering the technology curriculum: six case studies in primary and secondary schools*. Stoke-on-Trent: Trentham Books.

Eggleston, J. (1996) *Understanding design and technology*. Buckingham: Open University Press.

Gillard, D. (2011) *Education in England: a brief history*. Available at: www.educationengland.org.uk/history (Accessed 29 December 2011).

Hardy, A.L. (2013) 'Starting the journey: discovering the point of D&T', *PATT27: Technology Education for the Future: A Play on Sustainability, Christchurch, New Zealand, 2-6 December 2013*. University of Waikato: Technology Environmental Science and Mathematics Education Research Centre, pp. 222–228.

Hardy, A.L. (2016) *What's the point of D&T?* [online]. STEM Learning Ltd. Available at: https://www.stem.org.uk/blog/what%E2%80%99s-point-design-and-technology (Accessed 12 July 2016).

Hardy, A.L. (2017) 'How did the expert panel conclude that D&T should be moved to a basic curriculum?', in Norman, E.W.L. and Baynes, K. (eds.), *Design epistemology and curriculum planning* (pp. 18–21). Loughborough: Loughborough Design Press.

Hardy, A.L. (2018) 'Defining the value of a school subject', *PRISM: Casting New Light on Learning, Theory and Practice*, 1(2), pp. 55–82.

Harris, M. and Wilson, V. (2003) 'Designs on the curriculum? A review of the literature on the impact of design and technology in schools in England', *Journal of Design and Technology Education*, 8(3), pp. 166–171.

Kimbell, R. (1999) 'Coming of age', *Journal of Design and Technology Education*, 4(1), pp. 3–4.

Kimbell, R. and Perry, D. (2001) *Design and technology in a knowledge economy*. London: Engineering Council.

Kingsland, J.C. (1969) 'In search of an alternative road' in Baynes, K. (ed.), *Attitudes in design education* (pp. 9–20). London: Lund Humphries.

McCormick, R. (1990) 'Technology and the National Curriculum: the creation of a 'subject' by committee?' *The Curriculum Journal*, 1(1), pp. 39–51.

McCormick, R. (2002) 'The coming of technology education in England and Wales', in Owen-Jackson, G. (ed.), *Teaching design and technology in secondary schools: a reader* (pp. 31–47). London: RoutledgeFalmer.

McGimpsey (2011) *A review of Literature on Design Education in the National Curriculum*. London: RSA Design and Society.

Mulberg, C. (1992) 'Beyond the looking glass: technology myths in education', in Bedgett-Meakin, C. (ed.), *Make the future work*. Essex: Longman.

NCC (1991) *Aspects of National Curriculum design and technology*. York: National Curriculum Council.

Norman, E. (ed.) (1990) *Teaching design and technology 5-16*. London: Longman.

Paechter, C. (1995) 'Subcultural retreat: negotiating the design and technology curriculum', *British Educational Research Journal*, 21(1), pp. 75–87.

Penfold, J. (1988) *Craft, design and technology*. Stoke-on-Trent: Trentham Books.

Qualifications and Curriculum Authority (1999) *Design and technology: the National Curriculum for England*. London: DfEE/QCA.

Qualifications and Curriculum Authority (2007) 'Design and technology: programmes of study for key stage 3 and attainment targets', in *The National Curriculum: statutory requirements for key stages 3 and 4*. London: Qualifications and Curriculum Authority, pp. 50–59.

Rutland, M. (2009) 'An MA student's critical evaluation of D&T', *Design and Technology Teaching*, 25(2), pp. 25–28.

Smithers, A. and Robinson, P. (1992) *Technology in the National Curriculum: getting it right*. London: Engineering Council.

Wright, R. (2008) 'The 1992 struggle for design and technology', *Design and Technology Education: an International Journal*, 13(1), pp. 29–39.

# 2 International perspectives on technology education

*Frank Banks and P. John Williams*

## Introduction

In this chapter we are going to consider the content of the design and technology (D&T) curricula across the world. By looking at other countries, it enables us to 'hold up a mirror' to our own D&T curriculum and feeds into the debate on the content of our own school's technology/engineering curriculum and how it could develop. The creative designing-and-making area of a school's curriculum has different names in different countries and different roots of development. What has developed over the years, and what is possible in the future, is enabled or constrained by a country's wider school systems. Some countries have a very well-established vocational school strand with different traditional expectations of the purpose of a technology curriculum compared to the general schools. Many, perhaps most, current technology curricula have their roots in the craft tradition when the production of 'quality products' were paramount. Some have had a design element included for many decades. Some curricula exist as a spin-off of an applied science approach, and even if not formally considered part of STEM (science, technology, engineering, mathematics), many technology curricula now incorporate the 'S' and the 'M' into the design and development of solutions to problems. Most significant of all, however, the wider context of society and the workplace in which the school curriculum is being shaped have undergone some profound changes. Before we look in detail at specific countries, let us consider some of these worldwide contextual issues.

## The changing context

This chapter is being written in 2021 by two authors, one who lives in the UK and the other in Australia. When the first edition of this book was published in 2013, no one would have thought then that the climate emergency would lead to such devastating wildfires in Australia and California and other extreme weather events worldwide. The relentless encroachment, cultivation, and exploitation of wildlife in formerly remote regions of our interconnected world have led to a global pandemic and so many COVID-19 deaths in the UK. Across Europe and North and South America, 2020–2021 has

DOI: 10.4324/9781003166689-4

witnessed the many months-long closures of schools, the cancellation of school examinations and, for students of all ages, 'remote learning' at home. Practical subjects such as D&T presented a particular challenge for home learning, and even when some in-school face-to-face contact was possible, social distancing made it difficult to teach as normal.

As we look to the future, we need to widen the debate beyond the parameters of the past. In all counties, the technology/engineering part of the curriculum has, at least, a nod to relevance in the 'real world' and vocational usefulness. But what will that future 'real world' be like? And how should the design and technology curriculum change?

> We are currently preparing students for jobs that don't yet exist, using technologies that haven't been invented, in order to solve problems, we don't even know are problems yet.
> (Gunderson *et al.*, 2004: 13)

> We are in a uniquely exciting time. We understand how to engage kids. We need to give them real-world challenges, have them work with other kids, and provide them with the right kind of adult support. Project-based learning is how people work in the real world. We need to let our kids create portfolios of joy.
> (Lyons in Dintersmith, 2018: 18)

> In a survey by the National Association of Colleges and Employers (NACE, 2017), more than two-thirds of employers reported that they look for employees who demonstrate strong creative problem-solving, teamwork, and communication skills. For the United States to remain competitive in the 21st Century, our citizens must be equipped with creative problem-solving skills.
> (Duyar et al., 2019: 2)

There is clearly a need to consider how the D&T curriculum and even aspects of schooling itself will need to adapt in the face of the rapid changes taking place as society adapts to future challenges: a massive rise in online retail and the decimation of big high-street stores, 'white-collar' home working supplemented with video 'office' meetings, the development of new entrepreneurial 'cottage industries', and the increased automation in manufacturing industries. If there really is a need to consider vocational usefulness as an aspect of curriculum development, how are countries around the world responding to the new challenges? Are different countries' D&T curricula able to adapt to the new vocational context?

## What lessons can be learnt from other countries?

We have selected a range of countries for you to consider which represent some of the diversity of technology education throughout the world. As you look at the Technology curricula of the different countries bear in mind the possible adaptability that is needed to 'future-proof' what is taught, the extent to which the curriculum allows pupils or groups of pupils the autonomy to choose what they learn, design and make. Finally, consider each country's wider society and school organisational system that provides the rationale for how technology is framed and taught.

## Australia

Arguably the most significant date in the history of technology education in Australia was 1987, when all state and federal ministers of education agreed on the National Goals for Schooling in Australia. As part of this, they declared that the curriculum was composed of eight learning areas, one of which was technology.

This declaration had profound outcomes. First, in secondary schools, the subject areas from which technology education developed were located within the elective areas of the curriculum. The implication was that these subjects provided learning experiences relevant only to specific groups of students with particular interests or career destinations in mind, but now this area was important for all students. Second, in primary education, technology had not generally been part of school programmes, and primary teachers had little experience to draw on to develop programmes. The challenge for technology education was to determine the learning experiences that are essential for all students and are unique to technology education.

The states have traditionally been responsible for education and curriculum, but after a number of attempts, in 2014, a national curriculum, 'Technologies' was published. This curriculum is composed of two distinct, and mandatory, subjects, with Design and Technologies emphasising 'design thinking' as students engage in design and 'making' processes and Digital Technologies emphasising 'computational thinking' with the use of digital systems to create solutions.

What has been a strength of past Technologies curricula developed by the various states and territories has been the explicit encouragement of experiential learning pedagogies (Kolb, 1984) and constructivist epistemologies (Dewey, 1997; Piaget, 1977; Pinch & Bijker, 1994) to engage students in the development of skills and knowledge. The new national curriculum continues to encourage these approaches, ensuring student experience and understandings have 'real-world relevance' (Lombardi, 2007). It seems that the new National Curriculum: Technologies has broadened this trend to develop values and address real-world issues, with a focus on the development of thinking skills and values as well as the expected practical skills to contribute to 'sustainable patterns of living' (ACARA, 2014).

The scaffolding of content is clear throughout the developing stages of the curriculum. Students aged 4 to 6 years experience a guided design process and are made aware of the needs and concept of the environment. Seven- to 9-year-old students are encouraged toward a more outward orientation in developing cognitive outcomes from exercising a design process. They take more responsibility for project management and planning for design solutions. Ten- to 12-year-old students, in middle or high school, are in the final stage of the mandatory curriculum. They are given greater access to a diverse range of equipment and tools for the realisation of designed solutions. As a result, the expectations of their engagement with these resources are that these students will be able to design, plan and manage projects safely. In the later years of schooling, the individual states offer a range of technology subjects which specialise more in design, engineering, or specific materials technologies.

It has been noted that there has been a shift in the focus of the curriculum from an economic orientation of developing the individual as a future worker to the development of the individual to contribute to bettering the three pillars of society, the economy, and the environment (Williams et al., 2019). What is explicitly expected in the National Curriculum: Technologies is the development of the individual to competently design and engage in an increasingly rigorous process to develop solutions to satisfy identified needs.

The Technologies curriculum is unique: no other area of the Australian curriculum seeks to develop within its learners' purposeful technological self-actualisation, informed by contextually validated knowledge to integrate social, technical, and environmental systems through various creative modes of applied design (Williams et al., 2019: 180).

## China

China has a history of significant technological inventions, of which it is proud – from paper and gunpowder to satellites, nuclear energy, superconductors, high-energy accelerators, advanced computers and robots. In 2021, President Biden pressured Apple Inc. to return production of the iPhone out of China and back to the US. Apple's response was that China had a skilful workforce that worked long hours and for lower wages. Interestingly, however, although technology education as education for production was a strong rationale in many Marxist-driven economies, that rationale is prevalent in the US too. Gu, Wang, and Fujita (2018: 225) noted:

> In the 1950s and 1960s, the People's Republic of China integrated technology education and labour education in order to cultivate students' positive attitude towards labour and technology, as well as to teach students labour techniques. In 1958, the government advocated that education should work for politics and should integrate with production and labour.

China has a long involvement in vocational and technical education, and 'Integrated Curriculum of Practical Activity' has been part of the curriculum since the early 1900s. In recent years, information technology and community service have developed alongside the labour-technical education. Information technology has developed into a subject in its own right.

Again, like the US, STEM has received a boost in recent years, but in contrast, China's centralised system has had a larger and more uniform impact. In 2017, the Chinese National Institute of Education Sciences published '2017 China STEM Education White Paper' (Yang and Ke, 2020) emphasising that STEM education is in line with China's economic development plans and its desire to improve the nations skills' base. Science and mathematics have traditionally been important and high-status subjects, but practical work has been less prevalent. Through an integrated approach to STEM, the Ministry of Education hopes to encourage students to solve real-life problems. However, the enormity of implementing any new technology curriculum via STEM or modifying labour-technical education in a country with more than 300 million students should not be underestimated.

### *Germany*

The education system is funded by both federal and state governments, but responsibility for education is devolved to the 16 state governments. There are many similarities however because of federal regulations, inter-state cooperation and national projects.

There are generally three types of secondary schools in Germany: *haptschule* (general secondary school, apprenticeship preparation), *realschule* (general comprehensive school), and *gymnasium* (high school, university preparation), and about one third of all pupils attend each type of school. Technology education hardly exists in the gymnasium which has a strong tradition of a liberal arts curriculum, although technology has now made some inroads at the lower secondary level. Technology education is well established in the realschule, and in the later years it may be an alternative to a second foreign language (Mammes et al., 2016).

The aims of technology education are to provide a functional knowledge about technical devices and processes; teach technology-specific methodologies, for example creativity, cooperation, and communication; and develop evaluation and assessment capabilities.

Not all state systems, however, have technology as a compulsory subject at all levels. For example, technology subjects may be called Technik (process and systems, consequences of technology), Technisches Werken (skill development through making), or Arbeitslehre (careers, technology and economics).

An example of a Technisches Werken curriculum is that from the state of Schleswig-Holstein which has taken the lead in technology education since 1992. In this case, the curriculum spans secondary school years 7 to 10 and covers

- machine and production technology,
- transportation and traffic,
- electrical engineering,
- construction and the built environment,
- supply and waste management, and
- information and communication.

The methodologies involved in teaching technology include

- instruction, how to do something;
- design exercises;
- manufacturing exercises, planning of the production process;
- technological experiments;
- technological analyses;
- technological exploration, outside of school; and
- technological assessment and evaluation.

In summary, the technology curriculum in general education is different across the German states and between the different secondary schools. Technology is taught in the general comprehensive schools but in the gymnasiums, in only 5 of the 16 federal states: a patchwork of curriculum provision within a patchwork of school organisation. For a country with such a reputation for technological innovation, this is surprising. Not so surprising are recommendations for improvement:

- Implement a compulsory and consistent offer of technology education in all types of school and all school levels. Introduce mandatory educational standards.
- Ensure better harmonisation between vocational and general education.
- Improve the training of technology teachers and the expansion of technology didactic research at universities. (Mammes et al., 2016: 34)

*Israel*

Israel has a population of 8.6 million, 1 million people fewer than London. It is a similar size to Wales, and yet this small country has an enviable tradition in education generally and technology education in particular. There are different types of schools, or 'tracks', that pupils follow, both secular and religious, but the secular state schools are attended by the majority of pupils. It is possible that high school students choose not to attend a conventional school but instead study for a trade at an approved vocational school. These apprenticeships are provided by the Ministry of Industry, Trade, and Labour, following a pattern of two years of classroom study followed by one/two years during which students study three days a week and work at their chosen trade on the other days. Trades such as hairstyling, cooking, mechanics and word processing are available.

There has been a long focus on science, technology, and society since its introduction into junior high schools in 1995. In 2014, Israel launched a new national curriculum which is intended to focus on the needs of students trying to cope with the challenges ahead in the 21st century through active experiential learning, group work, critical thinking and research.

Dagan (2020) notes that there are 32 study pathways in high school technology education. These are divided into three categories: (a) science-based technology tracks, (b) technology tracks and (c) vocational tracks. In the science-based technology tracks, some of the science, technology and engineering subjects are integrated, for example the biotechnology, electronics, mechatronics, environmental sciences and scientific engineering tracks. The students study in technology tracks for three years. In their first year, they have to study either physics or technology sciences. During the second and third years, they have to choose topics from their chosen track and develop projects in which they design and make solutions to everyday problems and present them to the external examiners.

There is an informality in Israeli schools which extends to teachers being called by their first name and pupils being encouraged to be fully involved in the problems posed to them and for which they are encouraged to engage in appropriate research. This is particularly noteworthy in 'Obshchestvo Remeslenava Truda' (ORT) schools which have been innovating the technology curriculum across the world. ORT, which is often translated from Russian as 'Association for the Promotion of Skilled Trades', was founded in St Petersburg in 1880 to provide employment skills for Russia's impoverished Jews. The organisation began to support training programs in Jewish schools and establish its own vocational schools in the early 20th century. By 2003, ORT was teaching 90,000 students in Israel in 159 schools, colleges, and institutions. It estimates that it is educating 25% the country's high-tech workforce.

A particular ORT initiative is ISTEAM (innovation, science, technology, engineering, art, mathematics). Following the thrust of the new national curriculum, students bring together the different disciplines to work on a major project matching the developmental needs of the individual learners and of the society to which they belong, a clear problem-based learning approach in which the students work on something that interests them to take a real-world issue, blurring the boundaries between subjects.

While acknowledging the worth of these types of integrating initiatives, Dagan (2020) notes:

> Nevertheless, an integrative study subject that combines Science, Technology, Engineering and Mathematics into a unique program is still very rare. Although at the national levels there are declarations about the importance of STEM education, the changes that have taken place mainly involve reinforcing each discipline, rather than instilling integrative teaching of the STEM disciplines as a unified subject.

## *South Africa*

Although apartheid ended in 1994, the education system is still changing in many ways in South Africa, particularly in relation to curriculum planning. Education traditionally reflected the pre-1994 system of government with separate departments for each racial group, overseen by the Department of National Education, with patterns of demographics, subjects studied and the proportions of students proceeding onto higher levels varying, with only 35% of blacks compared with 98% of whites passing matriculation. Expenditure on black education was about one quarter that spent on white education, with very poor facilities for blacks. It was a massive task to equalize the educational system with over 12.3 million students, 386,000 teachers and 48,000 schools.

The first national curriculum was implemented in South Africa in 2006 and consisted of eight compulsory learning areas, one of which was technology, based largely on the English D&T model. However, being a new learning area, there were no teachers trained in technology and so the first teachers were co-opted from other areas until cohorts of rapidly requalified teachers were able to complete short courses.

The degree of implementation of technology in schools varies remarkably, from independent (private) schools whose technology facilities would compare favourably to any in the world to some state schools which have no electricity or water and for whom, consequently, technology as a subject is not a priority. There were many difficulties in implementation in schools in rural areas:

- a lack of appropriate resources (classrooms, workshops, tools, equipment, materials)
- insufficiently stocked libraries and media centres
- overcrowded classrooms
- inappropriate and insufficient furniture
- a lack of space to store materials, tools, and projects in progress
- insufficient time allocation for technology education in timetables.
(Potgieter, 2004)

The 2014 curriculum review resulted in some major changes in technology. In particular, the removal of the ambitious outcomes-based learning (OBL) which was set in place after the new political dispensation was elected in 1994. However, it was mainly contextual and practical factors that placed major demands on and posed challenges to the implementation of a new education system, aligned with a new ideology. Due to these challenges the country now finds itself moving back towards content-based education (Ankiewicz, 2020).

In 2014 the Department of Basic Education (DBE) launched a strategy to reposition technical schools and schools of specialisation (engineering; mathematics, science and information and communication technology [ICT]; sport; arts; commerce and entrepreneurship) as a part of orientating the upper high school years (Grades 10–12 – ages 15–17) as a basis for human resource development. The objectives for this strategy include the following:

> The repositioning of technical schools and schools of specialisation to be able to respond to the needs of the country and the demands of the modern economy as identified in the National Development Plan (NDP; National Planning Commission, 2012)

Strengthening/broadening the curriculum to provide more areas of specialisation which will lead to more participation of students.

Restoring partnerships between industry or business, technical schools and schools of specialisation in preparing students for the world of work.

In 2020, Ankiewicz noted that the reformed content-based curriculum involved the upgrading of workshops, replacement and supply of tools and equipment and in-service training to teachers currently teaching these subjects. The expansion of the curriculum implies the introduction of areas of specialisation within the following:

Civil technology, namely civil services, construction and woodworking
Electrical technology, namely electrical, electronics and digital electronics
Mechanical technology, namely automotive, welding and metalwork, as well as fitting and machining

(Ankiewicz, 2020)

The South African technology curriculum is unique in that it includes a specific outcome focused on Indigenous technology. The government has attempted to support schools' and teachers' development in this area for a number of reasons. Most of the technology curriculum reflects 'Western' views about technology, and a focus on Indigenous technologies is an attempt to rectify that, with a more 'African' perspective. In addition, in a context of a large number of extremely resource-poor schools, teaching about technology through a historical and Indigenous context may be the only realistic option.

Despite the severe difficulties surrounding its implementation, teachers and students remain committed to the opportunities presented by 'doing technology'.

## *Sweden*

In Sweden, the subject is called technology and is a mandatory subject in compulsory schooling (6–16 years). Similar to Finland, Sweden has a traditional technical education history: a vocationally oriented craft technology for boys and a home economics–type subject for girls, with students often also reflecting social class distinctions.

In the early 1960s, there was for the first time in Sweden a technology subject in general education, Technological orientation (*Teknisk orientering*), which was not mandatory but designed primarily for boys who would neither go on to higher education nor do a purely vocational course, a group of pupils which belonged to what in the USA was called "the new 50 percent" owing to the size of this group. This was not a subject aimed at technological literacy however, because it was rooted in a vocational tradition and focused on the technical skills necessary for work in industry (Drawing, Materials science, etc.).

(Hallström et al., 2014: 124)

Since the 1980s, politicians have been concerned about the importance of technology in society and the need for education to prepare students adequately; in 1994, it was made a core compulsory subject), and this remains the case. The Swedish school curriculum was revised in 2018, with some modifications in 2021. The aims set out for technology follow:

- Teaching in technology should aim at helping the pupils to develop their technical expertise and technical awareness so that they can orient themselves and act in a technologically intensive world.
- Teaching in technology should essentially give pupils the opportunities to develop their ability, for example, to identify problems and needs; use concepts and expressions of technology; and study how cultural attitudes towards technology have an impact on men's and women's choice of occupation and use of technology. (Skolvoket, 2018: 296–297)

The 2018 curriculum supports teachers in suggesting content and providing brief 'performance targets'. A school system that requires all students to study technology needs to give scope for a range of interests given the different backgrounds. A systemic problem could be that if the compulsory technology curriculum is spread widely it becomes every teacher's problem and, in consequence, no teacher's problem. Taking an analysis of the 2021 technology curriculum (Nordolf et al., 2021: Table 3) and looking very selectively at some of the content required in the final years of compulsory education, it includes the following.

*Technological solutions*

Included are technical solutions such as for controlling and regulation by means of electronics and various types of sensors and how technical solutions that utilise electronics can be programmed.

*Working methods for developing technological solutions*

Included are items such as different phases of technical development are included: identification of needs, investigating, proposing solutions, construction, and testing and how different phases in the work process interact in the students' own work and in technology development work in society, for example in architecture and public transport.

### Technology, human, society and the environment

Included are concepts such as considering the internet and other global technical systems; the benefits, risks and limitations of these systems and the relationship between technological development and scientific progress; how technology has enabled scientific discoveries; and how science has enabled technological innovations.

By Grade 9 (age 16), pupils to be able to, for example,

> [c]arry out simple work involving technology and design by studying and systematically testing and retesting possible ideas for solutions and also design well developed and well planned physical or digital models. During the work process, pupils formulate and choose action alternatives that lead to improvements. Pupils draw up well developed documentation of the work using sketches, models, drawings or reports where the intention of the work is well documented.
>
> (Skolverket, 2018: 302–303)

It is a tall order to construct a compulsory technology curriculum for all across all compulsory school ages (see Taiwan), and it is a small wonder that much of the curriculum can be explored through information technology. But it is interesting to note that in Sweden, the environmental and social impact of technology is so explicit.

### Taiwan

Taiwan's plan for a 12-year compulsory education was fully implemented in July 2020. In the new curriculum, technology was a newly added learning area. Technology in Taiwan has echoes of the original 1990 'Technology' national curriculum in England and Wales, which embraced both D&T and information technology (IT), but in Taiwan the two curriculum strands are living technology (LT) and IT.

While cautioning that simply enacting a compulsory national curriculum does not necessarily imply change will actually happen, Fujita and Lee (2018: 118) note: 'The newly added Technology learning area aims to develop students' capabilities of "doing, using, and thinking" in an adaptive and friendly learning environment so as to have the technological literacy required in the 21st century' A diagram illustrating the LT curriculum is shown in Figure 2.1.

In the past, the technology curriculum has been part of natural science and living technology (NS&LT), which science has tended to dominate.

LT in senior high schools builds on the curriculum framework of junior high schools, and problem-solving and active learning predominate. There is an integrated approach building on the background and interests of the pupils. Topics such as 'Technology and Life' and 'Information and

*International perspectives on technology education* 37

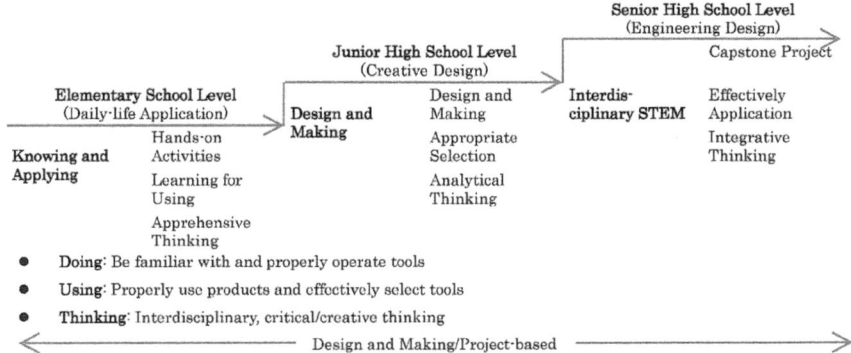

*Figure 2.1* Diagram showing the structure of the technology curriculum across compulsory school in Taiwan (Kuen-Yi, 2017).

Communication' are taught in the first school year, and 'Construction and Manufacturing' and 'Energy and Transportation' in the second. IT, graphical communication, construction and manufacturing and conceptual aspects of energy and power are integrated into the topics. This integration is common, and some suggest that it could be extended to STEM too (Kuen-Yi & Yu-Jen, 2020).

The politics of curriculum change are significant in Taiwan. Science and technology are important drivers of the economy, and a compulsory curriculum from Grades 1 through 12 demonstrates a keen imperative to provide value-added services and manufacturing through a well-educated workforce. Technology as a new curriculum area; it is distinct from the former close association and dominance of science is contrary to the developments in many other Far East countries. It will be interesting to see if it continues in such a political culture to remain distinct from STEM.

## UK

The British government of the late 1980s introduced a prescribed curriculum into state schools in England, Wales and Northern Ireland, and for the first time, technology became a compulsory subject for all pupils from the ages of 5 to 16 years. However, the nature of the school subject of technology is not the same, in terms of content and ethos, across the UK. There have been many curriculum changes and school system changes since then. The most significant has been the greater devolution of responsibility for education to the four countries of the UK in 1998, creating a patchwork of different educational provision not dissimilar to the arrangements in countries such as Germany, although not such a formal federal system. Consequently, over the years, the national variations across the UK in what is embraced by the school subject area of 'technology' has become more marked.

### England

A key development in England, which has also been seen in other countries, is a move away from a detailed prescription of what should be taught to a slimmer national curriculum. Coupled with this has been developments in the school system including 'Academies' and 'free schools' which are non-profitmaking, state-funded schools which are free for pupils to attend but are not subject to local government scrutiny (although they are subject to inspection by the Office for Standards in Education) and may opt out of the national curriculum. The creative curriculum in general has suffered in recent years due to the creation of the English Baccalaureate (EBacc). The EBacc is restricted to English, mathematics, the sciences, history or geography and a language. Students may take other subjects including music, art or D&T, but they do not count in the all-important ranking of schools. Secondary schools are measured on the number of pupils that take General Certificate of Secondary Education (GCSE; examinations usually taken at 16) in these EBacc subjects and in how well their pupils do. The downplaying of D&T in this formal way has reduced the number of pupils electing to study the subject after the age of 14. But as the subject association for D&T teachers points out, from 11 to 14

> [a]s students progress through this phase, they may be given the opportunity to focus on specific aspects of the subject such as product design, food technology, engineering, systems and control, electronics, textiles and graphics. However, at its core is creativity and imagination. Students learn to design and make products that solve genuine, relevant problems within different contexts whilst considering their own and others' needs, wants and values. To do this effectively, they will acquire a broad range of subject knowledge and draw on additional disciplines such as mathematics, science, engineering, computing and art.
>
> (DATA, 2021)

### Northern Ireland

In Technology and Design, as it is named in Northern Ireland, the aim is to enable pupils to become confident and responsible in solving real-life problems, striving for creative solutions, independent learning, product excellence and social consciousness. There are nine curriculum areas in Northern Ireland, with Technology and Design strand as part of the Science and Technology area, there is a strong 'applied science' thrust, and at the age of 14 pupils learn about

- design,
- communication,
- manufacturing, and
- control.

Technology and Design encourages pupils to develop creative thinking and problem-solving skills by evaluating design proposals and selecting and using materials that are fit for purpose. The intended learning outcomes are

- demonstrate practical skills in the safe use of a range of tools, machines and equipment;
- research and manage information effectively to investigate design issues, using Mathematics and ICT where appropriate;
- show deeper understanding by thinking critically and flexibly, solving problems and making informed decisions, using Mathematics and ICT where appropriate;
- demonstrate creativity and initiative when developing ideas and following them through;
- work effectively with others;
- demonstrate self-management by working systematically, persisting with tasks, evaluating and improving own performance;
- communicate effectively in oral, visual (including graphic) written, mathematical and ICT formats showing clear awareness of audience and purpose. (CCA, 2021)

These learning outcomes are achieved mainly through the designing and making of products in resistant materials, 'product design' or 'systems and control' in which the emphasis on electronics is unusual and sophisticated compared to other areas of the UK.

*Scotland*

In 2011, Scotland implemented the 'Curriculum for Excellence' (CfE), which lacks the prescription of the curriculum in England and Northern Ireland, and like Wales, schools are encouraged to design their curriculum to suit local needs. However, the CfE includes an area called 'Technologies', and it aligns with creative, practical and work-related activities. As in many countries, however, the examination system has a hold on the extent of the freedom schools have for curriculum design and there are two examinations, D&T and Design and Manufacture, that are of particular interest.

'Design and Technology – The aims of the Course are to enable learners to:

- develop skills in producing and interpreting sketches, drawings and diagrams;
- develop skills in practical model making and construction;
- develop skills in testing and simple evaluation of models;
- apply safe working practices in a workshop or similar environment to develop knowledge of basic engineering ideas.

Design and Manufacture – The aims of the Course are to enable learners to:

- develop skills in the design and manufacturing of models, prototypes and products;
- develop knowledge and understanding of manufacturing processes and materials;
- develop an understanding of the impact of design and manufacturing technologies on our environment and society.

Also of interest in Scotland is a number of so-called practical courses, such as Practical Electronics. The aims of this course are to enable learners to develop

- knowledge and understanding of key concepts in electronics and apply these in a range of contexts;
- a range of practical skills in electronics, including skills in analysis and problem solving, design skills, skills in the safe use of tools and equipment, and skills in evaluating products and systems;
- awareness of the importance of safe working practices in electronics;
- an understanding of the role and impact of electronics in changing and influencing society and the environment'. (CfE, 2021)

Interestingly, in Scotland, there are also popular courses simply called 'Practical Skills' available in woodworking, metalworking and cookery.

## Wales

In April 2019, a curriculum was launched in Wales built around 'areas of learning and experience'. Known as a Curriculum for Wales 2022, the need for a coordinated approach is built into the curriculum design. For example, one area of learning is 'Mathematics and Numeracy', and another, 'Science and Technology', and the curriculum stretches across the whole school-age range of 3 to 16. Looking at 'Science and Technology', one can see that it includes the following:

> Design thinking, and engineering offer technical and creative ways to meet society's needs and wants:
>
> By applying their experiences, skills and knowledge, learners can design and shape innovative engineered solutions. Being part of a user-centred design process will encourage them to use creativity to develop ideas, manage and mitigate risks, and minimise complexities. When engineering products, services and systems, they will need to understand and control the interactions between materials, structures, components and users. The application of engineering processes allows learners to develop accuracy, precision, dexterity and craftsmanship. By designing and engineering outcomes in response to needs and wants, learners can become enterprising problem solvers.
>
> (Hwb, 2021)

## United States

The educational system in the US is decentralised, with each state responsible for its own education, although the federal government provides some general control through funding guidelines. Some states pursue curriculum development and implementation at the state level, and others give broad guidelines with the actual curriculum work done by local school districts. This results in great variety.

This diversity in the US makes it difficult to generalise, but the US has a long history of seeing technology education as needing to reflect the changes in society and in work practices. For example, manual training in the 1870s, a skills-based approach through 'industrial arts' has developed in the modern era into technology and engineering education in most states. In many states, developments have been configured as part of a move to adopt an integrative approach to STEM and influenced by the makerspace movement (Moye et al., 2019).

Technology education in the US has struggled for many years (as in many other countries) with public misconceptions about the nature of technology education, most commonly confused with IT and computing. The move to engineering was intended to overcome this as the general population has a clearer conception of engineering than of technology. Many states adopted engineering, including engineering design. In the latter part of the 20th century, there was a concerted effort in the US to develop standards in different subjects. This is not a national requirement, certainly not a national curriculum but, rather, a setting out of good practice and aspirations. The Standards for Technological Literacy: Content for the Study of Technology in 2000 and updates in 2002 and 2007 (ITEEA, 2007), and now the Standards for Technological and Engineering Literacy (ITEEA, 2020), have been very influential in making clear what the technology curriculum should look like.

The other rationale for including engineering is the STEM movement. This is a politically supported attempt to address the declining number of students studying science and engineering at university and the presumed consequential decline in economic activity. However, as many states insist teachers have a high subject-specific education, in some areas, it is difficult to recruit teachers with a wide subject background suitable for STEM. This could be ameliorated by teachers of the different STEM subjects 'looking sideways' and collaborating in their teaching as advocated strongly by Banks and Barlex (2021).

Developments in the US are often the result of deliberations of higher education and the academic community rather than from grass-roots developments. This means that it takes longer for new initiatives to become common practice than if teachers were more involved in the curriculum development process. However, recent developments in STEM and engineering at the elementary level have led to some interesting initiatives and joint projects across educational levels (see Wells, 2020).

In very few areas in the US does technology constitute part of the core curriculum, which means it has to compete with other electives for students.

Integrated STEM, despite the teacher shortages, seems to ensure, like in England, mathematics and science will be drawn on increasingly in technology and engineering.

## Conclusion

During the 2020 global pandemic, many schools were closed, affecting 1.6 billion children in 192 countries. Robert Halfon (2020), the chair of the cross-party education select committee of the UK parliament, said, 'The coronavirus outbreak is going to have a deep and long-lasting impact right across the education sector'. In 2021, the source of the pandemic is still being investigated, although it is generally thought to have crossed over to humans from bats either directly or via an intermediary animal, perhaps in a so-called wet market containing exotic animals or through human in-roads into formerly remote underdeveloped geographical areas. What has all this to do with technology education in schools?

The pandemic's origins are likely to be due to the same exploitation of the environment as is the cause of global warming. Bill Gates (2021), founder of Microsoft, suggests that solving climate change would be 'the most amazing thing humanity has ever done. By comparison, ending the pandemic is very, very easy'. The pandemic that has directly and profoundly affected the life chances of so many young people is intimately linked to the future of the planet, and the solution to these problems is not only through learning to change our behaviour but also through the development and use of new technologies. The rationale for a school technology curriculum, as we have seen in the examples from different countries, is widening the pupils' understanding of the impact of technology on society, creating appropriate artefacts to meet particular needs and focusing on real-life problems. Given this rationale, using sound reasoning and evaluating the facts, and using skills gained through technology education, global issues such as the COVID-19 pandemic and climate change can be rationally addressed. Some countries, taking an appropriate approach to their pedagogy are allowing pupils to directly address their deep concerns about their future.

## Questions

1. Looking across the world, what would you wish to take and include in the technology of your country? And why?
2. What do you think is the best rationale for compulsory technology in the curriculum?
3. What do you see as missing from the different curricula?
4. What changes to technology curricula and pedagogy deemed suitable for the 20th century are needed to meet the changing priorities and the new needs of society in the middle of the 21st century?

# References

ACARA (2014). *Technologies*. Retrieved from Australian Curriculum: Available from: https://www.australiancurriculum.edu.au/f-10-curriculum/technologies/

Ankiewicz, P. (2020) Technology education in South Africa since the new dispensation in 1994: An analysis of curriculum documents and a meta-synthesis of scholarly work. *International Journal of Technology and Design Education*. doi:10.1007/s10798-020-09589-8

Banks, F. and Barlex, D. (2021) *Teaching STEM in the Secondary School: Helping Teachers Meet the Challenge* (Second edition). London: Routledge.

CCA (2021) *Council for the Curriculum, Examinations and Assessment*. Available at: https://ccea.org.uk/ [Accessed 13 February 2021].

CfE (2021) *Education Scotland*. Available at: https://education.gov.scot/education-scotland/ [Accessed 13 February 2021].

DATA (2021) *Design and Technology Association: Secondary*. Available at: https://www.data.org.uk/for-education/secondary/ [Accessed 13 February 2021].

Dagan, O. (2020) STEM or S T E M in Israel. Available at: https://dandtfordandt.wordpress.com/papers/stem-across-the-world/ [Accessed 22 August 2022].

Dewey, J. (1997) *Experience and Education* (1st Touchstone edition, Vol. Kappa Delta Pi Lecture Series). New York: Simon & Schuster.

Dintersmith, T. (2018) *What School Could Be*. Princeton, USA: Princeton University Press.

Duyar, I.T., Mina, D.K. and Owoh, S.J. (2019). Promoting student creative problem-solving skills: Do principal instructional leadership and teacher creative practices matter? In Tuncer Fidan (ed), *Vocational Identity and Career Construction in Education* (78–99). IGI Global.

Fujita, S. and Lee, L.S. (2018) Curriculum revival?: Revisiting technology education in Taiwan. *Journal of the Japan Society of Technology Education*, 60(2), pp. 116–120.

Gates, W. (2021) 'Solving Covid Easy Compared with Climate': BBC. Available at: https://www.bbc.co.uk/news/science-environment-56042029 [Accessed 20 February 2021].

Gu, J., Wang, J. and Fujita, S. (2018) Evolution of technology and engineering education in Chinese primary schooling. *Journal of Japan Society for Technology Education*, 60(4), pp. 255–258.

Gunderson, S., Jones, R. and Scanland, K. (2004). *The Jobs Revolution: Changing How America Works*. Canada: Copywriters Inc.

Halfon, R (2020) 'The impact of COVID-19 on education and children's services': UK Parliament. Available at: https://committees.parliament.uk/work/202/the-impact-of-covid19-on-education-and-childrens-services/news/114704/the-impact-of-covid19-on-education-and-childrens-services/ [Accessed 20 February 2021].

Hallström, J., Hultén, M. and Lövheim, D. (2014) The study of technology as a field of knowledge in general education: historical insights and methodological considerations from a Swedish case study, 1842–2010. *International Journal of Technology and Design Education*, 24(2), pp. 121–139.

Hwb (2021) *Curriculum for Wales: Science and Technology*. Available at: https://hwb.gov.wales/curriculum-for-wales/science-and-technology/statements-of-what-matters/ [Accessed 13 February 2021].

ITEEA (2007) Standards for Technological Literacy: Content for the Study of Technology. Available at: https://www.iteea.org/42511.aspx [Accessed 26 July 2021].

ITEEA (2020) *Standards for Technological and Engineering Literacy*. Available at: https://www.iteea.org/ [Accessed 22 February 2021].

Kolb, D.A. (1984) *Experiential Learning: Experience as the Source of Learning and Development*. New Jersey: Prentice-Hall.

Kuen-Yi, L. (2017) *New Paradigm or Old Wine? The Development of STEM Education and Maker Education in Taiwan*. Keynote Address at TENZ-ICTE Conference, October 8–11, 2017, Christchurch, New Zealand.

Kuen-Yi, L. and Yu-Jen, S. (2020) *STEM in Taiwan*. Available at: https://dandtfordandt.wordpress.com/papers/stem-across-the-world/ [Accessed 22 February 2021].

Lombardi, M.M. (2007, May). Authentic learning for the 21st century: An overview. In D.G. Oblinger (ed.), *Educause Learning Initiative*. Available at: https://www.researchgate.net/profile/Marilyn_Lombardi/publication/220040581_Au [Accessed 22 August 2022].

Mammes, I., Fletcher, S., Lang, M. and Munk, D. (2016) Technology in Germany. In M.J. de Vries, S. Fletcher, S. Kruse, P. Labudde, M. Lang, I. Mammes, C. Max, D. Munk, B. Nicholl, J. Strobel and M. Winterbottom (eds.), *Technology Education Today* (pp. 11–38). Munster: Waxmann.

Moye J.J., Reed, P.A., Barbato, S.A. and Fujita, S. (2019) Technology education in the United States. *Journal of the Japan Society of Technology Education*, 61(4), pp. 333–341.

NACE (2017) 'The Key Attributes Employers Seek on Students' Resumes'. Available at:https://www.naceweb.org/about-us/press/2017/the-key-attributes-employers-seek-on-students-resumes/ [Accessed 26 July 2021].

National Planning Commission (NPC) (2012) *National Development Plan 2030: Our Future – Make It Work*. Pretoria: Presidency of South Africa.

Nordolf, C., Norström, P., Höst, G. and Hallström, J. (2021) Towards a three-part heuristic framework for technology education. *International Journal of Technology and Design Education*. doi:10.1007/s10798-021-09664-8.

Piaget, J. (1977) *Le comportement, moteur de l'evolution*. Paris: Editions Laffont.

Pinch, T. and Bijker, W.E. (1994) The social construction of facts and artifacts: Or how the sociology of science and the sociology of technology might benefit each other. In W.E. Bijker, T.P. Hughes and T.J. Pinch (eds.), *The Social Construction of Technological Systems. New Directions in the Sociology and History of Technology* (pp. 17–50). Cambridge, MA: MIT Press.

Potgieter, C. (2004) The impact of the implementation of technology education on in-service teacher education in South Africa (impact of technology education in the RSA). *International Journal of Technology and Design Education*, 14(2), pp. 205–218.

Skolvoket (2018) *Curriculum for the Compulsory School, Preschool Class and School-age Educare*. Available at: https://www.skolverket.se/ [Accessed 23 July 2021].

Wells, J.G. (2020) *STEM Education in U.S. Secondary Schools*. Available at: https://dandtfordandt.wordpress.com/papers/stem-across-the-world/ [Accessed 22 February 2021].

Williams, P.J., Ellis, D., Pagram, J., Macgregor, D., Seeman, K. and Fujita, Shinichi. (2019) A critical perspective on technology education in Australia. *Journal of the Japan Society of Technology Education*, 61(2), pp. 169–171.

Yang, C. and Ke, S. (2020) *The Development of STEM Education in China*. Available at: https://dandtfordandt.wordpress.com/papers/stem-across-the-world/ [Accessed 22 February 2021].

# 3 How do we do race in design and technology?

*Bhavna Prajapat, Rose Sinclair, and Alison Hardy*

## Introduction

This chapter deliberately takes a different format to others within this book. The authors and contributors have come together to co-author and collaborate on this work, which we think breaks new ground within design and technology. For the contributors, we are drawing on the teacher as researcher and the teacher as reflexive practitioner; the authors are drawing on their lived experiences to explore the question, How do we do race in design and technology? and begin the road to exploring some possible answers.

We also wondering: Who are the voices that have shaped the design and technology curriculum around race? Who are the voices that currently shape the design and technology curriculum around race, issues of decolonisation, definitions and clarifications?

The chapter starts with an overview of decolonisation and diversity in design and technology and then broadens out into understanding the language around race and diversity. The design discourse takes us to globalisation and cultural values and the monolithic space taken by only structuring the current design and technology curriculum with a Eurocentric modelling of design history. The narrative voices of teachers then provide the backdrop to the rest of the chapter; their voices speak to the differing experiences, their perspectives as reflective practitioners are there to offer thoughts and reflections and they do not yet provide answers. The chapter ends with a call to reclaim the curriculum and bring the marginalised voices in from the margins.

## Decolonisation and diversity: an overview

'Decolonising the curriculum', 'race', 'racism', 'anti-racism', 'diversity' and the 'global contribution to knowledge' are words, phrases, labels and terms that need unpicking for design and technology education. This is complex and not without some discomfort to black, brown and white people for different reasons (Eshun, 2021; Joseph-Salisbury, 2021). Debates on issues of race and racism have been going for many years, and we are still talking

DOI: 10.4324/9781003166689-5

about it (Gillborn, 2008; Sherrington, 2020; Joseph-Salisbury, 2021). We can look back to Beryl Gilroy's vivid documentary in her book *Black Teacher* (1994) in which she detailed her experience of racism in both teacher training and securing her first teaching placement; Beryl became one of Britain's first black headteachers in 1969. The wider experience of black male teachers in the east end of London in the 1960s was showcased in film *To Sir with Love* (1959) based on the experiences of E.R Braithwaite, who would go on be one of the founders of the Caribbean Artist Movement (CAM). (Note: CAM explored what is a Caribbean aesthetic in art and design and how to engage in new directions for Caribbean arts and culture that would have a direct impact on the Caribbean community [Walmsley, 1992] after centuries of European domination in the field arts and culture.)

Rollock and Gillborn's (2011) use critical race theory (CRT) to make sense of racism by explaining how racism is so normalised that most people do not even notice it, and some deny its existence or some try to silence the voices, as experienced by Sam Mikinde's account later in this chapter. CRT is based on personal narratives and advocates that racism is not just overt acts of violence. Lander (2021, slide 12) explains how 'racism is prevalent through inaction, silent act of omission, deletion, exclusion, apparent innocence or polite inclusion'. On occasions, Bhavna and Rose (two of the chapter's authors) and the four contributors have experienced the social unacceptance of racism and the subtler forms of racist behaviour, such as microaggression, ambivalence and ignorance.

Unless the root and impact of racism are fully understood by teachers, there will continue to be a cursory approach to addressing issues of race and racism (Hardy, 2022). For example, many teachers' response to decolonising the design and technology curriculum, as discussed later by Richard Harris, is about including images of designers who are not white, to represent diversity, which is necessary but, in our view, insufficient. Decolonising the design and technology curriculum is a process whereby there is a need to reorder, reclaim, reconnect, reapply and regain the use of methodologies, and design practices, that have been submerged or hidden or marginalised because of the community from which they come from.

There is a danger of tokenistic decolonisation if the focus is just on including designers and technologists only because of the colour of their skin. It may be a start, but the focus needs to be on putting design heritage first which is interlinked with cultural capital and design capital, acknowledging whose culture has capital and the technological engagement; if race is put at that forefront, it foregrounds the colour of the person, not the designs they create or the tangible heritage or knowledge contribution. Pran Patel, a teacher and secondary school senior leader, shared his experiences as an Asian pupil (TEDx, 2019) and of not having that interlinked cultural capital seen in his own British education. He explains how he could not answer to himself how his heritage's worth and contribution to the world or how the Eurocentric curriculum disadvantaged him, as he knew only white scholars and scientists and no one from other cultures. He argues that decolonising the curriculum is important and everyone knowing about sources of knowledge and acknowledging contributions from all over the world benefits all pupils, including learning that knowledge is not Eurocentric.

How can design and technology education can move away from a Eurocentric model of education and more toward understanding the diverse world we live in. What does a diverse design and technology curriculum look like? Bury and Marr (2021) point out that technological progress, achievements and advancements have advanced through multicultural exchanges of knowledge, skills and understanding. They outline a global trade that involved buying various materials and processing materials to form new materials taking place as far back as 2000 BCE in countries of the East and South. Also, some of the sophisticated remains of civilisations that were unearthed by archaeologists and the knowledge that was passed on by traders and invaders from far-away countries eventually reached the West. All this can be referred to in the content of teaching design and technology to dispel the myths about other races and cultures being 'uncivilised'. Knowledge from indigenous cultures and the involvement of minorities have contributed towards technological advancement (see Chapter 8 for more detail).

In this chapter, the authors and contributors introduce and raise issues that go beyond the curriculum that affect and effect how we understand and talk about race in design and technology. We are mindful that race sits alongside other issues of intersectionality and equality and social justice, for which this chapter is too short to explore, but as the issues about race develop, we want these other issues to also be explored by us and by others. As Rose wrote to Alison in response to the podcast episode *Decolonising the D&T curriculum* (Hardy, 2020):

> This discourse is wider than just 'decolonising the curriculum. It's about the internal and external structures and systems that are faced at each step to get to the classroom. It's about who has the knowledge, what knowledges are valued, how these knowledges are valued, and whose role is valued. It is more than just replacing books, and this is where the discourse about decolonising needs to change.
>
> (Sinclair, 2020)

There are numerous reasons why these discussions need to be had, and we believe this chapter to be one of the first formal discussion spaces where issues pertaining to race in design and technology have been brought together. A key aspect is the health and well-being of ethnic minorities who work with, teach and who are part of our community. Some minorities suffer from trauma as result of racism and racially motivated microaggressions, behaviours that derogate, undermine, invalidate, intimate, dismiss, belittle and many more that are often delivered to disadvantaged groups, and these behaviours can lead to a feeling of oppression and self-deprecation and sometimes result in mental health issues (Chakraborty and McKenzie, 2002; Sue, 2010). Bignall et al. (2019) state that black and minority ethnic people have a higher percentage of depression and mental illness, as well as poorer treatment and outcomes, disproportionally compared to white British.

Joseph-Salisbury (2021) and Sherrington (2020) provide some reasons as to what teachers will gain from increasing their racial literacy:

1. a depth of understanding about race and racism
2. the impact of racism
3. how race and racism work in society
4. language and skills for the classroom
5. knowledge to diversify the curriculum

This approach supports education policymakers to create a framework approach to diversity which has tended to homogenise race and colour offering a tokenised approach as discussed which could be symbolised through the trope of the three 's's': 'saris, samosas and steelbands' (Troyna in Modood and May, 2001). This tokenises race in the classroom rather than addressing the issues of how race can be researched and discussed within the confines of curriculum and how the lived experience of the school community could be formed through a progressive narrative.

The language of race and diversity is one that we feel is rarely, if ever, discussed in the design and technology curriculum but remains seated in wider school policy documents. Language around race and diversity and its use in design and technology still remain couched in terms related to cultural constructs than it is to the heritage or specifics of a design or the designer. To therefore start to understand how race can be discussed an understanding of the terms used and that are ascribed to race are briefly discussed.

## Understanding the language

We recognise that language and terms are loaded with history, meaning and offence. Here we discuss some terms and words used to talk about race. Language is contentious and you may disagree with the definitions below and our decisions. We expect that our decisions today will also be looked at in years to come as offensive and misguided. All we can say here is that we have made the best decisions we can, given our current knowledge, experiences and understanding.

The Law Society (2022) have comprehensive guidance on terminology and identifies the categorisation of race as

> rooted in White supremacy and effort to prove biological superiority and maintain dominance over others. . . . It's now widely accepted that race is a social construct. However, having been racialised and shared common experience of racism, racial identity is important to many and can be a basis for collective organising and support for racially minoritised individuals.

There is debate about which words, phrases and acronyms to use when talking about ethnicity and race. Blakemore (2019) unpicks and explains race, ethnicity and racism by first presenting a dictionary definition of *race* as 'a category of humankind that shares certain distinctive physical traits' (Merriam-Webster in Blakemore) which she says are 'usually associated with biology and linked with physical characteristics such as skin or hair'. She continues with the dictionary definition for *ethnicity* as 'large groups of people classed according to common racial, national, tribal, religious, linguistic, or cultural origin or background, [i.e.] cultural expression and identification, asserting that 'neither race nor ethnicity is detectable in the human genome'.

Gabriel (n.d.) explains why terms like BAME (Black, Asian and Minority Ethnic), BME (Black and Minority Ethnic) and people of colour (PoC) are problematic and reduce difference in addition to reinforcing racial inequality by excluding white as an identity; she suggests the term 'racialised minorities'. The UK government explains its reasons for the discontinued use of BAME, which placed the focus on race rather than heritage, and issued a guide to support those wanting to write about ethnicity in December 2021. Malik et al.'s (2021) report on the terminology review gives a comprehensive insight into why these terms are offensive and confusing; they offer the term *black* and *global majority* as an alternative that has its own limitations. The UK government argue that the term *ethnic minorities* draws attention to racialised and marginalised people and sums up the default meaning of any appellation being assigned, thus including white minorities such as Gypsy, Roma, Traveller and Irish, who also have a history of being marginalised people.

In this chapter, we use the term *ethnic minorities*; however, where the contributors have chosen to use other terms, we respect their decision.

## Designing for all – global inclusion

Why is design for all and global inclusion an issue? Here are a few examples which we think demonstrate why it is an issue:

- 'The Racist Soap Dispenser' (Futureism, 2017) that only dispensed soap to a white-skinned hand and not a black-skinned hand (this video went viral on YouTube).
- The Kodak photography company categorising light skin as normal. Any other skins colours came out as overexposed, and only when pressurised by the furniture and chocolate industries did Kodak address this issue (Seth, 2021).
- The beauty, film and theatre industries showing up as having a deficit when they only employ white make-up artists. Many white make-up artists do not know how to work with varied skin tones or varied hair types whereas black make-up artists learn about all skin colours and hair types (Fetto, 2019; Mohammed, 2021).

- Deodorant advert showing a woman turning from black to white (Oakes, 2017)
- Artificial intelligence (AI) face recognition. Amnesty International (2021) calls to 'ban dangerous facial recognition technology that amplifies racist policing' as it amplifies and misdirects towards racialised and marginalised communities as more likely to be in the wrong – stereotyped negatively.

These designs and marketing reinforce the message that lighter skin is more desirable. For some minorities at the receiving end of this form of racism there is pain, hurt and an erosion of self-esteem. Racism can become an internalised and self-deprecating practice, and regardless of race, people can become conditioned into a racialised way of thinking about skin colour, developing low self-esteem in people of colour; this is well documented by the doll experiments of Dr Kenneth and Mamie Clark in the 1950s (Agabond, 2008a, 2008b, 2009). Drs Clarke carried out studies with children aged three to seven using four dolls that were identical except for their colour. The children were asked about the race and colour of the dolls and which they preferred. The white dolls came out as the most preferred dolls, and most children associated the best traits with white dolls (LDF, 2020).

In this section we have provided a brief overview of some of the challenges caused by the design and marketing world that have supported the idea that light and white is best. If nothing else, we have provided some examples to use in design and technology classrooms, but we think if you stop here and read no further, then you are potentially taking the tokenistic route which was discussed earlier in the chapter. Next, we introduce our contributors who have shared their experiences and thoughts with us and you.

## Design and technology teachers of colour

Our teachers' narratives are their first-hand stories, their perspectives, and just like Gilroy and Braithwaite, they offer a new voice for a new generation of teachers. First, we hear from Richard Harris, who trained here in the UK and then worked abroad before returning to take up a position in a London school as a head of department, an award-winning teacher who writes from a personal perspective about how people of colour are represented in design and technology.

This is Richard's personal account of a moment of serendipity when his daughter asked him, 'Are all artists white?'

> Teachers observe that children will learn from each other and from what they see. It could be said that children aspire only to the careers that they know exist. Being a mixed-raced educator of design and technology, with a career of 17 years' experience, imagine my dismay when

my six-year-old daughter asked me the question, 'Are all artists white?' I promptly answered, 'No, anyone of any race may be an artist if they so wish'. During my daughter's parents' evening at her school, I noticed a poster of famous artists: all white, all male artists. My daughter's query now made sense, and the realisation of it hit hard. The message interpreted from a simple poster and its potential to create barriers to opportunities and careers made me think of my subject and what practices design and technology teachers use to represent people of colour in the subject.

Holly (2021) writes about people's perception of engineers as white men. In the curriculum we are taught that Thomas Edison invented the light bulb in 1879, but nobody teaches about Lewis Latimer, a black engineer who created the carbon light bulb filament in 1881 that made the light bulb durable. This is an example of a white, Eurocentric history teaching disregarding the black contribution to science (Science Council, 2019).

Although now we have positive initiatives instigated by Black History Month in schools, that raise awareness of people of colour in engineering and design-related industries. I work in a mixed state school in London, where the senior leadership team supported the decolonisation of the school curriculum where we could create a D&T [design and technology] curriculum that represents the famous black engineers and artists. The Royal Academy of Engineering (RAE, 2018), support the idea of diversity initiatives and emphasise how this is the responsibility of all teachers to make a real difference to children who need to see role models from a range of backgrounds and to raise the aspiration for all children.

RAE (2018) and the Design Council (2018) report that the design economy employs a higher proportion of minority groups compared to other industries and acknowledge that teachers have a role in making the design and engineering profession a career option. Ekeke (2021) reported that there is still much work to do as black people make up only 3% of the UK tech workforce.

It was good to see McFarland's (2021), feature in The Sunday Times of the African-American designer Virgil Abloh (1980–2021) [Note from Rose: Abloh went on to be the first African American to be an artistic director at the French luxury fashion house Louis Vuitton, then became the CEO of Off-White and is credited with linking street fashion with haute couture. He was noted as one of the top 100 influential people in *Time* magazine in 2018]. The media has the power to counteract harmful stereotypes, and present positive role models of successful black and ethnic minorities, thus creating a future where young children will not ask questions relating to race and careers.

Just as Richard Harris raises questions of visibility, the wider design canon shows that the invisibility of any narrative related to the black experience of design is detrimental to a broad understanding of the history of design as subject.

Victor Margolin, the design historian, highlighted the need to broaden the 'canon' in design history to include the marginalised but consistently came up against a lack of existing narrative through which he could frame and discuss ways in which design history, itself, could and should highlight the notion of a range of contributions to the grand narrative. Sylvia Harris (a black graphic designer) posits that for many black designers in the design industry, 'we are taught to follow historical trails laid out by Eurocentric modernists and American traditionalists. I began to realise there is not a monolithic/white style' (Berry et al. 2022: 35). Smith (2012) and Tunstall (2013) highlight the scarcity of history in trying to locate a linear narrative of those who are marginalised in the wider discourses of design. Tunstall (2013: 236) frames this within the grand narratives that 'ignores non-Western ways of thinking rooted in craft practices that predate yet live alongside modern techniques' alongside the domination of 'how-to guides' that perpetuate the narrative of the dominant Western design ideology, design thinking and problem-solving grounded in linear and rational approaches to design but that ignores local knowledge, misunderstand ethnicity, undermining local people, cultures and practices (Smith, 2012; Tunstall, 2013; Manthalu and Waghid, 2019).

Next Sam Makinde, a design and technology teacher, shares his experiences and thoughts when he asked design and technology teachers for ideas.

> With diversity on my mind, I went online to a design and technology teachers community page, requesting project ideas that are culturally inclusive. I was hoping that other colleagues might have successfully completed one they might share. Almost immediately, a reply was posted that appeared to challenge my request and argued for design and technology focus to be on culturally neutral projects and that anything else was divisive. This was quickly followed by similar comments. Although this might not have been the view of everyone, there were no other comments to support my request.
>
> Despite the initial reaction that almost silenced me, I persisted and pointed out the need for teachers to start considering inclusion for all and received some supportive responses.
>
> My experience of the lack of visibility of black engineers and designers makes it difficult for teachers to generate representative/diverse teaching materials and this can appear as a lack of appreciation of the other cultures and non-acknowledgement of the contribution of black designers and engineers. My awareness of the Eurocentric content in

> the design and technology curriculum accentuates the same tradition of non-inclusive ideas, materials, or topics that bears little resemblance to diversity thus, undervaluing contributions of other cultures or a possibility of subconscious bias that they are of a lower calibre when compared to the British made ones.
>
> I base this on my experience of social media, where I have noticed that people are often quick to respond without thinking and can come across as thoughtless, defensive or deliberately offensive. For example, how everyday products such as televisions, light bulbs and phones that are made in China, Taiwan or India often have disparaging comments, some of which have racial undertones and implications of being bad or faulty design due to the country of origin.
>
> All the same it was great to see the emerging evidence of black faces such as a Nigerian-born designer's exhibition at the Design Museum (2020) which launched a schools' competition event. Exhibitions that reflect global representations go in tandem with change in attitudes and conceptions as well as theoretical, cultural and practical inclusion of ideas, products and materials that have been the privilege enjoyed by white designers for many years.

What emerges from these two distinct dialogues and narratives are notions of absent voices, plus a call to reclaim and reposition the voice of design and design heritage and retell new stories. The inclusion of this voice, however, needs to start before students start secondary education, as Richard Harris points out – his six-year-old daughter has already surmised that all artists are white because that's all she's seen.

Building on Sam's experience, we suggest that the starting point is to challenge and reclaim the stories to broaden the canon and refresh and redress the existing dialogues of design thinking, knowledge and understanding. The lack of historical reference to black British-based designers is telling. We would need to go back to 1957 to reference one of the first designers of Caribbean heritage making their mark on British postmodern design, Trinidadian designer Althea McNish (1924–2020), but she and others do not feature in the design and technology textbooks or exam specifications. We are aware this is changing but it leaves us with a dilemma of how to map the design legacy for people of colour from 1957 to 2021 and beyond in order to bring it into the design and technology curriculum.

The good news is that minorities and women are achieving more recognition in the workspace. In some classrooms, there is evidence of diversity and teachers are working to include everybody. Leila Marr, an advanced skills teacher with 10 years' experience in the classroom, shares her perspective as a female teacher of colour.

Being a black female design and technology teacher has a real status of its own. It represents positivity and a strong role model for all students, schools and the D&T community. Unfortunately, the School Teacher Workforce data from the DfE (2021) show that representation of teachers from an ethnic background continues to be very low and out of teachers whose ethnicity was known:

- White British people made up 92.7% of head teachers, 89.7% of deputy or assistant head teachers and 84.9% of classroom teachers
- 0.1% of classroom teachers were Mixed White and Black African – the lowest percentage out of all ethnic groups in this role
- 0.1% of deputy and assistant head teachers were from the Mixed White and Black African, and Chinese ethnic groups – the lowest percentage out of all ethnic groups in this role

It would appear that the ethnicity data of subject specialisms teachers in the UK is not collected by the DfE or by the subject organisations. Hence, the picture presented is not clear, and from this, we cannot then tell how with the subject any inconsistencies can be addressed.

Studying in the 1980s, I was taught materials by white males and home economics and fashion and textiles by white females. This perception didn't change when I was training as a design and technology teacher in the 1990s. Black and ethnic minority design and technology teachers in my own education were rare.

After a lesson observation, I was in conversation with the Hertfordshire County advisor for design and technology, who encouraged me to apply for the role of an advanced skills teacher (AST). Not once did I think this was about my race or gender as it was a moment of my excellent practice being recognised, seen and heard. I was the first AST specialising in graphic products. I did occasionally think about what some teachers would feel about a black female AST coming in to support them. Fortunately, that there was never a problem, but it does indicate the thought process of a black person. This is an example of white privilege and not having to think about who you are culturally.

I was an AST for design and technology for ten years, and my role was to support a range of schools in Hertfordshire, which is a predominantly white area. I worked with few non-ethnic and non-white heads of departments (HoD) and newly qualified teachers (NQTs). The low numbers made me reflect that this is just not enough to make a difference for ethnic minority students in some areas.

Years of observing structural racism and inequalities have an impact and for me it interferes with my thinking about myself. Although,

I was, encouraged to apply for the HoD position, I questioned myself about being a black female, my experience, my subject expertise and whether I would be accepted against a young white male, who would be cheaper and fit in with an all-boys school. I wonder if any other black and ethnic teachers have similar thoughts and go through same processes in which the 'ethnic' identity takes up a large thinking space and often is perceived as a barrier to progress.

To understand specific barriers to recruiting a diverse workforce in the motoring industry, The Hamilton Commission (set up by Sir Lewis Hamilton) reported that '[a] lack of black teachers and leaders in schools [limited] the number of positive role models' (2021, p.18) Ethnic minority students need visible role models, that is people who look like them to inspire them. I feel, that as design and technology teachers, we need to show young students from ethnic minority communities, that they can be and are part of history in design, technology and the wider industries to promote change and make a difference for our future.

My own experience of being a black design and technology teacher has been positive and I can incorporate as much cultural inspiration as possible. Sharing the lived experience from different backgrounds and using the history of a range of iconic designers is a celebration of change and part of the future curriculum. I know that wherever you come from, in design and technology, culture can be embedded throughout the curriculum, and not in a tokenistic way.

The representation of people of colour matter in the content of teaching of design and technology, and we need to be seen, heard and recognised. We need to make visible the black and ethnic designers, engineers and much more to give young students an incentive to believe they can succeed. Where better to start than to show students that they are open to all possibilities regardless of what background they come from.

The consistent message from the teachers' narratives is that we need to see more examples of designers and engineers who look like us in the materials we use to present to the diverse student population that we all teach. More than that, we need to be able to provide those pupils and the other teachers we work with examples they can draw on to support a more inclusive curriculum, with an aspirational cultural curriculum, that is not embedded within a tokenistic framework. The lack of ethnicity data in relation to teachers, however, from both the DfE and other professional subject associations, increases the challenge to providing meaningful strategies to support teachers from ethnic minorities, at all stages of their career progression. What begins to be apparent that for students to thrive and engage teachers of colour build schemes of work that draw on cultural heritage.

## A way forward?

The final voice we hear is that of Marlene Wylie, who shares her experiences within the art and design education community. As we write this chapter, Marlene is the president elect of NSEAD (National Society for Education in Art and Design), the subject association for art and design. We asked Marlene to contribute because she is a colleague of colour involved in leading a creative subject. We had heard about her work at NSEAD and wanted to share it as a way that one group have decided to take to begin to develop an anti-racist creative curriculum. Much has been done in history education to decolonise the curriculum (see work led by Dr Marlon Moncrieffe at the University of Brighton for examples) but not so much as far as we can see in creative subjects. NSEAD's work may provide a template for design and technology, if not some thoughts for reflection.

> **Call to Action**
>
> The blatant killing of George Floyd, witnessed globally is, in my view, the physical manifestation of why we as educators need to be deeply immersed in reflection and introspection on race. Systemic racism is still undeniably prevalent in organisations today, and by admission NSEAD, with social justice at its core, has recognised that despite our deeply committed mission since 1888 to improve art, craft and design education for everyone there is still much work to do.
>
> I have been an enthusiastic and committed member of NSEAD for 25 years and have served two terms as vice president. My call to leadership as president elect during this term, 2022, as a woman of colour, has proved to be highly significant. I am acutely aware that the successes that I have achieved in my career over the years are a result of a variety of quite complex navigations.
>
> Often the only person of colour present around the table has been my experience for much of my creative and professional life. My journey as an artist, designer and educator has left me with complete conviction that we have to support one another in understanding where we are in terms of our racial literacy and recognise that there is still work to do to challenge the current colonial and Eurocentric educational landscape.

> **Anti-Racist Actions**
>
> Immediately following the toppling of the monument to the British slave trader Colston by protestors in Bristol, swift action was taken to respond to this moment by the NSEAD general and assistant general secretary. Supported by the council and prompted by our enthusiastic members, we wasted no time in setting out how as a society we would seek to disrupt racism in our subject. It was felt that we could not

watch this moment in the history of art in silence. Much discussion took place at a strategic level about the importance of how we set out to achieve this disruption.

In early June 2020, we published our resolve, making clear what we wanted to achieve in five days, five weeks, five months, and five years. Our call to be a collective voice in ensuring we are an anti-racist organisation. By way of creating a task force, we set out to identify what actions we needed as interventions to ensure that our subject, art educators and policy makers are anti-racist in actions and intentions. We stated clearly in our communications that our strategic plan over the next five years had to deliver on our promise to address equality, diversity and inclusion throughout the organisation and beyond.

**Formation of our Anti-Racist Art Education Checklist and Support**

The instigation of our Anti-Racist Art Education Action Group in July 2020 as our task force was integral to the development of a series of materials to support the changes we need to see. This group contributed a combination of expertise and lived voice to create three Anti-Racist Art Education Checklists to support art educators and partner organisations in the review of their curriculums, publications and resources. Although we have used the term *checklist*, they are to be considered more a tool to open up conversation, support questioning and review current provision. We want to make clear that the support materials are not created as a linear 'to-do' list but rather as a means by which one can actively engage in the process of critically reviewing our decision-making, actions and language. The philosophy and recommendations on how to use the checklists are provided by NSEAD through a specially designated area on our website (search for 'Anti-Racist Art Education (ARAE) Resources' on the NSEAD website). We expect these support materials to evolve over time as we continue our journey of learning and unlearning. We believe that it is only through constant reflection, questioning, feedback and collaboration that we can become actively anti-racist.

As president elect of NSEAD for 2022, I am encouraged that we as a society recognise that we have a duty to be part of true and lasting change. We are aware that we have reached a tipping point in ensuring that we up our game in working towards achieving our mission. As a result of new insights, academic research and lived voice, it would be true to say that this endeavour will be forever ongoing as we respond to shifts in our thinking and experiences. We could say that there are many priorities in our work and one of our imperatives now has become to actively address how we would seek to become an actively anti-racist association.

## Conclusion

If race and racism are to become things of the past, then the issues pertaining to race and racism become the responsibility of all teachers as educators seek to provide an anti-racist approach to the curriculum. But it is important to flag a potential problem with this. Leonardo and Porter (2010: 139) outline the conflict as, on one hand, creating a 'safe' place, where 'whites can avoid publicly 'looking racist', which then overwhelms their reasons for participating in racial dialogue', and, on the other, denying a space for minorities to have an honest dialogue about race, racism, inequality and injustice and those that speak out not to 'become overt targets of personal and academic threats [or at] at risk of violence' (p. 14). When debating the editorship and contribution of this chapter, we wanted to create a safe space for everyone involved, where the one white editor, Alison, was not denying space for the other two, nor was she been provided with a space to avoid 'looking racist'. Instead, the editors and contributors have worked as allies to begin this conversation and debate about the issues that arise from a Eurocentric curriculum, with few voices heard or seen from ethnic minorities in design and technology. We hope this chapter models a safe starting point for how the whole design and technology community can address the question, How do we do race in design and technology?

The need therefore to reclaim, recall and offer an opportunity to thrive in the space is essential for teachers of all colours. The advancement of our subject demands a new reading of design as heritage and design as cultural construct that draws on all our heritage and knowledge in a combination of ways and through learning. The narratives in this chapter seek to capture what is still missing and start to open discussion on what could be potential new futures to open doors that invite communities to thrive.

## Questions

1. Why are conversations around race difficult when deconstructing design and technology education? What is at the root of this difficulty?
2. How do you define *inclusive design*? How does your definition differ from the discussions in this chapter?
3. How can different narratives be used in creating design briefs that invite a global approach to designing and making?
4. How can design and technology visualise (educate about) the idea of a global citizen?

## References

Agabond, J. (2009). *The Clark Doll experiment. Agabond* [online blog], 29 May. Available at: https://bit.ly/38idzYF [Accessed 22 November 2021].

Agabond, J. (2008a). All Whites are racists. *Agabond* [online blog], 6th August. Available at: https://bit.ly/3qJQvYY. [Accessed 22 November 2021].

Agabond, J. (2008b). All Blacks are racists. *Agabond* [online blog], 8 August. Available at: https://bit.ly/3IREeYK [Accessed 22 November 2021].

Amnesty International (2021). *EU: Proposed legislation on artificial intelligence 'falls short'* [online]. Available at: https://www.amnesty.org.uk/press-releases/eu-proposed-legislation-artificial-intelligence-falls-short [Accessed 25 March 2022].

Berry, A.H., Collie, K., Laker, P., Noel L., Rittner, J. and Walters, K. (2022). *The Black Experience in Design*. New York: Allworth Press.

Bignall, T., Jeraj, S., Helsby, E. and Butt, J. (2019). *Racial disparities in mental health: Literature and evidence review, Racial Equality Foundation*[online]. Race Equality Foundation. Available at: https://bit.ly/3qOSXxh. [Accessed 22 November 2021].

Blakemore, E. (2019). Race and ethnicity, explained. National Geographic [online], 23 February. Available at: https://www.nationalgeographic.co.uk/history/2019/02/race-and-ethnicity-explained. [Accessed 25 February 2022].

Bury, M. and Marr, L. (2021). Design and technology. In M. Cole (Ed.), *Equality in the Secondary School: Promoting Good Practice Across the Curriculum* (pp. 87–106). London: Continuum.

Chakraborty, A. and McKenzie, K. (2002). Does racial discrimination cause mental illness? *British Journal of Psychiatry*, 180(6), pp. 475–477. doi:10.1192/bjp.180.6.475. [Accessed 22 November 2021].

Department for Education (2021). *School Teacher Workforce*. Department for Education.

Design Council (2018). Does design have a diversity issue? Available at: https://www.designcouncil.org.uk/news-opinion/does-design-have-diversity-issue [Accessed 11 November 2021].

Ekeke, O. (2021). *Tackling tech's big diversity problem starts with education* [online]. The Wired. Available at https://www.wired.co.uk/article/racial-equality-tech. [Accessed 15 February 2022].

Eshun, E. (2021). *White mischief: The background hum*, 4th October [BBC Radio 4]. Available at: https://www.bbc.co.uk/sounds/series/m00106bz [Accessed October 2021].

Fetto, F. (2019). *The beauty industry is still failing black women*. The Guardian [online] 29 September. Available at: https://bit.ly/3NtYSln [Accessed 25 November 2021].

Futureism (2017). This 'Racist soap dispenser' at Facebook office does not work for black people. [YouTube] *Futureism* 18 August. Available at: https://www.youtube.com/watch?v=YJjv_OeiHmo [Accessed 25 March 2022].

Gabriel, D. (n.d.). Racial categorisation and terminology. Black British Academics [online]. Available at: https://blackbritishacademics.co.uk/about/racial-categorisation-and-terminology/. [Accessed 25 March 2022].

Gillborn, D. (2008). *Racism and Education: Coincidence or Conspiracy?* (1st ed.). Oxforshire, UK: Routledge.

Gilroy, B. (1994). *Black Teacher*. London: Bogle L'Ouverture.

The Hamilton Commission (2021). *Accelerating Change: Improving Representation of Black People in UK Motorsport*. Project Forty Four Limited.

Hardy, A. (2022). *How do we do race in D & T?* Nottingham Institute of Education [online blog], 18 February. Available at: https://bit.ly/36DJvpC [Accessed 25 March 2022].

Hardy, A. (2020). *Decolonising the D&T curriculum*. Talking D&T [podcast] Available at: https://dralisonhardy.com/tdt30-decolonising-the-dt-curriculum/ [Accessed 25 March 2022].

Holly, J. (2021). 3 Ways schools can improve STEM learning for Black students. *The Conversation* [online], 6 June. Available at: https://bit.ly/3IQl3yj [Accessed 25 February 2022].

Joseph-Salisbury, R. (2021). *Race and racism in English Secondary Schools a report.* Black History Month. Available at: https://bit.ly/35osNKt [Accessed November 2021].

Lander (2021). *Hopeful or hopeless? Teacher education in turbulent times,* [Powerpoint presentation] at *University Brighton, School of Education Research and Enterprise Conference,* 12th July 2021. Available at: https://bit.ly/3uFx0C3 [Accessed November 2021].

The Law Society (2022). A guide to race and ethnicity terminology and language. Available at: https://www.lawsociety.org.uk/topics/ethnic-minority-lawyers/a-guide-to-race-and-ethnicity-terminology-and-language. [Accessed 22 March 2022].

LDF (2020). A revealing experiment: Brown v. Board and 'The Doll Test' [online]. Available at: https://bit.ly/3tNrJJn [Accessed 14 February 2022].

Leonardo, Z. and Porter, R.K. (2010). Pedagogy of fear: Toward a Fanonian theory of 'safety' in race dialogue. *Race Ethnicity and Education,* 13(2), pp. 139–157, doi:10.1080/13613324.2010.482898

Malik, S., Ryder, M., Marsden, S. and Lawson, R. (2021). *BAME: A Report on the Use of the Term and Responses to It – Terminology Review for the BBC and Creative Industries.* Birmingham: Sir Lenny Henry Centre for Media Diversity, Birmingham City University.

Manthalu, C. H. and Waghid, Y. (2019). *Education for Decoloniality and Decolonisation in Africa.* [Online]. Cham: Springer International Publishing AG.

McFarland, J. (2021). The rise and the rise of Virgil Abloh. The Sunday Times [online] 21 May. Available at: https://www.thetimes.co.uk/article/the-rise-and-rise-of-virgil-abloh-05b3rph2z [Accessed 20 November 2021].

Modood, T. and May, S. (2001). Multiculturalism and education in Britain: An internally contested debate. *International Journal of Educational Research,* 35(3), pp. 305–317, doi:10.1016/S0883-0355(01)00026-X

Mohammed, S. (2021). Leomie Anderson has called out the lack of Black makeup artists in the fashion industry: 'Why do I look like I work in the mines?' [online]. Glamour Magazine. Available at: https://bit.ly/3qPMsdP [Accessed 25 November 2021].

Oakes, O. (2017). *Dove 'deeply regrets' campaign showing woman turning from black to white* [online]. PRWeek. Available at: https://bit.ly/3uIc4Kv [Accessed 15 February].

Rollock, N. and Gillborn, D. (2011). Critical Race Theory (CRT), British Educational Research Association online resource. Available at https://www.bera.ac.uk/publication/critical-race-theory-crt [Accessed 25 February 2022].

Royal Academy of Engineering (2018). Designing inclusion into education. Available at: https://bit.ly/382I0BI [Accessed 17 October 2021].

Science Council (2019). Black history month: Insight into the lives and scientific inventions of material marvels. *Science Council* [blog] 11 October. Available at: https://bit.ly/38dDrop [Accessed 20 November 2021].

Seth, R. (2021). 'If not for the internet...'. *Deccan Herald* [online], 21 November. Available at: https://bit.ly/3IRF4ES [Accessed 24 November 2021].

Sherrington, T. (2020). *Towards an antiracist Curriculum, Step 1, Reading.* Teacherhead [blog]. Available at: https://bit.ly/3uEvPCW [Accessed 10 November 2021].

Sinclair, R. (2020). *Decolonising Design Podcast and update.* 23 June. Email to: Alison Hardy.

Smith, L.T. (2012). *Decolonizing Methodologies: Research and Indigenous Peoples.* (2nd ed). Otago, New Zealand: Otago University Press.

Sue, D.W. (2010). *Microaggressions and Marginality: Manifestations, Dynamic, and Impact.* Hoboken, NJ: Wiley.

TEDx (2019). Decolonise the curriculum. Available at: https://bit.ly/3LsDZF4 [Accessed March 2022].

Tunstall, E. (2013). Decolonizing design innovation: Design anthropology, critical anthropology, and indigenous knowledge. In W. Gunn, T. Otto, and R. C. Smith (Eds.), *Design Anthropology – Theory and Practice* (pp. 232–250). London & New York: Bloomsbury Publishing Plc.

Walmsley, A. (1992). *The Caribbean Artists Movement 1966–72: A Literal and Cultural History.* London, UK: New Beacon Books.

# Part II
# Debates about design and technology

# 4 Why did design and technology education fail, and what might replace it?

*David Spendlove*

## Introduction

The Bramble Cay melomys can be regarded as a metaphor for design and technology (D&T) as it is acknowledged as the first mammal to be reported extinct due to human-induced climate change (Fulton, 2017). Whilst D&T may not yet be extinct and is equally not a rodent, few subjects in the history of formal education have experienced, in the way that D&T have, such a rapid rise followed by a dramatic threat to its existence. Across approximately a 30-year period, D&T examination entries in England have fallen by almost 80% since the start of the new millennium whilst the governance and infrastructure supporting the subject have equally withered. If we therefore consider parallel matters such as changing environments and evolutionary theory, we can contemplate how insufficient adaption to the significant and rapid changes in the external education ecosystem has led to the rapid demise of the subject. Likewise, it is regarded that the Bramble Cay melomys was a mammal that was 'allowed' to become extinct, 'because it was not a flagship species' (Fulton, 2017, p. 2), and in the same way, we can regard the demise of D&T in England occurring not necessarily through a single catastrophic event but rather through the series of unintended consequences that have 'allowed' a non-'flagship' subject to implode. However, like humanity itself, perhaps D&T evolved as a result of a set of unusual environmental factors that saw it come into existence and evolve rapidly, and as a consequence, we perhaps should not be surprised that it has remained more susceptible to threats and vulnerabilities than other curriculum areas.

In reading this introduction, you might therefore be tempted to consider that so far, this is all a bit downbeat and what has it got to do with you, particularly if you are just starting out in the subject? Well, the aim for this chapter is to not only capture something of the history of the subject in order to offer a personal perspective in order to contextualise how the subject got to where it is. However, in addition, hopefully reading this chapter are the future local, national and international leaders of the next iteration of the subject in which it will be essential to understand both the complexity of the D&T education ecosystem and the particular points of failure in the original version of the subject that will need attention in order to try to avoid repeating the same errors again. It should also be pointed out that whilst the focus of this chapter is primarily within the English education context, the political and educational themes are increasingly international and interchangeable and subsequently may help serve as a warning for those who have yet to be impacted by such challenges.

In this chapter, I therefore take a deliberately provocative position by considering how D&T as a subject has ultimately failed to sufficiently adapt to the changing environment in order to become an established 'flagship' curriculum subject in England's education system. In doing so, I explore how the ecosystem that should have sustained the subject also failed intellectually, pedagogically, politically and organisationally to preserve the subject and as a consequence how the subject entity has in itself failed to adapt in order to survive.

By identifying the interrelated double failure of both the subject and the ecosystem, I am attempting to do this through adopting a critical and designerly reflection in order to better understand not only how design and technology as a 'product' has been failed but also how the essential elements of the next incarnation may achieve a greater degree of success, increased robustness and a more sustainable future in any future iteration of the 'subject' – should the subject survive and evolve from its current predicament. In critiquing D&T, it is perhaps also important to provide some level of reassurance to the reader by stating that my starting position is based on my belief that a form of 'design and technology' education should exist within children's general learning entitlement, but sadly, we know good arguments alone will not secure the subject's future. Therefore, it is incumbent for those within the subject, who have sufficient domain-specific understanding, to be the subject's own fiercest critics. Ultimately, it is those within the subject who can comprehend the nuance and explore the interrelationship of the complexity of education sustainability and policy reform who are in a position to identify a better way forward for D&T.

In this chapter, I propose that D&T has been allowed to decline as a result of political neglect, bad timing and inconsistent and misjudged governance based on the following themes:

- Political disregard, educational change and school structures
- New teacher supply and development
- Governance and contradictions

I also examine the ecosystem that nurtured a potentially forward-thinking, interdisciplinary creative subject whilst examining how such distinctive qualities also contributed to the decline of D&T.

Finally, through examining what happened in the past, I speculate on what may happen in the future whilst also proposing alternative ways for unique aspects of D&T to thrive.

## Political disregard, educational change and school systems

The biggest impact accelerating the recent collapse of D&T came from the 2010 Conservative party election win and the formation of a coalition government with the Liberal Democrat party spearheaded by Michael Gove as secretary of state for Education implementing a radical change agenda. Whilst it could be argued that the subject was already in decline and that D&T lacked the robustness to adapt to a change in the political climate, it remains clear that D&T was not at the forefront of ministers' minds when they engaged in a period of rapid and radical educational reform. Therefore, rather than through a deliberate and purposeful act, I would argue that primarily through negligence, disregard and unintended consequences D&T was 'allowed' to rapidly deteriorate primarily due to both the radical restructuring of school governance alongside the privileging of particular ideologies within the curriculum that typically excluded the subject in the following ways.

### Structural reform of schools

The Conservative-led coalition government significantly promoted and incentivised a changing school structure, including extending the Academies Programme that had previously been introduced under New Labour (1997–2010). Ironically design and technology had been a beneficiary of a previous restructuring of schools when the City Technology Colleges were introduced in 1986 following the emergence of specialist technology 'colleges' in 1992. However, the 2010 incarnation of Academies and 'free schools' were to be publicly funded schools but which operated with increased autonomy existing outside local authority control. This last point is particularly significant as pockets of effective D&T often existed within local education authorities which frequently had effective and forward-thinking subject advisory services.

In many respects, the national network of advisers was a cornerstone of the subject and along with those involved in initial teacher education had very much been a key element of developing the subject in the 1970s and 1980s. Therefore, the emergence and establishment of multi-academy trusts effectively removed the network of advisors for the subject. In addition, the freedoms that came with 'Academisation' also gave headteachers the opportunity to significantly reduce the amount of time provided for design and technology which for reasons of cost, time, difficulties in recruitment of teachers, performance measures or weak departments has often resulted in many schools significantly reducing their provision of the subject. Subsequently whilst pockets of provision have been created and sustained across some multi-academy trusts ultimately the structural reform of schools has accelerated the fragmentation of D&T.

### Curriculum reform

Central to the 2010 coalition government's mantra was a prescriptive and narrow focus on a rigorous 'knowledge rich' cultural literacy based on the work of E. D. Hirsch et al. (1988), which manifested itself through radical changes to both the national curriculum and General Certificate of Secondary Education (GCSE). In addition, the English Baccalaureate (EBacc) further privileged a number of GCSE 'academic subjects' which would be used as a measure of a school's performance in relation to how many pupils were studying History or Geography, English, Mathematics, Science and a Modern Language. The introduction of the EBacc therefore marginalised particular subjects, as well as emphasising specific pedagogies and forms of assessment that would promote a 'neo-traditional' view of schooling driven by the schools minister Nick Gibb. The schools minister's distain for anything considered creative, enquiry-based or constructivist is evidenced by his recollection of an early experience of problem-solving which made little sense to him as he recalled the 'absurd lesson' in geography when he was asked to justify where to put a capital city on a 'blank, made-up island', as well as 'another lesson where he was told to 'make the mess of wires, batteries and bulbs he was given, work' (Gibb, 2018). One does wonder what would have happened if those activities had been appropriately scaffolded for the young Gibb!

Unfortunately, the rapid structural and curriculum changes, whilst promoted by the government as the restoring of rigour and autonomy, created the additional impact of marginalising subjects such as D&T. These increasingly radical reforms to teacher preparation and pedagogy, through a populist ideology centred on neo-traditional anti-progressive (Craske, 2020) approaches, have therefore further destabilised the shallow foundations of design and technology. As a result, the profound curriculum reform encompassing the national curriculum, Progress 8, EBacc alongside the marginalisation of creative subjects saw GCSE examination entries for design and technology fall by two thirds from 270,000 in 2010 to 90,000 entries in 2020.

## New teacher supply and development

The much-paraphrased McKinsey and McKinsey (2007) statement of 'the quality of an education system cannot exceed the quality of its teachers,' is probably best regarded as a metaphor rather than a statement of fact. However, the assertion does provide a useful lens through which we can consider the demise of D&T, as the reality is that the future development and aspirations for D&T would not only be contingent on maintaining the supply of high-quality teachers but also be dependent on the ongoing and continuous professional development of an entire workforce. Such professional development can also be considered as particularly significant given that D&T has always been a subject undergoing rapid transformation in both content and pedagogy.

In many respects, the ongoing transformation of the D&T community has been one of the major challenges for those involved in the development of D&T teachers as there has rarely been a genuine consensus as to what the best pathway of development for teachers should be. In addition, new teachers have often been straddling multiple identities in trying to align themselves with past, present and future orientations of the subject. As a teacher educator, I would often be involved in the selection and training of new teachers from a variety of subjects, and although it is a generalisation, I would suggest that the background, trajectory and perceptions of D&T trainee teachers were often the most diverse when compared to other subjects. Likewise, the variety of experiences that new teachers would engage with as part of their teaching practices would be incredibly different given the variations of status, history and expertise that exists across different D&T departments.

This multitude of experiences and diversity of D&T provision can also be considered to have increased significantly from 2010 onwards and as previously alluded, we saw both a radical shake-up of the structure of schools, the transformation of the curriculum and significant change in initial teacher education. Accordingly, not only were there changes in the national curriculum, GCSE and A Levels but also how and where new teachers were trained was also transformed through moving teacher training to an increasingly 'school-led' system that provocatively offered 'the best schools and leaders control [over] which teachers are recruited and how they are trained' (DfE, 2016, p. 24) whilst allowing schools potentially a greater say in shaping what teachers should learn.

Although the government rhetoric and posturing around a 'school-led' approach were effectively an artificial binary, given that schools had operated in well-established partnerships with universities for many years, the combination of reduced financial incentives to train as a teacher in D&T, the uncertainty over the curriculum and the increased diversity of routes into teaching has ultimately had a destabilising impact on the subject. Hence, the number of teachers recruited in D&T has fallen approximately two thirds from circa 1200 in 2010–2011 to less than 400 in 2019–2020. This dramatic reduction also corresponds with an incentivised growth in the number of teacher education 'providers', including 'school-led' provision with the inevitable impact of more providers training fewer trainee teachers and a significant loss of the critical mass and community amongst cohorts. This has also had the impact of increasing volatility within the university sector, resulting in not only a significant reduction in full-time academics working in higher education but also the knock-on impact of reduced curriculum development, scholarship and research capacity across the sector.

Once again, we can see that a further combination of factors has had a dramatic impact on D&T, and whilst it could be argued that the subject was merely a victim of a series of unintended consequences, the changing environment for teacher training and development has had a destabilising impact on the subject. Therefore, in returning to the initial McKinsey quote, the extensive deregulation, a loss of expertise and critical mass mean that the quality of D&T teachers can no longer be assured to the extent that is required, and because of this, the future quality of the D&T education system cannot be sufficiently guaranteed in the absence of an appropriate infrastructure.

## Governance and contradictions

In examining the relatively short history of D&T as a formal area of the curriculum, it is useful to consider the key role of governance and associated organisations that have played a part in both the establishment and subsequent unravelling of the subject. Within this context perhaps the central organisation throughout the life span of the subject has been the Department for Education, which has existed in numerous incarnations often representing different political priorities of the time. For example at the start of the inception of the national curriculum around 1988 the name was the Department of Education and Science (DES), whilst from 1995–2001 'employment' was prioritised by the Labour government through the Department for Education and Employment (DfEE) before changing to an emphasis on skills as the Department for Education and Skills until 2007. Reflecting a broader cultural change and emphasis on families, the Department for Children, Schools and Families was operational until the following Liberal and Conservative governments removed this emphasis, reverting back to the DfE in 2010.

As noted, these changes of name should not be considered insignificant as they have coincided with major reforms that have had a profound influence on the ecosystem within which design and technology has either thrived or been denied influence. Likewise the changing political parties in power have equally used policy to promote and deny the growth of the subject with perhaps the most significant being the Conservative Education Reform Act 1988 which established 'Technology' as a Foundation National Curriculum Subject (1988, DES). It is therefore ironic that design and technology can be seen to have both been nurtured and dismantled by Conservative governments.

### *Quasi-Autonomous Non-Governmental Organisation*

A further key aspect of governance aligned to government influence has been through those organisations that have been established or supported by the government previously in the form of quangos (quasi-autonomous non-governmental organisations) to facilitate the growth and development of subjects. As such, up until 2010, D&T can be considered to have benefitted from these organisations in particular through the Qualifications Curriculum Development Authority (QCDA) and the Training and Development Agency (TDA) for schools. Both organisations, whilst not without their problems, had a supportive and considered approach in encouraging the development of the subject. The closure of these organisations at the start of the Conservative and Liberal coalition government in 2010 therefore meant that key allies within these organisations were lost. This may well not have been deliberate, but the rapid dismantling of quangos and the swift replacement with alternative forms of government organisations and structure have meant that D&T has often been overlooked and neglected. We can therefore certainly point to the period from about 2010 as to when key government policy and governance were no longer proactively supporting the growth and development of D&T.

## Higher Education Institutions

A further key stakeholder group that can be considered as part of the intellectual governance of the subject came from universities operating within the higher education institution (HEIs) infrastructure. This group, which would have included researchers, those involved in initial teacher education, members of schools of education and design departments and those funded by organisations to promote and develop the subject, formed and supported a network of academics interested in better understanding and clarifying the phenomenon of D&T education.

Similar to the government quangos, HEIs also became increasingly fragmented and marginalised from 2010 onwards as the combination of reduced project funding, disruption of the curriculum and fragmentation and turbulence within initial teacher education preparation created a 'perfect storm', which meant the research momentum that had been building within England was severely disrupted. In some respects, the disruption in the academic sector, particularly to those involved in teacher preparation programmes had been occurring for some time due to the reduced demand for design and technology teachers alongside the natural churn of those academics who had been influential in the inception of the subject moving on or retiring. However, the additional significant disruption to teacher preparation programmes and a shift to a 'school-led' system of teacher development further accelerated the demise of the subject. As a result of this significant turbulence in the system, working in higher education, particularly within D&T, has become increasingly precarious. Therefore, the resulting attrition and contraction of academics across the last decade has had a significant impact in reducing the critical mass of individuals able to be involved in both research and curriculum development, contributing further to the demise of the intellectual governance of D&T.

## The Design and Technology Association

A cornerstone within the governance of design and technology has been the Design and Technology Association (D&TA) which, like the subject itself, has prospered and declined in parallel, with the significant changes over a relatively short period since its inception in 1989. Through the stewardship of a number of chief executive officers, the subject association had, up until 2010, maintained a healthy and active membership, often only second in size to the Association of Science Educators, as well as a commercial viability along with curriculum influence whilst maintaining a conducive political dialogue with those in government. However, one of the challenges for the association has been in navigating the balance between reflecting its members' needs and wishes alongside its own commercial ambitions without being compromised by both demands. The governance and leadership of the association have subsequently, at times, appeared confused and in a state of paralysis as it has tried to appease both extremes of a traditional and progressive membership whilst also attempting to maintain integrity alongside resolving commercial tensions. The DT&A could therefore be characterised as a force for good that became overwhelmed with managing multiple stakeholder interests which subsequently made it difficult to articulate a clear vision for the subject. As such, the subject association has not been able to exert the influence required when it most mattered, and like the subject itself, the DT&A has also had to contract and adapt whilst looking for new commercial and political allies.

This phenomenon is not unique to the DT&A as many organisations become compromised by prioritising meeting their own objectives and future security followed by addressing the expectations of their multiple stakeholders. What may have been different for the association was that given the rapid development and shifting identity of the subject, the leadership of the association have rarely been able to confidently articulate what the subject actually was or indeed how it should be taught without fear of marginalising commercial or membership interests. As a result of this impotence, when combined with the fragmentation of governance across other organisations, it has meant that D&T have become increasingly vulnerable and exposed.

## *Offices for Standards in Education*

The final aspect of governance that is worth considering is from the Offices for Standards in Education (Ofsted) who since the 1992 Education Act have inspected and reported on state schools in England. In this capacity, Ofsted became the barometer for indicating the quality of D&T through its monitoring and annual reporting. It can be argued that up until 2011, Ofsted had maintained its independence from government and its adherence to being impartial by inspecting without 'fear or favour'. However, under the leadership of Sir Michael Wilshaw Ofsted underwent something of an identity crisis both in relation to how it engaged with both the sector and the government. Central to this was a shift in focus away from school inspections, providing a broad overview of the curriculum towards a much narrower view of pupil and teacher performance. Given that D&T was no longer a key area of inspection, whilst many teachers may have welcomed this, it also meant that headteachers were also less likely to make the subject a priority given the reduced scrutiny. Therefore, over time, Ofsted no longer had the expertise, political motivation or capacity to make significant recommendations or to be influential within D&T.

In summary, there are many other key agents of governance such as examination boards, local education authority advisors, charities, consultants and various key stakeholder groups who will have contributed to the initial growth and infrastructure supporting D&T. However, through fragmentation and change of government, the network of governance that initially sustained D&T ultimately dissipated and subsequently contributed to the rapid implosion of the subject.

What is apparent is that whilst D&T has experienced significant turbulence, particularly in the last decade, in parallel, the governance structures have equally undergone their own rapid transformation and demise. As a consequence, it could be argued that due to the embryonic nature of D&T, the subject had a greater reliance and dependency on a broad governance network. In particular, the subject was overly reliant on key individuals who had been very much part of the evolution and growth of the subject and who occupied strategic and influential positions in the DT&A, Ofsted, HEIs, government organisations and the advisory service. As such, the departure of these key individuals, the changing structure of governance organisations and a period of rapid government reform may, through a combination of bad timing and political machinations, have resulted in a rapid destabilisation of the subject's governance.

## The future – design thinking and rethinking design and/or technology

As a result of the significant structural reform across the last decade in how schools are operated, managed and funded along with how teachers are trained and undergo professional development has meant the ecosystem in which D&T originally evolved is no longer in existence. Subsequently, D&T will not be resurrected in the same way it was created, if it can re-emerge at all. Inevitably such reflections might be considered bleak but in the true sense of 'wicked' (Rittel and Webber, 1973) design problems it is essential that we understand and problematise the extent of the challenge ahead whilst considering the multiple stakeholders involved in order that we can identify a new way forward, which I propose as Design and/or Technology 2.0.

### *Design and/or Technology 2.0*

I have written elsewhere about Design and/or Technology 2.0 (Spendlove, 2017) so I will summarise the key premise, which uses the concept of software and product upgrades to suggest that what whilst this chapter has identified how Design and Technology version 1.0 may have failed, or has been failed, a significant upgrade of the architecture to a future iteration, such as version 2.0, 2.1, 2.2 (and so on) may help us intellectually reconceive what a future version of the subject may be. Within this context, there are two further dimensions to emphasise.

### *And/Or*

A fundamental issue that exists with the current iteration of design and technology is that there remains a lack of clear understanding what it actually is.

Both the word *design* and the word *technology* have clear definitions; however, when these words are combined into a single entity by the use of *and*, we have the beginnings of a semantic, philosophical and pedagogical discussion as to what 'D&T' actually is. Previously I have written about this confusion (Spendlove, 2015) which is compounded by *design* being used as both a verb and a noun whilst the word *technology* is often used in education spheres to denote a curriculum subject that may or may not specifically include design.

Unfortunately, I do think that the confusion over the naming of the subject has contributed to the demise of design and technology and any future iteration of the subject has to consider this issue. In the context of my 'And/Or' proposal, I am therefore seeking conceptual clarification as to whether the subject is both two entities combined, as in 'design AND technology', or whether it is two single entities as in 'design OR technology', where the subject seamlessly flips from one domain to another. Inevitably in proposing a future alternative iteration of the subject, it is acknowledged that if the 'And' version of the subject is retained, then we maintain the conceptual issues that currently exist, which may not be insurmountable but that do present a significant barrier to the future existence of the current subject incarnation.

*Design Thinking*

Related to And/Or is that a recognised weakness of D&T has often been the capacity to authentically develop design capability in pupils. The reasons for this are multifaceted and long-standing but will likely remain in any future iteration of the subject. However, within this context, an opportunity also exists to adopt and take ownership of the increasingly used term of *design thinking* as a catalyst for use within a 2.0 model of design and/or technology education. Inevitably, this is unlikely to be straightforward given the existence of the prevailing difficulties that traditional notions of design have had in becoming established in practice in the 1.0 version.

Nevertheless, whilst 'design thinking' is itself a term struggling to both be defined and an activity that can increasingly be located within the different parts of the curriculum, there would appear to be an opportunity for the D&T community to show the same tenacity as was apparent in the emergence of design and technology 1.0, in capitalising on a window of opportunity that may exist for embracing design thinking as a central feature of a new iteration of the subject. In doing so, it would be essential to emphasise the cognitive and reflective aspects of design thinking which distinguish it from forms of design which primarily prioritise the creative and aesthetic elements of process.

**Rethinking Design Education**

In a short chapter, such as this I am inevitably trying to cover a lot of ground at the expense of the depth required to fully explore the various topics.

Nevertheless, I want to signpost that in thinking of ways forward related to design and/or technology 2.0 and design thinking – the common theme of 'design' is itself continually undergoing a global process of rethinking and redefining.

In previous work, I have positioned that design education, within the primary and secondary phases of education, situated as a predominantly creative, material, 'product'-orientated and aesthetic activity may be a dated concept. Likewise a 'human-centred', Western, colonized, capitalist model of design education which has permeated the English curriculum may ultimately be the opposite of what is needed for a sustainable planet. Therefore, whatever version of the subject materializes, there is a significant need to reconceive many outdated and taken-for-granted conceptions of the subject. This is a significant challenge but perhaps serendipitously given the contraction of the subject now may be the perfect time to reinvigorate a new version of the subject given it is perhaps now at a manageable scale.

## Conclusion

In this chapter, I have offered a snapshot of both the demise and a possible re-emergence of how design and/or technology 2.0 may offer a way forward for the subject. However, any future iteration of the subject will still be highly dependent on successful alignment with new and emerging structures related to teacher development, governance of the subject and political will.

There is little doubt that D&T is undergoing an existential crisis having experienced the most rapid emergence and implosion of all subjects on the curriculum with the 2020 GCSE entry of approximately **90,000** students being only 23% of the 2000 entry of 404,000. Likewise, the number of new teachers training to teach the subject has also dropped dramatically whilst the supporting infrastructure and governance have equally become fragmented. Inevitably, what is clear is that on its current trajectory the subject is not sustainable.

Furthermore, with the dismantling of the infrastructure from which design and technology emerged, attempting to rebuild the subject in its current form would appear both regressive and potentially futile. There should, however, be optimism that an opportunity does exist to reimagine what might be possible, to learn from the past and to create something that more closely matches the aspirations that many in the subject have aspired to but which have failed to materialise or be sustained. Similarly, a post-COVID-19 society needs a D&T literate society that can understand, interrogate, critique and take action to hopefully create a 'better future'. As such, a new generation of educators now has an opportunity to be the new activists who employ the very skills, knowledge and capabilities that they aim to engender in their pupils in order to promote the existence of new forms of D&T education.

Ultimately a form of high-quality D&T education can offer a way to a better understanding of the world, as well as an education on how to take considered ethical action within a future society that will continually face ecological, political, biological and economic challenges. If developed and implemented successfully Design and/or Technology 2.0 is an activity that is entirely distinct from anything else on the curriculum, that is intellectually rigorous, inclusive, deliberately speculative, imaginative, creative, technical, challenging and highly stimulating. However, conversely, if mundane versions of the original incarnation of design and technology are perpetuated and resuscitated then the subject can no longer justify its existence within the school curriculum.

## Questions

1 What are the current and future political priorities that D&T might align with that you consider would also benefit the future development of the subject?
2 What threats and opportunities exist within your school (or other organisational groupings) that may enhance or pose a threat to the future of D&T?
3 What is your vision for the future of D&T? Is your vision sustainable, and how might it be developed into a reality?

## References

Craske, J. (2020). Logics, rhetoric and 'the blob': Populist logic in the Conservative reforms to English schooling. *British Educational Research Journal*, 47(2), pp. 279–298.
Department of Education and Science (DES)/Welsh Office (1988). *National Curriculum Design and Technology Working Group: Interim Report*. [The Parkes Report.] London: HMSO.
DfE (2016). *Educational excellence everywhere. Presented to Parliament by the Secretary of State for Education by Command of Her Majesty*. Available at: www.gov.uk/government/uploads/system/uploads/attachment_data/file/508447/Educational_Excellence_Everywhere.pdf [Accessed 3 January 2020].
Fulton, G.R. (2017). The Bramble Cay melomys: The first mammalian extinction due to human-induced climate change. *Pacific Conservation Biology*, 23(1), pp. 1–3.
Gibb, N. (2018). *ResearchED speaks to … the RT Hon Nick Gibb MP, Minister of state for school standards*. Available at: https://researched.org.uk/2018/09/26/tom-bennett-speaks-to-nick-gibb-2/ [Accessed 15 January 2021].
Hirsch Jr, E.D., Kett, J.F., and Trefil, J.S. (1988). *Cultural literacy: What every American needs to know*. New York City: Vintage.
McKinsey, C. and McKinsey, M.M. (2007). *How the world's best performing school systems come out on top*. London: McKinsey.
Rittel, H.W. and Webber, M.M. (1973). Dilemmas in a general theory of planning. *Policy Sciences*, 4(2), pp. 155–169.
Spendlove, D. (2015). Developing a deeper understanding of design in technology education. In P.J. Williams, A. Jones, and C. Buntting (eds.). *The Future of Technology Education* (pp. 169–185). Singapore: Springer.
Spendlove, D. (2017). Design Thinking: What is it and where might it reside? In E. Norman and K. Baynes (eds.). *Design Epistemology and Curriculum Planning* (pp. 39–42). Loughborough: Loughborough Design Press.

# 5 What's so special about design and technology anyway?

*Matt McLain*

## Introduction

Within the wider context of technology education, design and technology (D&T) involves problem finding and problem-solving, typically focusing on the designing, making and evaluating of products, systems or environments. D&T emerged as a subject in the National Curriculum for England from the largely gendered craft disciplines, where practical education for girls traditionally educated them for the home, developing skills with food and textiles, and for boys for manufacturing, developing skills in wood and metal work (Atkinson, 1990). The latter decades of the 20th century saw the introduction of new, more design-oriented curricula around the world, reflecting changes in both society and industry. This movement sought to unite the former material-defined subjects, replacing craft with design. Where the role of materials has been secondary to that of design, creativity and innovation, this transition has been more successful. However, as Paechter (1995) described at the beginning of the D&T story, teachers' subcultural retreat into craft- and material-centric mindsets has arguably hindered the subject in achieving these aims to the present day. In this chapter, I explore D&T through the lens of signature pedagogies, both recognising and challenging current practice, speculating on the future of teaching and learning in the subject. A key point in this debate is the role of making in the contemporary and future D&T paradigms.

Unlike so-called traditional academic subjects, D&T is a subject concerned with doing and developing pupils' capability, as opposed to learning a defined and bounded body of descriptive knowledge (Bell et al., 2017; Bernstein, 1971, 1975, 1990; McLain et al., 2019). Technology is constantly changing and developing, so the knowledge used in the design and technology classroom[1] is (or should be) different today than it was a decade ago. For example, when I began teaching, my specialist area was 'systems and control technology', and I taught through decades when electronic circuits were designed and built using discrete components to the introduction of programmable components, such as the microcontroller. During this time, it

DOI: 10.4324/9781003166689-8

was common for pupils to design and make customised circuit boards, learning to fabricate (using photoetching) and populate (by soldering components) these boards. These were seen as important skills. However, the last decade has seen plethora of prepopulated microcontroller boards tailored to a range of budgets, questioning the relevance of pupils producing circuits from scratch. Advances in technology have meant that the function of a circuit can be designed by programming rather than by configuring discrete components. If D&T is not primarily about teaching a timeless body of knowledge about technologies but about using knowledge to design and make, then we ought to question what the subject is for. This has curricular and pedagogical implications for policymakers and educators.

Therefore, we might ask ourselves, Is the purpose of D&T to learn about specific technologies and processes or to use appropriate technologies to prototype design solutions to real problems? I argue that it is the latter – putting design at the centre as the uniting factor between the often competing 'material' or making technologies. I do not deny that there is value in pupils learning established technologies (such as soldering), as they can help develop hand–eye coordination and provide them with the opportunity to use more accessible tools and resources that are used in industry. However, to hold certain practical skills and processes as essential, or sacrosanct, risks turning the subject into modern craftism – making the technological tail wag the design dog! We must ask ourselves whether the pedagogies and approaches that we used last decade (or even last year) remain fit for purpose. Accepting that technologies are in a constant state of flux, another aspect of the debate is What is at the heart of D&T if not design?

Currently in England, and other Western nations, the notion of powerful knowledge has risen to the fore (Gibb, 2017; Muller & Young, 2019; White, 2018; Young, 2008), with a focus on traditional academic subjects. This has been mirrored by a decline in examination entries for almost all practical and creative subjects, including D&T in England (e.g. Busby, 2019; Flaig, 2020; Whittaker & Allen-Kinross, 2019). However, there seems to be a growing acknowledgement that a narrow curriculum is an impoverished curriculum, which fails to meet the needs of all learners (HOC, 2021; Spielman, 2019). When discussing intelligence in the context of knowledge and curriculum, it is easy to focus on crystalised intelligence, which refers to accumulated knowledge. This is easier to define and test than fluid intelligence, which describes the ability to think and act flexibly (Horn & Cattell, 1966). However, more recent research by Sternberg (2005) identifies three distinct facets of intelligence, which challenge the knowledge bias: analytical, creative and practical. Through its fundamental activities of ideating, realising and critiquing (McLain, 2021b), D&T education not only contributes to the more obvious practical and creative intelligence but also develops the analytical. A key area where these intelligences are fostered during project-based learning, is where pupils are designing, making and evaluating. Therefore, good D&T has the power to enable pupils to draw on and apply knowledge from other subjects, developing so-called 21st-century skills, including empathy, creativity and problem-solving (Joynes, Rossignoli & Amonoo-Kuofi, 2018). Whilst it may be the case that D&T has a weaker epistemological[2] basis (DfE, 2011), as compared to more established subjects (which, having been part of the curriculum for much longer, are more clearly defined and understood), it has a rich ontological[3] foundation. Arguably, D&T makes a valuable contribution to the curriculum, with its focus on capability and working with uncertainty, which is a key feature of a signature pedagogy (McLain, 2021b). However, this is only true where there are genuinely uncertain outcomes in at least some D&T projects – that is pupils have the opportunity to work with autonomy and determine the outcome of a design process. An over-emphasis on making 'take home' projects or focused practical tasks masquerading as design and make undermines efforts to develop creative, design and innovation skills. Projects focusing on made artefacts have their place and value in a broad D&T curriculum, but in the light of the wicked problems facing society, surely D&T should espouse sustainable approaches, such as approaches to designing that minimise or eliminate waste in the face of climate change or is more inclusive of a diverse community, adopting a pedagogy of transformation and rehabilitating the D&T project. We might ask ourselves how we would respond if the outcome of a pupil's design process suggested that a system or service is more appropriate than a made product and what the implications would be for our practice and how D&T is assessed.

## Reframing D&T subject knowledge

Reflecting on the nature of D&T education, I suggest there are three fundamental activities – ideating, realising and critiquing – and two key processes – communicating and knowing (McLain, 2021b). In using the relatively unfamiliar terms *ideating, realising* and *critiquing* (rather than the more familiar *designing, making* and *evaluating*), my intention is to disrupt your thinking and preconceptions. Both *design* and *technology* are words with multiple meanings in their common usage. The word *design* can refer to anything from the act of drawing to a complex construction. And *technology* can refer to objects, activities, knowledge or volition (Mitcham, 1994). Adopting the terms *ideating, realising* and *critiquing* enables us to focus on the fundamental activities of D&T and avoid potential confusion and misconceptions – as well as blur the boundaries between designing, making and evaluating.

No doubt, there are other important aspects of D&T and there are different versions of the subject being successfully taught in many countries (see Table 5.1). However, right at the heart of the concepts of both design and technology lies the idea of the transformation of human wants, needs and desires into artefacts – products, systems, services or environments – using the resources available (Morrison-Love, 2017).[4] This drive to transform is fundamentally human, giving rise to the technologies that marked the prehistoric ages of human activity – each new technology standing on the

*Table 5.1* Global Design and Technology Curricula

| Country | Purpose Statement Excerpts |
| --- | --- |
| Australia (ACARA, 2014) | "The practical nature of the Technologies learning area engages students in critical and creative thinking, including understanding interrelationships in systems when solving complex problems. A systematic approach to experimentation, problem-solving, prototyping and evaluation instils in students the value of planning and reviewing processes to realise ideas." |
| England (DfE, 2013) | "Design and technology is an inspiring, rigorous and practical subject. Using creativity and imagination, pupils design and make products that solve real and relevant problems within a variety of contexts, considering their own and others' needs, wants and values… Pupils learn how to take risks, becoming resourceful, innovative, enterprising and capable citizens." |
| Hong Kong (EB, 2016) | "Technology Education (TE) is the study of the purposeful application of knowledge . . . , skills and experiences in using resources to create or add value to products and systems to meet human needs. . . . TE subjects are introduced at different points of time with varying emphases to cope with the social, economic and technological development both locally and globally. |
| New Zealand (TKI, 2017) | "Technology is intervention by design. It uses intellectual and practical resources to create technological outcomes, which expand human possibilities by addressing needs and realising opportunities. Design is characterised by innovation and adaptation and is at the heart of technological practice. It is informed by critical and creative thinking and specific design processes." |
| South Africa (DoE, 2002) | "Technology has existed throughout history as an activity in which people use a combination of knowledge, skills and available resources to develop solutions to meet their daily needs and wants. Some of these solutions are in the form of products while some solutions involve a combination of products to make systems. . . . However, the knowledge, skills and resources used today are different because of the accelerating developments in technology. Today's society is complex and diverse." |
| Sweden (Skolverket, 2018) | "Teaching in technology should aim at helping the pupils to develop their technical expertise and technical awareness so that they can orient themselves and act in a technologically intensive world. . . .Teaching should help pupils to develop their knowledge on how to solve different problems and satisfy needs with the use of technology. Pupils should also be given the preconditions to develop their own technical ideas and solutions." |
| United States of America (ITEEA, 2021) | "In order to be a technologically literate citizen, a person should understand what technology is, how it works, how it shapes society and in turn how society shapes it. Moreover, a technologically literate person has some abilities to 'do' technology that enables them to use their inventiveness to design and build things and to solve practical problems that are technological in nature." |

shoulders of the last at an exponential rate enabled by access to more efficient or plentiful energies. Somewhat late, there is an increasing awareness and acknowledgment of the fragility of our climates and ecosystems, yet the demand for energy and resources continues. As a result, the need for a conscious and critical awareness of the impact that our socio-technological activity is arguably more important than ever. Rather than continuing to contribute to conspicuous consumption and the production of waste, D&T must take stock and embrace a critical approach to designing (and making), fostering responsible, sustainable and inclusive design. However, due its inherent focus on knowledge *for action* – as opposed to *for recall* – D&T have the potential to offer an alternative approach to that of other subjects in school curricula; for example whilst science seeks to eliminate extraneous variables to focus with greater resolution on the object of its enquiry, design (and technology) embraces the whole context in order to find the problem it will then seek to solve. If we simply focus projects on the skills necessary for the production of objects in a school workshop, "we run the real risk of preparing them to live lives that work against the Earthly conditions necessary to sustain their lifestyles" (Petrina, 2000).

## Signature pedagogies

In response to studying learning in the professions, Lee Shulman (2005) introduced the term 'signature pedagogies' into the educational lexicon. Signature pedagogies are 'characteristic forms of teaching and learning' (p. 52) within a particular discipline. These are not necessarily the most effective approaches, but they are the most widely used ones. There are several features of signature pedagogies, including the importance of knowledge in and for action and the role of uncertainty. Therefore, a signature pedagogy can be defined by how a discipline applies its body of knowledge in contexts where the outcome is not predetermined. In D&T, this is seen most clearly in 'the project', where the assessment focus is as much on the process than on the product.

This way of looking at pedagogy built on Shulman's earlier work (1986) on pedagogical content knowledge (PCK), which focused on the complexities of teacher knowledge (for a D&T perspective, see Banks et al., 2004). Whilst PCK is interested in the relationship between subject content, pedagogy and curriculum and how particular concepts and processes are taught, signature pedagogies focus on the pedagogical approaches that are pervasive across a discipline (i.e. common approaches that can be seen in from school to school). Whereas PCK is concerned with teachers' knowledge of how to teach subject content, including awareness of the associated difficulties and misconceptions associated with a particular area and the curriculum resources available to teach it, signature pedagogies focus on the activities of teaching and learning themselves. Both PCK and signature pedagogies have value in teacher education and professional development. In this chapter, I use *signature pedagogies* as a means to examine our teaching methods and question whether they are fit for purpose in addressing the underpinning and implicit structure of D&T – that is are they coherent with the assumptions that we make about the best way of teaching the subject and do the develop the attitudes, values and dispositions associated with D&T education.

Signature pedagogies are concerned with learning to *think*, learning to *perform* and learning to *act with integrity* – sometimes referred to as dispositions of head, hand and heart. As D&T are subjects that are predicated on capability and knowledge for action, the triple concern with knowing, doing and valuing has resonance with how it is taught around the world through various curricula (Table 5.1).

As illustrated in Table 5.1, the fundamental activities of ideating, realising and critiquing are at the heart of design and technology around the world (also see Chapter 2). Key themes are evident throughout the excerpts in the table, where the attitudes and dispositions associated with designerly and technological knowing (thinking, doing and valuing) are fostered in versions of various national curricula.

Shulman also described signature pedagogies as being composed of three layers, or structures: surface, deep and implicit (Table 5.2). The *surface structures* are the teaching methods employed in the D&T classroom. These include a range of pedagogical approaches, from the demonstration of practical skills through to the facilitation of creative and innovative problem-solving. Within Shulman's description of 'approaching and withdrawing' (p. 54) is an implied continuum of relatively restrictive approaches that narrow learners' focus on specific tasks or procedures to more expansive approaches that encourage autonomy and creativity, such as generating innovative solutions in response to a design context and problem. Extending our analysis from the *surface* to the *deep structures*, the curricular frameworks cited in Table 5.1 emphasise 'doing' and project-based learning involving ideating, realising and critiquing (albeit stated in terms of designing, making and evaluating).

There are various ways of configuring the three fundamental activities, one of which (a four-fold pedagogical model for D&T) is outlined in the next section. The *implicit structure* can be looked at from both a personal and a curricular perspective. There are many different values that are (and can be) ascribed to D&T, which can be influenced by who is doing the valuing and

*Table 5.2* The Structures of Signature Pedagogies (Shulman, 2005, pp. 54–55)

| | |
|---|---|
| **Surface Structure** | "…concrete, operational acts of teaching and learning, of showing and demonstrating, of questioning and answering, of interacting and withholding, of approaching and withdrawing…" |
| **Deep Structure** | "…, a set of assumptions about how best to impart a certain body of knowledge and know-how…" |
| **Implicit Structure** | "a moral dimension that comprises a set of beliefs about professional attitudes, values, and dispositions…" |

what the assumed purpose of the subject is. As discussed earlier, the origins of D&T are in craft and making, which holds the public imagination, as reflected in recent television programmes such as *The Great British Sewing Bee*, *Handmade: Britain's Best Woodworker* and *The Great British Bake Off*, in the UK. There is also a psychomotor argument for teaching practical skills, such as the declining dexterity of surgeons (Coughlan, 2018). However, it is arguable that a contemporary and relevant D&T curriculum should focus on the transformational nature of the subject through ideation, realisation and critique.

Design projects are ideal spaces for knowledge to be applied in contexts where the outcomes are uncertain – that is the *deep structure*. This provides opportunities to develop resilience and autonomy, alongside creativity and innovation. The role of learning environments and teachers are also important features of signature pedagogies, with specialist facilities, resources and expertise at the heart of how D&T is taught (and learnt). Four further features emerge from signature pedagogies for design education, which reinforce these notions:

- Design thinking (praxis, thinking/doing, capability, etc.)
- Design studio (learning environments, ways of working, etc.)
- Design 'crit' (critique, assessment, formative, feedback, etc.)
- Design project (design and make, project-based learning, etc.)

It is the thesis of this chapter that the design project is a (if not *the*) deep structure of D&T, and the best way to develop the subject's body of knowledge – including ways of knowing that are conceptual (drawing on abstract ideas), procedural (applying knowledge and processes) and strategic (deliberate and autonomous; McCormick, 1997; McLain et al., 2019). The epistemological basis of design and technology has been debated and questioned (e.g. DfE, 2011), but the changing nature of technology means that any technological body of knowledge will evolve and change over time. However, this is only problematic when considering the temporal nature of resources (materials and components) and tools (hand, machine and computer-based), rather than knowledge of how these 'technologies' are used to solve problems and address the needs and wants of human beings (not to mention with wider realms of flora, fauna, the environment and society). In making, for example, the principles of addition, subtraction, deformation and reformation categorise a wide range of material-specific techniques.

In the recent review of the General Certificate of Secondary Education (GCSE) qualifications, taken at the age of 16 in England, the D&T subject content (DfE, 2015) attempted to define a body of knowledge that was not built on discrete material classifications that characterised the previous syllabi – that is electronics, food, graphics, resistant[5] materials, systems and control and textiles. Technical principles covered the knowledge pupils need "to make effective design choices in relation to which materials, components and systems" (p. 5), which included properties of materials and processes for realising them into prototypes. Design and making principles focused on how technical knowledge are used in action, including strategies for ideating, critiquing, communicating and knowing. This was a significant change to the D&T paradigm. Possibly a step to far for some, but it is an essential step in consolidating the material schisms of the previous decades.

## A four-fold pedagogical model for D&T

In my earlier work (2021b), I describe a four-fold pedagogical model (Table 5.3) that has emerged in D&T (e.g. D&TA, 2019), balancing the fundamentals of ideating, realising and critiquing (Figure 5.1). This model draws on the work of Alison Hardy and Sarah Davies at Nottingham Trent University which was derived from work by Trebell (2009) and Barlex (2011). The model builds on research and scholarship on *designing without*

*Table 5.3* A Four-Fold Pedagogical Model for Design and Technology

| Approach | Description | Benefits | Limitations |
| --- | --- | --- | --- |
| Designing and making (DM) | Often referred to as *design, make and evaluate assignments (DMEA)*, this involved pupils following a design process from a set context, problem or brief. They involve ideating, realising and critiquing. | DM activities provide pupils with the opportunity to work with varying degrees of autonomy on a design project. They can be used to develop creativity, project management and resilience. | DM activities are limited by the time, resources, facilities and expertise available to pupils. Pupils may (and often do) come up with ideas that they are unable to realise. Furthermore, they do not have access to a wide range of different users and contexts. |
| Mainly designing (MD) | These activities focus on ideating activities but can involve limited realising or critiquing. They may involve modelling of prototypes, but typically not making using materials or components. | MD activities enable pupils to focus on the skills of designing creativity and innovation, without the constraints of having to make a prototype. Ideations can be speculative and address so-called wicked problems, using approaches like design fiction. | Designing without making limits opportunities for pupils to work creatively within constraints and realise their ideas using real materials and components. Unless pupils' creativity is fostered, and design skills are taught, they may struggle to be innovative. |

(*Continued*)

Table 5.3 (Continued)

| Approach | Description | Benefits | Limitations |
|---|---|---|---|
| Mainly making (MM) | These are similar to activities that have been described as *focused practical tasks (FPT)*. They are concerned with developing the skills related to making and involved realising activities. | MM activities enable pupils to develop skills and procedural knowledge, using tools and equipment to shape materials and components. The act of making is good for developing hand–eye coordination and well-being. | Working with real materials and components takes time and can potentially dominate the curriculum. Focusing on specific material areas and resources can also limit creativity and the consideration of alternative solutions to a problem. |
| Exploring technology and society (ETS) | There are some similarities to activities that have been labelled *investigate, disassemble and evaluate activities (IDEA)*, but also embrace wider aspects of critiquing the impact of technology and society on each other. | ETS activities provide opportunities for learners to focus on the impact of technology and society and the mediating role of design. A focus on critiquing enables pupils to explore issues and values, as well as simply analyse or evaluate products and systems. | Focusing on solely on issues of technology and society may inhibit designing and making activities, particularly where pupils are not supported to make decisions on next steps. An over-emphasis on ETS activities could limit design and technology to a cerebral social science. |

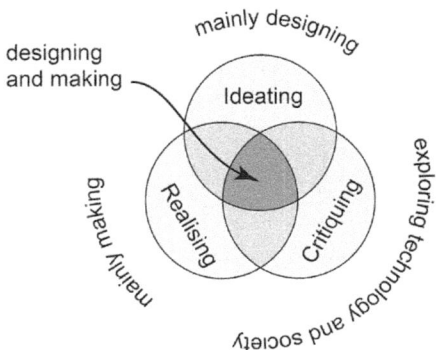

*Figure 5.1* Four-fold model of D&T pedagogy related to D&T fundamental activities.

*making* (e.g. Barlex & Trebell, 2008), *making without designing* (e.g. Banks & Owen-Jackson, 2007) and exploring technology and society (e.g. Barlex, 2003), which builds on the traditional *designing and making* paradigm (e.g. DfE, 2013).

Each of the four approaches reflects one or more of the three D&T fundamental activities: ideating, realising and critiquing. However, the fundamentals cannot (and should not) be treated in isolation – hence the 'mainly' appendage in the mainly designing (MD) and mainly making (MM) approaches. Furthermore, I would suggest that the four approaches themselves should be treated as having fuzzy boundaries, to be used as a guide rather than a rigid categorising of practice.

Earlier descriptions of D&T pedagogical approaches were limited to design-and-make assignments (DMAs), focused practical tasks (FPTs) and investigate, disassemble and evaluate activities (IDEAs), which did not include the option for a focus on designing without making. As indicated earlier, the inclusion of 'mainly' emphasises the fact that designing and making cannot (and should not) be entirely separated but that designing or making can become the main focus of a project rather than work within the restrictions imposed by designing and making in the school setting, where time, resources, expertise and facilities impose restrictions on pupils' design decisions. On the other hand, projects involving exploring technology and society sidestep the restrictions posed by designing and making, focusing on critiquing the role and impact of technologies on society (and vice versa). Adopting each pedagogical approach affords a different set of benefits and limitations. A school curriculum balancing projects (or schemes of work) that utilise all four provides the best opportunities to foster an authentic D&T experience. However, a well-designed D&T curriculum should also employ pedagogical approaches that are nuanced, acknowledging the 'mainly' appendage rather than doing designing *or* making and recognising that there can be more to critiquing when *exploring technology and society*. For example, a critical use of design fiction, to image future scenarios that explore intractable and 'wicked' problems[6] (Churchman, 1967) through the use of writing, discussing or acting, could act as a springboard into ideating design solutions. The four-fold model is a starting point to help teachers name their practice and should be adopted and adapted by schools to suit their local needs, with a blend of restrictive and expansive (see the following discussion) experiences.

## *Examples of projects*

In this section, I explore examples of D&T projects using the four-fold pedagogical model, considering more expansive and restrictive approaches. A beauty of D&T projects is that there are a plethora of different starting points and foci for delivering the learning outcomes. Not only do we have a range of material (e.g. food, metal, polymer, textile, wood, etc.) and component (e.g. electronic, mechanical, microcontroller, pneumatic, etc.) options and combinations, but we also have varying design contexts and challenges, which can include clients, environments, scenarios, situations, users and other factors. Whilst this makes the subject vibrant and dynamic, it can also be confusing for beginning (and even experienced) teachers, whose attention can become fixated on an artefact (made outcome), the resources (materials and components) or the technologies rather than on the learning intentions or outcomes, thus, incorrectly, prioritising the *product* over the *process* in teaching, learning and assessment. Therefore, we need to acknowledge that having 'the project' as a deep structure of our subject's signature pedagogy can potentially distract us from making intelligent decisions about our curriculum design should we conflate the project with its end product (i.e. the artefact).

The following examples are drawn from the D&T Association's Key Stage 3 (lower secondary) project bank of teaching resources (D&TA, 2019). Projects are (by necessity) limited by factors such as the available time, resources (materials and equipment), teacher expertise and the wider school curriculum, as well as age-related expectations and pupils' own capability.

As discussed before, DM projects provide pupils with the opportunity to ideate, realise and critique products or systems. Typically, they involve the production of an artefact, responding a design problem or a need. Hats are a popular option for textiles-focused projects, as they are relatively economic in terms of materials and are gender-neutral. DM project 32 focuses on festival headgear. A more expansive interpretation of this project would encourage pupils to do things like question the very notion of what 'headgear' means allow them to research real festivals (maybe even an educational visit to one!) and interact with clients and potential users; select from a wide range of materials (not just fabrics) and equipment; make principled design decisions; conduct user testing and evaluation. However, the D&T teacher must balance the limiting factors, considering their school context and the wider curriculum. More restrictive approaches might include limiting the project to focus to a particular festival and/or user profile; providing a simulated client's design brief;[7] limiting the choice of materials, equipment and/or processes; or focusing more heavily on one of the three fundamentals (i.e. ideating, realising or critiquing). A key question for the teacher is, "What is a quality outcome for this project?" Working with limitations and positioning the project along an expansive-restrictive continuum, the quality of the idea versus the product is necessarily going to be in tension.

MM projects focus more on the fundamental activity of realising, with the learning outcome focusing on a made artefact, with limited or no ideating or critiquing. The MM project allows pupils to focus on skill development, and the question of quality is much simpler than for the DM as pupils tend to be producing the same object to varying degrees of accuracy, assembly and finish. The safe use of tools and equipment is a common focus in food lessons, particularly at the beginning of a programme of study. MM project 5 focuses on building practical skills, including hygiene, routines and food preparation. Whilst an MM food project will more than likely focus on the use of set recipes and methods, a more expansive approach might include pupils selecting from a limited range of recipes; demonstrations that encourage pupils to draw on prior knowledge or to speculate using questioning, rather than straightforward explaining and modelling by the teacher; limiting the detail included in the method. By their very nature, MM projects tend to be more restrictive, as the teacher deliberately is focusing on a narrow range of skills and procedures. However, more restrictive approaches to this project might include breaking complex procedures down into mini 'demo and do' activities, with checkpoints on progress; videos, rolling slideshows or job cards to remind pupils of the key stages and correct procedures after demonstration; and, when using a knife to preparing ingredients for a fruit salad, providing templates or 'go/no-go' gauges to test the accuracy of cutting. As with DM projects, the teacher should make intelligent decisions on where to restrict or expand learning, taking into account the prior learning and capability of their pupils.

Conversely, MD projects tend to minimise the role of realising and critiquing. This removes some of the limitations that are inherent to making artefacts in a school D&T classroom, enabling pupils to be creative and think about possible, rather than necessarily achievable, ideas. DM project 42 focuses on designing an electronic toy for a child.[8] This project includes aspects of product design and systems and control. More expansive approaches to this project could include exploration of the design context, including observing children playing; defining the design problem and writing a design brief; using design thinking tools to defer judgement, challenge design fixation and promote divergent thinking; creating quick sketch models or prototypes of ideas for testing; working collaboratively in teams; and presenting online or recording a video outlining design ideas to a client. Using MD projects is a great way to introduce tools for innovation – it is important, however, that they do not focus narrowly on design communication skills (e.g. sketching, computer-aided design, etc.) to the exclusion of activities that foster creativity and provide opportunities for pupils to innovate. Conversely, it is also important to remember that working with restrictions and crossing boundaries are also an important part of being creative, so carefully planned restrictions can enhance creativity. Restrictive approaches might include providing a user profile or research data (e.g. video footage of children playing), forcing random combinations of features or characteristics, changing the client brief part way through the project, and focusing on the analysis of existing products.

Finally, *exploring technology and society* (ETS) projects typically step away from the design–make–evaluate paradigm, and offer an alternative range of methodologies. ETS project 41 focuses on the future and possible product evolutions. Whilst the project bank description suggests evaluating existing household products, more expansive approaches might include speculating on possible futures using design fiction to write or create an audio-visual recording of imagined scenarios (the film *Minority Report* is an interesting example of this); questioning assumptions about what a product should look like and/or do; addressing cultural assumptions and product evolution (e.g. the origins of QWERTY keyboard); using design strategies like the '5 whys' to systematically question assumptions and discover root problems; and using 'abductive' approaches to draw inspiration from unexpected places (e.g. using biomimicry to see how nature deals with similar problems). More restrictive approaches might include using or creating case studies of product evolution over time, analysing existing products, providing a set design fiction scenario for the pupils to work in, and using frameworks such as the circular economy to rethink product life cycles. The ETS project differs from the other three pedagogical approaches as it does not necessarily focus on pupils producing artefacts, but it enables them to think about the impact that technology has on society (and vice versa).

Together, the four-fold pedagogical model for the teaching of D&T, applied with the concept of an expansive-restrictive continuum, provides a rich framework for engaging and inclusive curriculum design. In the next section, I explore the concept of signature pedagogies as a tool for teachers to think and talk about how we teach D&T.

## Using signature pedagogies to talk about D&T

Developed from my work on the demonstration in D&T (McLain, 2018, 2021a), I combined the signature pedagogy structures with a dimension that draws on Fuller and Unwin's (2003) idea of an expansive-restrictive continuum. This continuum adds an extra dimension to the three structures (surface, deep, implicit) described by Shulman, recognising that some activities will be more directed and teacher-led (and therefore restrictive), whereas others are more open-ended and student-led (and therefore expansive). Both are important, and there is growing research evidence to support the use of direct or explicit instruction, which, by its very nature, tends to be more restrictive. However, a curriculum experience devoid of open-ended and autonomous learning deprives learners of the opportunity to make design choices, apply knowledge and grapple with uncertainty (Sahlberg & Doyle, 2019). Making a deliberate choice to either restrict or expand learning activities, ensures that the teacher is conscious of the benefits and limitations of the approaches they adopt – provided one is not favoured to the exclusion of the other. Some research suggests that more structured approaches can be more appropriate for younger, low-attaining and low-socio-economic-status learners (e.g. Reynolds et al., 2014). However, it is important to note that even in structured approaches, like direct instruction, independent practice is viewed as essential (Hattie, 2008).

In my research, participating D&T educators' views on demonstration revealed a tendency to prioritise subject expertise and classroom management over the consolidation of learning and facilitation of autonomy. This suggested that the *surface structure* (Table 5.2) of demonstration was inherently suited to the teaching of procedural knowledge (typically making skills), where the pupils replicate what the teacher models in the demonstration.

Therefore, when selecting pedagogical methods (surface structures), the teacher should consider the outcomes that they aim to achieve. For example, to encourage pupils to generate a range of ideas in response to a design context or brief, it is more effective for the teacher to model techniques for generating a range of ideas – such as the 6–3–5 Matrix, SCAMPER and others (see DfES, 2004) – rather than to demonstrate how they would design for the specific design problem/context. Demonstration is a form of teacher modelling, that is relatively restrictive and ideal for the transmission of technical skills, but it is less suited to innovation and origination whereas collaborative and discovery learning – such as the tools employed in design thinking (e.g. IDEO, 2021) – is more expansive and better suited to developing confidence and problem-solving strategies.

The fundamental activities of ideating, realising and critiquing run through each layer of D&T's signature pedagogy structure, emerging from the implicit attitudes, values and dispositions that the subject seeks to foster and underpinning the deep structures of the design project. As discussed earlier, the four-fold model provides a framework for integrating ideating, realising and critiquing into D&T projects in the classroom. The surface structures are the teaching (and learning) methods that teachers employ to instruct pupils and foster learning; being selected with due care and consideration of meeting the learning intentions and balance scaffolded approaches with those that encourage consolidation and autonomy.[9]

Figure 5.2 illustrates how signature pedagogies can be used as a discursive framework for design and technology educators to think and talk about how the subject is taught. The vertical dimension adds depth, diving below the surface pedagogical methods employed in the classroom. Whilst I propose that the implicit structure of D&T begins with the three fundamental activities, more could be added to broaden the discourse and recognise the multifaceted nature of the subject. Alternative, it may be convenient to focus on a single fundamental activity and how it features in the school curriculum (long-term planning) or across individual 'units' and 'schemes' of learning (medium-term planning). The example above limits the number of pedagogical approaches to four, both for convenience and acknowledging that it

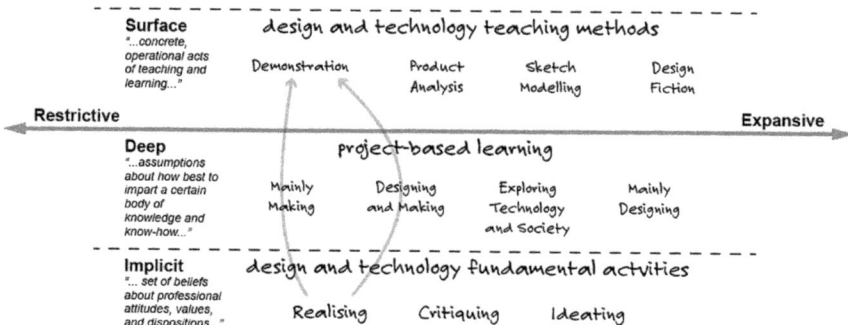

*Figure 5.2* A design and technology signature pedagogy framework.

is currently the prevailing model being presented in England. But these could (and should) be expanded to include a diverse range of methodologies that are (or should be) used in D&T lessons. In this case, the connections are 'bottom up', thinking about what deep and surface structures build on a particular implicit structure. But the framework could be used 'top down' to explore the deep and implicit structures that support the surface structure. Incorporating the expansive-restrictive continuum adds breadth to the framework, and the individual items can (and should) be moved left or right to encourage discussion on the level of scaffolding that is desirable in different contexts to adapt and optimise the learning experience for year groups, classes, groups and individuals.

To adopt an expansive-restrictive dimension to the selection of pedagogical approaches helps to avoid an overly linear approach to teaching D&T that (incorrectly) assumes that pupils must be taught skills before they are 'let loose' on creative and open-end activities. The four-fold model should be seen as being 'flat' or non-hierarchical, with each approach having equal value. The progression in learning comes from the scaffolding (restriction) and fading (expansion) of support for pupils, where *fading* is the term used to describe the removal of scaffolding (McLain, 2021b). Whilst the aim is for learning to become more expansive over time as pupils become increasingly capable, it is not as simple as moving from high levels of scaffolding to low and then none. Think of it like a receding tide, where water level drops (scaffolded learning) progressively, exposing more of the beach (autonomous learning), with waves continuing to crash on the beach, like micro-scaffolding being introduced and faded. And, of course, the tide will rise again, as does the level of scaffolding when pupils move from one phase of education to the next.

## The future D&T classroom

If 'the project' is the deep structure of D&T education's signature pedagogy, we must begin by asking whether this remains fit for purpose in the 21st-century curriculum. An approach to project-based learning that is flexible and allows pupils to experience learning by doing in authentic settings, can enable them to apply knowledge and develop autonomy. To ensure that D&T education remains current, as a community, we need to continually evaluate and reassess our approaches, asking ourselves whether it is fit for purpose, in the light of the following quote:

> "To prepare for 2030, people should be able to think creatively, develop new products and services, new jobs, new processes and methods, new ways of thinking and living, new enterprises, new sectors, new business models and new social models. . . . The constructs that underpin the competency include adaptability, creativity, curiosity and open-mindedness.
>
> (OECD, 2018, p. 5)

The Future of Education and Skills 2030 project was set up by the Organisation for Economic Co-operation and Development (OECD) to address the social, economic and environmental challenges presented by globalisation and technological developments. D&T, as a school subject, was conceived to meet these needs in the latter decades of the 20th century (e.g. DES/WO, 1988) and certainly has a role to play in developing children's and young people's "adaptability, creativity, curiosity and open-mindedness" – identified as underpinning competencies in the OECD's 2018 position paper.

Summarising the range of approaches and interpretations of 21st-century skills around the world, Joynes, Rossignoli and Amonoo-Kuofi (2018) identify five key professional attributes about which there is some consensus: communication skills, collaborative skills, individual learning approaches, individual autonomy, information and communication technology and digital literacy. These are skills that D&T and project-based learning are well placed to develop in children and young people. There is international research suggesting that design learning – that fosters autonomy and collaboration, in response to contexts, problems and needs/wants – applies and unites the STEM disciplines (e.g. English, 2019), which tend to be emphasised in the literature on 21st-century skills, alongside literacy and numeracy. Questions we need to ask ourselves include the following:

- Do our D&T projects need to be rehabilitated to better prepare children and young people for possible futures that we have not previously imagined?
- Does our curriculum need to be refocused wion th an emphasis the fundamentals of ideating and critiquing through a more strategic use of the MD and ETS approaches?
- Do we need to challenge the dictum of the 'take home' product at the end of each project?

Personally, my answer to all three is 'Yes!' What is yours?

## Conclusion

In this chapter, I have explored how a hybrid of the concepts of signature pedagogies and an expansive-restrictive continuum might provide a framework for professional dialogue around how D&T has been, is currently and might be taught. Arguing that more emphasis and curriculum time be given to projects taking MD and ETS approaches. Different D&T traditions have evolved around the globe, but there is a common thread through much of the current literature emphasising the importance of design and project-based learning. Whether the focus is on integrated approaches to interdisciplinary STEM (iSTEM), more craft or design-oriented iterations, the fundamental activities of ideating, realising and critiquing have a place in how the curriculum is conceived in policy and enacted in schools.

Considering the changes in technology and society, signature pedagogies are powerful tools for promoting talking and thinking about the D&T curriculum and pedagogy. Providing opportunities to name our practice, and both celebrate and challenge it, to ensure that it is fit for purpose in the 21st century. Given that we are educating children and young people for lives, relationships and jobs that do not currently exist, D&T education's policy-makers, leaders and teachers must learn to become agile and responsive. Learning from, but not being bound by, past and current practices and beliefs.

## Questions

1. Thinking about your experience with the design and technology classroom, what are the surface structures (teaching methods) that you used most in your teaching?
2. How do ideating, realising and critiquing figure in your lessons? Which are more evident than others? Why might that be?
3. What are the benefits and limitations of 'the project' as a means of delivering the design and technology curriculum? Is 'the project' the only deep structure?
4. What other attitudes, values and dispositions (implicit structures) underpin D&T education?
5. What does D&T offer to future learning, work and life?
6. What new pedagogies should the D&T education community adopt, and which should we discontinue? Why?

## Notes

1. The 'classroom' in design and technology, including a range of environments including kitchens, laboratories, studios and workshops.
2. Epistemology is the study of the world around us, including the definition and limits of human knowledge.
3. Ontology is the study of existence or being, including the nature of objects (things), how they are structured and how we experience them.
4. Morrison-Love proposes that transformation is at the heart of the subject, in the same way as the experiment is with science, and the proof with mathematics.
5. A prime example of unrefined committee driven curriculum design, if ever there was one!
6. Wicked problems are challenges or situations that are difficult (or impossible) to solve, due to changing, complex and/or competing demands. They appear to resist solutions, involving tensions and complicated social or systemic relationships. Examples include environmental change, where a solution to one factor can have negative effects on others, but where taking no action will also be detrimental.
7. A good design brief should avoid limiting the potential design outcomes, by defining a specific product, but should focus on the needs of the user and the problem that is to be solved.

8 By way of critique, the array of projects in the D&TA project bank, the examples of mainly designing projects is relatively weak and restrictive, in comparison to the others. I would encourage readers to critically engage with this, and similar, resource.
9 Note: the opposite of scaffolding (i.e. the removal of structures to support learners) is called fading - remember that, just like for a building, scaffolding is temporary and is removed when the structure is complete and stable.

# References

ACARA. (2014). *The Australian Curriculum: Technologies Introduction*. Available at: https://bit.ly/3LDBaRX [Accessed 30 March 2022].

Atkinson, S. (1990). Design and Technology in the United Kingdom. *Journal of Technology Education*, 2(1). Available at: https://bit.ly/3iZtw7O [Accessed 30 March 2022].

Banks, F., Barlex, D., Jarvinen, E., O'Sullivan, G., Owen-Jackson, G., & Rutland, M. (2004). DEPTH – Developing Professional Thinking for Technology Teachers: An International Study. *International Journal of Technology and Design Education*, 14(2), 141–157. doi:10.1023/B:ITDE.0000026475.55323.01

Banks, F., & Owen-Jackson, G. (2007). The Role of Making in Design & Technology. In D. Barlex (Ed.), *Design and Technology for the Next Generation* (pp. 186–197). Whitchurch, UK: Cliffe and Company (Advertising and Marketing) Ltd.

Barlex, D. (2003). Considering the Impact of Design and Technology on Society – The Experience of the Young Foresight project. Paper presented at the The place of design & Technology in the Curriculum PATT Conference, Glasgow.

Barlex, D. (2011, 19–21 May). An International Perspective on Design & Technology: Lessons for the Road Ahead. Paper presented at the *National Association of Advisers and Inspectors in Design and Technology Annual Conference: Design and Technology for all our Futures*, Winchester, UK.

Barlex, D., & Trebell, D. (2008). Design-without-make: Challenging the Conventional Approach to Teaching and Learning in a Design and Technology Classroom. *International Journal of Technology and Design Education*, 18(2), 119–138. doi:10.1007/s10798-007-9025-5

Bell, D., Wooff, D., McLain, M., & Morrison-Love, D. (2017). Analysing Design and Technology as an Educational Construct: An Investigation into Its Curriculum Position and Pedagogical Identity. *The Curriculum Journal*, 28(4), 539–558. doi: 10.1080/09585176.2017.1286995

Bernstein, B. (1971). On the Classification and Framing of Educational Knowledge. In M. Young (Ed.), *Knowledge and Control. New Directions for the Sociology of Education* (pp. 47–69). London: Collier-Macmillan.

Bernstein, B. (1975). *Class, Codes and Control: Towards a Theory of Educational Transmission* (Vol. III). London: Routledge.

Bernstein, B. (1990). *The Structuring of Pedagogic Discourse: Class, Codes and Control* (Vol. IV). London: Routledge.

Busby, E. (2019, Fri 24 May). Fewer Students Taking Design and Technology and Music at GCSE, Figures Reveal. Independent. Available at: https://bit.ly/38kTXD6 [Accessed 30 March 2022].

Churchman, C. (1967). Guest Editorial: Wicked Problems. *Management Science*, 14(4), B141–B142. Available at: www.jstor.org/stable/2628678

Coughlan, S. (2018). Surgery Students 'Losing Dexterity to Stitch Patients'. BBC News. Available at: https://www.bbc.co.uk/news/education-46019429

D&TA. (2019). D&T Key Resources – A Bank of Teaching Resources for Key Stage 3. Available at: https://www.data.org.uk/media/3249/ks3-dt-project-bank-2019.pdf [Accessed 22 August 2022].

DES/WO. (1988). National Curriculum Design and Technology Working Group Interim Report. Available at: https://bit.ly/394kvWA [Accessed 30 March 2022].

DfE. (2011). *The Framework for the National Curriculum: A Report by the Expert Panel for the National Curriculum review*. (DFE-00135-2011). London: Department for Education Available at: https://bit.ly/3ftmerm [Accessed 30 March 2022].

DfE. (2013). National Curriculum in England: Framework for Key Stages 1 to 4. London: Department for Education Available at: https://bit.ly/3qVHxrD [Accessed 30 March 2022].

DfE. (2015). Design and Technology GCSE Subject Content. (DFE-00283-2015). Available at: https://bit.ly/3781TqM [Accessed 30 March 2022].

DfES. (2004). Module 4: Teaching the Subskills of Designing. (0971-2004 G). Available at: https://bit.ly/3IY6nxe [Accessed 30 March 2022].

DoE. (2002). Revised National Curriculum Statement Grades R-9 (Schools). Pretoria: Department of Education of South Africa Available at: https://bit.ly/371wJ4e [Accessed 22 August 2022].

EB. (2016). Curriculum Development > Key Learning Areas > Technology Education. Available at: https://bit.ly/3uPmxUu [Accessed 30 March 2022].

English, L. D. (2019). Learning while Designing in a Fourth-grade Integrated STEM Problem. *International Journal of Technology and Design Education*, 29(5), 1011–1032. doi:10.1007/s10798-018-9482-z

Flaig, J. (2020). Engineering GCSE Entries Fall 31% Amid Poor Understanding of What Engineers Do. Engineering News. Available at: https://bit.ly/36Kej8c [Accessed 30 March 2022].

Fuller, A., & Unwin, L. (2003). Learning as Apprentices in the Contemporary UK Workplace: Creating and Managing Expansive and Restrictive Participation, *Journal of Education and Work*, 16(4), 407–426. doi: 10.1080/1363908032000093012

Gibb, N. (2017). The Importance of Knowledge-based Education: School Standards Minister Speaks at the Launch of the 'The Question of Knowledge' [Press release]. Available at: https://bit.ly/3tW6HIv [Accessed 30 March 2022].

Hattie, J. (2008). *Visible Learning: A Synthesis of over 800 Meta-analyses relating to Achievement*. Abingdon, UK: Routledge.

HOC. (2021). The Forgotten: How White Working-class Pupils Have Been Let Down, and How to Change it: First Report of Session 2021–22. (HC 85). London: Parliamenary House of Commons Available at: https://bit.ly/3wRSXAF [Accessed 30 March 2022].

Horn, J. L., & Cattell, R. B. (1966). Refinement and Test of the Theory of Fluid and Crystallized General Intelligences. *Journal of Educational Psychology*, 57(5), 253–270. doi:10.1037/h0023816

IDEO. (2021). Design Thinking for Educators. Available at: https://www.ideo.com/post/design-thinking-for-educators [Accessed 22 August 2022].

ITEEA. (2021). Technologically Literate Citizens. Available at: https://www.iteea.org/48897.aspx [Accessed 18 March 2022].

Joynes, C., Rossignoli, S., & Amonoo-Kuofi, E. F. (2018). 21st Century Skills: Evidence of Issues in Definition, Demand and Delivery for Development Contexts s (K4D Helpdesk Report). Available at: Brighton, UK: https://assets.publishing.service.gov.uk/media/5d71187ce5274a097c07b985/21st_century.pdf [Accessed 18 March 2022].

McCormick, R. (1997). Conceptual and Procedural Knowledge. *International Journal of Technology and Design Education*, 7(1), 141–159. doi:10.1023/A:1008819912213

McLain, M. (2018). Emerging Perspectives on the Demonstration as a Signature Pedagogy in Design and Technology Education. *International Journal of Technology and Design Education*, 28(4), 985–1000. doi:10.1007/s10798-017-9425-0

McLain, M. (2021a). Developing Perspectives on the Demonstration as a Signature Pedagogy in Design and Technology. *International Journal of Technology and Design Education*, 31(1), 3–26. doi:10.1007/s10798-019-09545-1

McLain, M. (2021b). Key Pedagogies in Design and Technology. In A. Hardy (Ed.), *Learning to Teach Design and Technology in the Secondary School* (4 ed.). Abingdon, UK: Routledge.

McLain, M., Irving-Bell, D., Wooff, D., & Morrison-Love, D. (2019). How Technology Makes Us Human: Cultural and Historical Roots for Design and Technology Education. *Curriculum Journal*. doi:10.1080/09585176.2019.1649163

Mitcham, C. (1994). *Thinking through Technology: A Path between Engineering and Philosophy*. Chicago: The University of Chicago Press.

Morrison-Love, D. (2017). Towards a Transformative Epistemology of Technology Education. *Journal of Philosophy of Education*, 51(1), 23–37. doi:10.1111/1467-9752.12226

Muller, J., & Young, M. (2019). Knowledge, Power and Powerful Knowledge Re-visited. *The Curriculum Journal*, 30(2), 196–214. doi:10.1080/09585176.2019.1570292

OECD. (2018). The Future of Education and Skills: Education 2030. Available at: Paris: https://bit.ly/3Duw3QS [Accessed 30 March 2022].

Paechter, C. (1995). Subcultural Retreat: Negotiating the Design and Technology Curriculum. *British Educational Research Journal*, 21(1), 75–87. doi:10.1080/0141192950210106

Petrina, S. (2000). The Political Ecology of Design and Technology Education: An Inquiry into Methods. *International Journal of Technology and Design Education*, 10(3), 207–237. doi:10.1023/A:1008955016067

Reynolds, D., Sammons, P., De Fraine, B., Van Damme, J., Townsend, T., Teddlie, C., & Stringfield, S. (2014). Educational Effectiveness Research (EER): A State-of-the-art Review. *School Effectiveness and School Improvement*, 25, 34.

Sahlberg, P., & Doyle, E. (2019). *Let the Children Play: How More Play Will Save Our Schools and Help Children Thrive*. New York: Oxford University Press.

Shulman, L. S. (1986). Those Who Understand: Knowledge Growth in Teaching. *Educational Researcher*, 15(2), 4–14. Available at: http://www.jstor.org/stable/1175860 [Accessed 22 August 2022].

Shulman, L. S. (2005). Signature Pedagogies in the Professions. *Daedalus*, 134(3), 8. doi:10.1162/0011526054622015

Skolverket. (2018). Curriculum for the Compulsory School, Preschool Class and School-age Educare. Available at: https://bit.ly/3NIZSCi [Accessed 30 March 2022].

Spielman, A. (2019). Amanda Spielman Speaking at the Victoria and Albert Museum (speech transcript). Available at: https://bit.ly/3LBZFPp [Accessed 30 March 2022].

Sternberg, R. J. (2005). The Theory of Successful Intelligence. *Interamerican Journal of Psychology*, 39(2), 189–202.

Trebell, D. (2009). Studying Classroom Interaction During a Design-Without-Make Assignment. *Design and Technology Education: An International Journal*, 14(3).

TKI. (2017). The New Zealand Curriculum Online: Technology. Available at: https://nzcurriculum.tki.org.nz/The-New-Zealand-Curriculum/Technology [Accessed 18 March 2022].

White, J. (2018). The Weakness of 'Powerful Knowledge. *London Review of Education*, 16(2), 11. doi:10.18546/LRE.16.2.11

Whittaker, F., & Allen-Kinross, P. (2019, Fri 24 May). GCSE Entries: Engineering and Design Technology Flop as EBacc Subjects Soar. Schools Week. Available at: https://bit.ly/3iUIAUA [Accessed 30 March 2022].

Young, M. (2008). From Constructivism to Realism in the Sociology of the Curriculum. *Review of Research in Education*, 32(1), 1–28. doi:10.3102/0091732X07308969

# 6 Does food fit in design and technology?

*Suzanne Lawson and Susan Wood-Griffiths*

## Introduction

Yes, it does. No, it does not. The debate here is not issues within the subject; the debate is the subject itself. Some argue design and technology (D&T) is not where food studies should be located in the school curriculum; others argue it is. This chapter looks at the debate around food within the D&T curriculum and considers the historical context and the evolution of the food curriculum. When D&T was established in the National Curriculum (DES 1990), the common thread defining the suite of materials studied was the design process. The various iterations of the National Curriculum from 1990 until 2013 (DfE 2013a) used common terminology and headings to define what should be taught whether working with food, textiles, resistant materials or systems and control technology. When writing this chapter in 2013 (Lawson 2013), it was argued food had to be in D&T to survive. This updated chapter hopes to offer a range of opinions so that you can draw your own conclusions and decide – does food fit in design and technology?

## The historical context

The introduction of 'technology' as a subject in the new English National Curriculum (DES 1990) in 1990 perhaps marks the start of the debate 'Does food fit?' Until this point, domestic science and home economics had evolved from subjects that arguably sat comfortably in the social climate of the early to mid-twentieth century supporting what Lawson (2013, p. 102) notes as a 'philanthropic-utilitarian function'. The subject's inclusion in technology meant home economics teachers became 'food technology' teachers and the emphasis moved from domestic production of meals to commercial production of marketable food products. Food teachers received no training and little support for teaching the industrial and commercial components of food production leaving many feeling alienated from a curriculum seeming to have little reference to food and containing words such as designing, artefacts, systems and mechanisms (Rutland 2006). The curriculum content of the subject changed with the introduction of vocabulary, including 'product development', 'sensory evaluation', 'food for a target market of consumers',

DOI: 10.4324/9781003166689-9

and the increasing demand for the use of industrial tools and equipment (DES 1990). At the time, the new subject 'technology' married together traditional craft subjects using textiles, wood, metal, plastic and food but appeared to be closer to the philosophy of the former craft, design and technology (CDT) specification than home economics. Did food, with its history of domestic study, fit this philosophy? Did it have anything in common with technological areas? While some teachers felt alienated by these changes in the subject, others saw the transformation as presenting new and exciting challenges, opportunities to move the teaching forward and the best opportunity for the future of food in schools.

Critics of food as part of the new Technology National Curriculum, most notably from the engineering community, did not think food belonged in the subject mix. Their arguments included that being able to cook is 'affected by technology but [is] not necessarily part of it' (Smithers and Robinson 1992, p. 15) and that the inclusion of food in technology was more about keeping home economics alive and making technology girl-friendly than its intrinsic value (Smithers 1993, cited in Fine 1994; Knight 1996). As Fine (1994, p. 41) noted: 'the gist of the anti-food lobby was that Technology was essentially about making, structures and artefacts so to include food would reduce its rigour and diminish its status'. It is debatable that the inclusion of food in technology meant that food (as home economics) lost its identity and became a part of every child's curriculum, albeit within the matrix of technology (Knight 1996). The British Nutrition Foundation (BNF) welcomed the new curriculum, noting that food technology should not be confused with cookery and arguing that food technology teaches pupils scientific principles (Fines 1994). Understanding and articulating this argument is central to the debate about whether food fits in D&T.

Revision of the National Curriculum in 1995, and the change in nomenclature from technology to design and technology (DFE/WO 1995), did nothing to help. Teachers wanting to teach food skills in a traditional context found themselves teaching pupils the, arguably worthless, activity of drawing food products and requiring them to complete paper-based 'design tasks' at the expense of providing opportunities to develop practical skills. Pressures on curriculum time for D&T meant that many schools adopted a 'carousel' approach, in which pupils spent just a few weeks each year in each of the D&T areas. This resulted in limited opportunities for pupils to cook, and these were then further restricted by demands to draw food products and packaging. Food teachers struggled with the conflicting demands of developing pupils' practical food skills as well as design capabilities. Ofsted (2002, 2004, and 2005) highlighted that some D&T teachers paid insufficient attention to the process of designing, limiting pupils' experience to a series of short, focused practical tasks. Without explaining why this was important in food technology, the Ofsted reports reinforced the idea that pupils should draw food design ideas, leaving many food teachers frustrated. The Key Stage 3 National Strategy 'Design and Technology Framework and training materials' (DfES 2004; government-produced materials intended to support teachers in the teaching of designing) provided a broader definition of the term *designing* offering teachers non-graphical examples of designing and modelling strategies, which could be used in food technology. Innovative strategies promoted creativity by providing pupils with a rubric for design ideas such as 'extending a product range' or working with peers to change key components in the design. This was helpful, but it still presented design work as a paper-based activity.

What seemed to have been lost at the time was the realisation that designing in food was not about drawing and that pupils need to understand key skills and scientific principles to adapt and develop recipes. Rutland and Barlex (2006, p. 6) argued that designing in food was different from other activities as it was 'simultaneous' involving brainstorming, customer opinion and attribute and product analysis, as well as modelling with food products for testing and development. This view was supported by Owen-Jackson (2007), who argued that designing with food was better referred to as 'food product development' and involved working with food ingredients rather than drawing food products. This was perhaps the 'golden era' of making food fit into the subject albeit if the fit always felt slightly incompatible.

Further revisions to the National Curriculum in 1995 (DFE), 1999 (DfEE/QCA), 2007 (QCA) and 2013 (DfE) all retained food within D&T. Of course, aspects of food education are covered in other subjects, notably personal, social, health and economics (PSHE) education; science; geography; and physical education (Reeves 2020), but it is the continued inclusion of food as a material in D&T that is central to the debate here. In the 2014 adaptation of the curriculum, all pupils aged 5 to 14 years in maintained schools were, and are, required to study 'Cooking and Nutrition' (DfE 2014). Whilst remaining under the umbrella framework of the Design and Technology National Curriculum Programme of Study, lobbying from many charitable organisations such as Jamie's School Dinners, the Let's Get Cooking Campaign, the Healthy Schools initiative and the BNF (Seabrook and Grafham 2020) resulted in a shift of focus back to cooking and nutrition. This iteration of the curriculum talked of teaching basic cookery skills, nutrition and healthy eating, as well as 'instilling a love of cooking' in pupils (DfE 2013a, p. 3). Influenced by the government commissioned 'School Food Plan' (DfE 2013b), the curriculum referenced the need to 'cook a repertoire of predominately savoury dishes' perhaps reflecting the authors, restaurateurs Henry Dimbleby's and John Vincent's, observations on school visits that found a proliferation of 'cupcake' making in many schools.

The 2013 National Curriculum document coincided with educational reforms that introduced a high-status English Baccalaureate (EBacc) into English secondary schools. As discussed in Chapter 1, the EBacc focused on a benchmark measurement that required secondary school pupils to take examinations in English, mathematics, science, a language and history or geography. This left very limited curriculum time for the 'creative subjects', including all aspects of D&T. So how did this impact food teaching in secondary schools?

The AKO Foundation charity, in a combined study by the Jamie Oliver Food Foundation, the British Nutrition Foundation, the Food Teachers Centre and the University of Sheffield, published the Fell Report in 2017 reviewing the state of food education in England. The report did not question, 'Does food fit?' but instead questioned 'Does food education happen?' It found a wide variation between schools in the quantity (duration and frequency), content and quality of what was being delivered, finding 'patchy' delivery of knowledge and skills, little application of the principles of a healthy diet in food choices and heavy constraints caused by a lack of time, budget and facilities.

For upper secondary English pupils, examination specifications in D&T: food technology was replaced with a new qualification in 'food preparation and nutrition' in 2013 (DfE). The removal of any reference to D&T in the titles fuels the argument that not only does D&T not fit but it has also now been removed.

This is also reflected in the Design and Technology Association (DATA) 'Career Profile for Teachers of Design and Technology: Subject Competencies' (2017) which omitted food entirely. DATA considered that the competencies for food teaching had already been defined by the framework of knowledge and skills documents for primary (Public Health England in 2015a) and secondary schools (Public Health England in 2015b), in collaboration with the British Nutrition Foundation. The BNF played a role in providing resources and training for food teachers, but a dedicated online platform called the Food Teachers' Centre began building momentum at the same time. The Food Teachers Centre, established in 2013, took the initiative to provide an online support network coupled with regional courses to provide members with shared ideas, resources and training. The Food Teachers' Centre perhaps took over the role of a subject association dedicated to food education in the UK. It could be argued that this was a defining period in the separation of food from design and technology although it was still a key material in the programme of study.

## Food and health

The English curriculum Design and Technology Programme of Study opens with a purpose statement that declares,

> Design and technology is an inspiring, rigorous and practical subject. . . . High-quality design and technology education makes an essential contribution to the creativity, culture, wealth and well-being of the nation.
> (DfE 2013b, p. 1)

Arguably, any discussion about food as a subject within the school curriculum debates well-being (Butler 2014), childhood obesity (Lawson 2013), school meals (Dimbleby and Vincent 2013) and, more recently, food poverty (Marsh 2018) and the impact these have on education. The COVID-19 pandemic further highlighted questions about well-being, school meal provision, the role food education plays in school and food eaten when not at school. Also illuminated was the wider role schools have in supporting pupils' well-being that extend beyond the formal curriculum, particularly for those pupils identified as being 'vulnerable' (Richardson 2020).

Concerns about childhood obesity and children's eating habits, spurred originally by Jamie Oliver's (2005) attempts to improve the quality and nutritional value of school dinners were reinforced by Dimbleby and Vincent (2013) in the School Food Plan, resulting in an arguably political focus on school food. Prominent food celebrities, such as Mary Berry (Nikkah 2012) and Prue Leith (Marsh 2018), joined debates on food in schools resulting in political interventions including the aforementioned statutory requirement to teach cooking and nutrition within the D&T curriculum in Key Stages 1 through 3 and legislation to define School Food Standards that apply to the provision of food in all maintained schools (DfE 2019).

Joining the food education for well-being debate, English professional footballer Marcus Rashford (BBC Sport 2020) challenged the government's support for poorer families highlighting the impact that poverty has on families in Manchester. Aware of the problems through his own childhood experiences and his family's reliance on free school meals, he used his profile to demonstrate philanthropy and influence government policy during the pandemic in 2020/21. Working with the charity FareShare, (https://fareshare.org.uk/) to deliver meals to children no longer receiving free school meals during school closures, he used his influence to highlight childhood food poverty. In June 2020, Rashford revealed the charity had reached 3 million children (BBC Sport 2020), a figure which rose to 4 million. Subsequently, he highlighted the extent of childhood poverty, and through his challenges in November 2020, the government extended the funding to support the cost of food and household bills for another 12 months (Richardson 2020). The relevance of Rashford's campaigning on the debate 'Does food fit?' raises the question: Is the food curriculum fit for purpose? The extent of the reliance of families for free school meals, in England in the 21st century, shocked many and the need for food lessons in the curriculum was once again debated but, this time, specifically focusing on disadvantaged families.

Social media carried pictures of 'unacceptable' food packages distributed to families by a private contractor to compensate families who, due to lockdown, could not receive free school meals. The contents of these packages, which were supposed to provide five days of lunches, caused widespread outrage, and Prime Minister Boris Johnson was forced to conduct a review. Rashford's work, and sharing of his own story, also exposed how children in families in which parents were holding down several low-paying jobs could become reliant on fast-food outlets (specifically chip shops) to curb hunger. This might provide an explanation for the prevalence of obesity in low-income families (Elliot 2020), who refers to research indicating a correlation between a rise in the number of fast-food outlets and increases in obesity between 2010 and 2018. This is certainly an important justification for teaching about food, but if this is a serious ambition, we return to the argument that food education needs to be resourced and funded properly.

Conversely, Owen-Jackson and Rutland (2017, p. 63) argue that recent political influences have been detrimental to the value of teaching about food and its potential to contribute to pupils' overall education as well as in defining what and where it can be taught in schools. Teaching pupils to make healthy food choices, particularly within school, does not require the facilities, resources or teacher expertise demanded by lessons in food preparation. There is, therefore, a dichotomy between food education for well-being and food education as part of an academic curriculum.

A barrier to food education in any curriculum is the supply of ingredients for practical lessons. Arguably, most schools require pupils to provide ingredients for food lessons with some providing basic ingredients for disadvantaged children who are eligible for free school meals. There is little acknowledgement of the challenges this presents for many families not entitled to free school meals but who nevertheless struggle. The COVID-19 pandemic highlighted the extent of food and fuel poverty and the reliance on food banks and free school meals. This is not a new issue. In 2014, the Trussell Trust (Butler 2014) reported the need to pack kettles and cold boxes of food for families with inadequate cooking facilities, these being boxes of food that need hot water alone or no heating. The exposure of this food poverty raises serious questions for food teachers and school leaders about what pupils should be taught to cook in school and the skills they need to eat healthily and economically.

Children's health and well-being are important, and education has a place in promoting healthy lifestyles. While these issues can serve to justify the importance of food education, they are complex and may distract from the opportunity to develop a food education framework with rigorous qualifications that support the subject's academic credibility. Education should arguably have a focus on local context and content as part of curriculum design. Curriculum content designed to challenge pupils to prepare healthy family meals from a food bank package, for example, would allow pupils to design and make for a domestic local context, supporting an argument that food fits in the D&T curriculum.

Food education that links school food provision, pupils' well-being and practical food preparation is seen by some as a utopia (Dimbleby and Vincent 2013). If this is to be achieved, food teachers, arguably, have the expertise to influence the transformation. If serious about food education, the recognition of the part schools can play in addressing the problem needs to go beyond defining ambitions for the subject and what needs to be taught. It requires adequate funding for the food curriculum so that the subject is inclusive and recognises the difficulties faced by many families as a consequence of austerity.

## How does the food curriculum in schools prepare young people for employment in food-related sectors?

The purpose statement the National Curriculum for D&T declares:

> High quality design and technology education makes an essential contribution to the creativity, culture, wealth and well-being of the nation', and also that 'pupils learn how to take risks, becoming resourceful, innovative, enterprising and capable citizens.
>
> (DfE 2013a, p. 1)

Although D&T is only compulsory in lower secondary school, the terms 'wealth' and 'enterprising' imply that the subject is preparing for future roles in society. This is a further justification for food education that extends its importance beyond the life skills and well-being arguments to supporting pupils to make a positive economic contribution in future life and to gain qualifications to do this. This requires studying the subject at the examination level with a progression to further studies.

Within the food, agriculture and hospitality sectors, there are many opportunities for young people. The food and drink industry is the biggest manufacturing sector in the country. Food and drink manufacturing contributes more to the economy (£28 billion) than all other manufacturing sectors, including automotive and aerospace, and provides employment for over 430,000 people with employment in the sector growing by 19 per cent over the last decade (Food and Drink Federation 2021). The employment opportunities within the food industry present a good argument for teaching food within a technology context as the industry endeavours to develop new products that are innovative and sustainable.

Besides this, the hospitality sector, and specifically the catering elements of hospitality, also provides employment opportunities for those looking to develop food preparation skills. The UK hospitality sector employs over 3.2 million people amounting to 10 per cent of the UK workforce (UKhospitality 2021). This was the justification schools used for teaching the former examination specifications in catering and the vocational hospitality and catering qualifications and is an argument for the new food preparation and nutrition qualification which has more emphasis on developing food preparation skills.

There is currently only one food qualification available in England at the General Certificate of Secondary Education (GCSE) level, this being the GCSE Food Preparation and Nutrition qualification that replaced previous GCSE qualifications in D&T Food Technology, Home Economics: Food and Nutrition and Catering. Specifications for teaching Food Preparation and Nutrition in England were developed from a common subject content framework (DfE 2015) by three of the examination boards: AQA, OCR and Eduqas. As education is devolved in the United Kingdom, separate specifications were developed for teaching in Wales and Northern Ireland. For the purpose of this discussion, we shall focus on the English specifications, which became available for teaching in September 2016, with the first examinations being completed in 2018.

The GCSE Food Preparation and Nutrition Subject Content Framework declared that

> GCSE specifications in food preparation and nutrition must equip students with the knowledge, understanding and skills required to cook and apply the principles of food science, nutrition and healthy eating. They should encourage students to cook and enable them to make informed decisions about a wide range of further learning opportunities and career pathways as well as develop vital life skills that enable them to feed themselves and others affordably and nutritiously, now and later in life.
>
> (DfE 2015, p. 3)

Supplementary to this, Ofqual (2015a) published the GCSE Subject Level Conditions and Requirements for the examination boards to address when preparing the specifications. This document set out the assessment objectives and requirements that the awarding bodies should address when writing specifications whereby 50 per cent of the award would be examined by a terminal written examination and 50 per cent through non-examined assessments. The non-examined assessments (NEA) consisted of two tasks: a food investigation task and a food preparation task with three dishes to be made within a single three-hour period. A consultation on these proposals was undertaken over a short period and an analysis of responses was published in August 2015 (Ofqual 2015b). While there was no consensus in the responses, concerns that were raised by multiple respondents included issues about accessibility for pupils with disabilities and learning difficulties and the cost of ingredients being a barrier for students from low-income families. Other responses expressed concerns about inclusivity including those who, for religious or ethical reasons, could not handle certain food products and the requirement to prepare a 'three-course meal' might disadvantage students from certain ethnic groups for whom this concept is not familiar. Additional concerns were raised about the 'cost' to schools of facilitating a four-hour practical examination (three-hour task plus preparation and assessment time) in terms of rooming, teaching staff and lost curriculum time for other pupils. These concerns did not result in any amendments and the aforementioned awarding bodies developed specifications to meet the Ofqual requirements.

Seabrook and Grafham (2020) compared the similarities in the specifications (a consequence of prescriptive guidance) and noted that Eduqas and OCR are more explicit about the food commodities to be studied. They also commented on the much greater emphasis on the development of food preparation skills suggesting that this has resulted in a deficit in food product development and the use of emerging ingredients and techniques when compared to the previous GCSE in Food Technology.

All examination boards produced supporting materials as guidance for teachers, these were in part a marketing exercise for the boards to induce schools to work with them but also illustrate the skill levels in food preparation required (AQA 2019) – for higher grades, pupils need to demonstrate complex skills. The skills are exemplified by examples of 'dishes', and a review of the list highlights that in order to demonstrate more complex skills more ingredients will be required at more expense. For example, cheese scones provide an example of a basic savoury dish and cheese souffle or lasagne made with fresh pasta are examples to demonstrate complex skills. Reviewing the list, it is not easy to find an example of a dish that would enable pupils to demonstrate complex skills for a low cost. This emphasis on 'skill level' is concerning and raises questions about the accessibility of specifications not only for low-income families, particularly where they are required to provide ingredients but also for schools that rely on resourcing ingredients from school funds. Indeed, it could be argued that the pupils from prosperous families with good access to well-stocked supermarkets will have a distinct advantage of being successful compared those who live in areas of deprivation. There is an inequality of opportunity if young people from low-income families are excluded from pursuing their interest in food, and potential employment, due to a lack of funding for ingredients in food lessons.

## Post-16

The age at which pupils are entitled to leave school is determined by the devolved governments of the United Kingdom. In Wales, Scotland and Northern Ireland, pupils can leave school when they are 16, although at what time in the school year is determined by birth date. In England, they can leave school at the end of the GCSE year, but they are required to remain in education or training until they are 18. This means either staying in full-time education, starting an apprenticeship or traineeship or working or volunteering for 20 hours or more while in part-time education or training.

Historically pupils who have been keen to pursue careers in catering have tended to leave school and move to colleges where they can study for a range of technical professional qualifications at different levels (e.g. City and Guilds [C&G] Professional Food and Beverage Service, C&G Level 2 Technical Certificate in Food Preparation and Service C&G Professional Cookery) or to apprenticeships in a setting which can provide a real working environment.

For those who are looking to stay in school to study for advanced academic qualifications, before progressing into higher education to study catering or a food-related degree, there are limited options. At the time of writing, the only level 3 qualification currently available is the Eduqas applied level 3 certificate in food and nutrition. Although at an advanced level, this is an applied course and is not perceived by some to have the same academic status as an A level. Furthermore, some teachers report that the qualification offers limited progression from the Food Preparation and Nutrition GCSE. Teachers lament the removal of the Food Technology A level (Rutland 2020) which would have offered progression and built on the new GCSE with a widened focus on industry and product development.

Furthermore, the lack of an A-level course is reported to negatively affect the status of food in schools (Ballam 2018). Rutland (2020) argues for the development of a new A-level food course if the subject is to have the status it deserves. It needs to be acceptable as an entry requirement for degree courses in higher education and develop pupils' interest in professional and research careers in the food sector. Without the progression of the subject as a post-16 subject the debate asking, 'Does food fit?' is limited to lower and upper secondary schooling, and there is currently no option for it to fit at advanced level with its natural progression to vocational career options.

## Conclusion

So, does food fit? The changes in school-based food education in the last 30 years have meant inevitable pedagogical evolution. Food educators who supported its inclusion in the D&T curriculum framework would argue that within this context food could offer more than the utilitarian 'craft skill' function of the former home economics subject content. In the early years of the National Curriculum, food education struggled to fit within D&T, mainly due to the formulaic and ritualistic interpretations of the requirements leading to pupils being asked to draw food solutions. It may be argued that the recent shift to food preparation and nutrition has resulted in food preparation for affluent children who develop advanced food skills with no progression routes to advanced study and meaningful employment. The debate 'Does food fit in design and technology?' has now shifted to 'Is food education fit for purpose?' The COVID-19 pandemic highlighted the need for policymakers, parents, headteachers and pupils to understand that modern, updated food education is worthwhile for all pupils. The debate now is how can food education be reimagined to be relevant, inclusive and challenging. This requires a curriculum that is properly resourced, develops life skills and has clear progression routes to advanced learning and career opportunities. We continue to need to educate a generation so that they are equipped with skills for life and skills for work.

## Questions

1 If you could write a food curriculum, what would be the key learning objectives and course content?
2 What does food have in common (if anything) with other technology material areas?
3 Is there a future for food education in schools?
4 Does a pupil's demographic and social background impact their ability to do well in the current food-related qualifications?
5 Should food education be compulsory for all, and if so, how should it be funded?

## References

AKO Foundation (2017) *The Food Education Learning Landscape Report (Fell Report)*. The Jamie Oliver Foundation, AKO.

AQA (2019) *Notes and Guidance: Skill Levels in Food Preparation*. Available at: https://www.aqa.org.uk/resources/food/gcse/food-preparation-and-nutrition/assess/notes-and-guidance-skill-levels-in-food-preparation [Accessed 21 February 2021].

Ballam, R. (2018). Editorial. Where next for food education? *The British Nutrition Foundation Nutrition Bulletin*, 43, 7–9. London, UK: British Nutrition Foundation.

BBC (2020) Sport 'I'll keep fighting' – Marcus Rashford on meals campaign. *BBC Sport*. 11 June. Available at: https://www.bbc.co.uk/sport/football/53014511 [Accessed 20 February 2021].

Butler, P. (2014) Food bank issues parcels for those too poor to heat dinner. *The Guardian*. 20 January. Available at: https://www.theguardian.com/society/2014/jan/20/food-bank-kettle-boxes-trussell-trust [Accessed 20 July 2021].

DES (1990) *Technology in the National Curriculum*. London: HMSO.

Department for Education (DFE)/Welsh Office (WO) (1995) *Design and Technology in the National Curriculum*, London: HMSO.

Department for Education and Employment (DfEE)/Qualifications and Curriculum Authority (QCA) (1999) *The National Curriculum*, London: HMSO.

Department for Education and Skills (DfES) (2004) *Key Stage 3 National Strategy: Design and Technology Framework and Training Materials*. London: HMSO.

Department for Education (DfE) (2013a) *Design and Technology Programmes of Study: Key Stage 3. National Curriculum in England*. Available at: https://assets.publishing.service.gov.uk/government/uploads/system/uploads/attachment_data/file/239089/SECONDARY_national_curriculum_-_Design_and_technology.pdf [Accessed 24 February 2021].

Department for Education (DfE) (2013b) *The School Food Plan*. Available at: http://www.schoolfoodplan.com/ [Accessed 24 February 2021].

Department for Education (DfE) (2015) *Food Preparation and Nutrition GCSE Subject Content*. Available at: https://www.gov.uk/government/publications/gcse-food-preparation-and-nutrition [Accessed 21 February 2021].

Design and Technology Association (2017) *Career Profile for Teachers of Design and Technology: Subject Competencies*. Available at https://www.data.org.uk/resource-shop/career-profile-for-teachers-of-design-and-technology-subject-competencies/ [Accessed 24 February 2021].

Dimbleby, H. and Vincent J. (2013). *The School Food Plan*. Available at: https://www.gov.uk/government/publications/the-school-food-plan

Elliott, L. (2020). *Poverty causes obesity. Low-income families need to be better off to eat well*. Available at: https://www.theguardian.com/business/2020/aug/09/poverty-causes-obesity-low-income-families-need-to-be-better-off-to-eat-well. [Accessed 23 August 2022].

Fine, G. (1994) Is there a future for food education in schools? *Design and Technology Teaching* 26(3), 39–44.

Food and Drink Federation (2021). *Statistics at a Glance*. Available at: https://www.fdf.org.uk/fdf/business-insights-and-economics/facts-and-stats/ [Accessed 21 February 2021].

Knight, P. (1996) Subject associations: The cases of secondary phase geography and home economics, 1976-94. *History of Education*, 25(3), 269–284.
Lawson, S. (2013) Does food fit? In G. Owen Jackson (ed.), *Debates within Design and Technology* (1st ed, pp. 101–114). Routledge: Oxon 101–114.
Marsh, S. (2018) *Prue Leith: Ban Packed Lunches and Teach Children to Cook*. Available at: https://www.theguardian.com/tv-and-radio/2018/aug/21/prue-leith-ban-packed-lunches-great-british-bake-off [Accessed 18 July 2019].
Nikkah, R. (2012) *Teach Cooking in Schools Says 'Queen of Cakes' Mary Berry*. Available at: https://www.telegraph.co.uk/foodanddrink/9432867/Teach-cooking-in-schools-says-Queen-of-Cakes-Mary-Berry.html [Accessed 18 July 2019].
Ofqual (2015a) *GCSE Subject Level Conditions and Requirements for Food Preparation and Nutrition July 2015*. Available at: https://assets.publishing.service.gov.uk/government/uploads/system/uploads/attachment_data/file/447469/2015-07-22-gcse-subject-level-conditions-food-prep-and-nutrition.pdf [Accessed 21 February 2021].
OfSTED (2002) *Report 2000/01*. London: HMSO
OfSTED (2004) *OfSTED Subject Reports 2002./03 - Design and Technology in Secondary Schools*. London: HMSO.
OfSTED (2005) *OfSTED Subject Reports 2003/04 - Design and Technology in Secondary Schools*. London: HMSO.
Ofqual (2015b) *Analysis of Responses to our Consultation on Conditions and Guidance for GCSE Food Preparation and Nutrition*. Available at: https://assets.publishing.service.gov.uk/government/uploads/system/uploads/attachment_data/file/454979/gcse-food-preparation-and-nutrition-analysis-of-responses.pdf [Accessed 21 February 2021].
Oliver, J. (2005) *Jamie's School Dinners* Channel 4 (1 February 2005–16 March 2005).
Owen-Jackson, G. (ed.) (2007) *Practical Guide to Teaching Design and Technology in the Secondary School*. London: Routledge.
Owen-Jackson G. and Rutland, M. (2017) *Food in the School Curriculum in England: Its Development from Cookery to Cookery*. Available at https://ojs.lboro.ac.uk/DATE/article/view/2159 [Accessed 24 February 2021].
QCA (2007) *The National Curriculum Key Stage 3*. London: HMSO.
Public Health England (2015a) *Food Teaching in Secondary Schools: A Framework of Knowledge and Skills*. London: PHE.
Public Health England (2015b) *Food Teaching in Primary Schools: A Framework of Knowledge and Skills*. London: PHE.
Reeves, S. (2020) Current research in nutrition in the school curriculum in England. In M. Rutland and A. Turner (eds), *Food Education and Food Technology in School* (pp. 229–242). Switzerland: Springer.
Richardson, H. (8 November 2020). Marcus Rashford: PM Climbdown over Free Meals in School Holidays. Available at: https://www.bbc.co.uk/news/education-54841316BBC [Accessed 20 February 2021].
Rutland, M. (2006) The inclusion of food technology as an aspect of technology in English school curriculum: A critical review. In M.J. de Vries and I. Mottier (eds), *International Handbook Of Technology Education – Reviewing the Past Twenty Years*. Rotterdam: Sense Publishers.
Rutland, M. (2020) Food teaching in upper secondary English schools: Progression into food-related undergraduate courses in higher education. In M. Rutland and A. Turner (eds), *Food Education and Food Technology in School* (pp. 289–302). Switzerland: Springer.

Rutland, M and Barlex, D. (2006) Developing a conceptual framework for auditing design decisions in food technology: The potential impact in initial teacher education (ITE) and classroom practice. In E. Norman and D. Spendlove (eds), *The Design and Technology International Research Conference Proceedings*. Wellesbourne: Design and Technology Association.

Seabrook, R. and Grafham, V. (2020) What is the current state of play for food education in English secondary schools. In M. Rutland and A. Turner (eds), *Food Education and Food Technology in School* (pp. 45–62). Switzerland: Springer.

Smithers, A. and Robinson, P. (1992) *Technology in the National Curriculum: Getting It Right*. London: Engineering Council.

## *Websites*

Fareshare Available at https://fareshare.org.uk/. [Accessed on 22 August 2022].

Trussell Trust Available at: https://www.trusselltrust.org/. [Accessed on 24 February 2021].

UK Hospitality Available at: https://www.ukhospitality.org.uk/ [Accessed 24 February 2021].

# 7 Role of making in D&T

*Mike Martin*

## Introduction

One of the key features of design and technology is the opportunity that it provides for pupils to see and touch, in three dimensions, the results of their own thinking and decision-making. The making aspect of the subject means that it provides a unique contribution to pupils' general education and a genuine link with the world of products and manufacturing outside the classroom. In my 30 years of experience, I have found that this aspect of the subject is by far the most interesting and rewarding, often providing good motivation and engagement to all that get involved. Yet we live in a world where pretty much anything is available to order, and all kinds of simple and complex products can be made in different countries and delivered to our door very quickly. If school education is a preparation for adult life, and the world of work, it could be argued that developing the skills of making with hand tools and machine tools is a waste of teachers' and pupils' time given that the era of craft apprenticeship (Penfold 1988) is long gone. Surely an awareness of what can be made with materials is enough? Pupils' education could then be focused on considering what they might design, to be made by others and what the consequences are of producing anything for ourselves, our community and the environment of which we are all part. This is a compelling argument and one possible future for the subject. If you disagree, then what really is the role of making in design and technology?

The answer to this question is not, as you can imagine, straightforward. Consequently, this chapter has been broken down into different sections that consider the varying roles that making can have within the subject. It considers the skills and knowledge that can be developed along with values and attitudes towards technology as a whole. In addition, factors affecting practice in school are considered and the chapter concludes with some questions about the future and the significant role that making might play in a subject that is very much at the heart of the relationship that there is between our made world and the natural environment. As Pavlova and Pitt (2007) discuss, the consideration of sustainability is an important aspect of design and technology education for now and the future.

## Making as a human activity

What better place to start than by considering the significance of making things for us as human beings? Making in all its forms is one of the things that sets us apart from other species on the planet and, if we consider human development, making shelters and increasingly more complex forms of technology have been an essential part of our existence. Through making processes we transform existing materials into something useful and in doing so we are realising in three-dimensional (3D) form something that will be of value to us. It is no surprise therefore that one of the first popular course books for the subject for the General Certificate of Secondary Education (GCSE) was called Design and Realisation (Chapman and Pearce 1998), supporting the idea that the subject is about realising in three dimensions what we have imaged in our minds – very much a natural human activity (Kelly et al. 1987). The Interim Report for Technology in the National Curriculum talked about developing 'capability to operate effectively and creatively in made world' (DES 1988: 3), and this is still one of the key drivers for design and technology as a subject within the National Curriculum (DfE 2013). Whilst making things can seem to be good for human beings, we also need to be conscious of the effects that this can have on the world around us. In the introduction his book *Technosystem*, Andrew Feenberg (2017) discusses the limits of human ambition (hubris) through technology and the need for us to take care not to destroy the very environment which supports us. In addition, we need to be aware of what Celia Lury (2011) describes as consumer culture and ask the question of whether design and technology education actually encourages consumption and should be removed from the curriculum as a result of its influence. A final thought in relation to making as a human activity is to consider the role of repair and maintenance alongside making things from new materials (Von Mengersen 2013). Given that the world has a finite amount of resources, it is likely that our ability to reuse and recycle what we have will be crucial in supporting our existence on the planet in the future.

Interestingly, in the lead-up to the current version of the National Curriculum for Design and Technology (DfE 2013), there was quite a bit of discussion about the role of the subject in providing opportunities to fix and repair things. As Hardy (2013) reported at the time, the draft curriculum document was poorly conceived and misguided, causing outrage across the teaching community. As a result, it took quite a while to refocus government thinking about the subject and take account of the views of those involved in the day-to-day teaching of pupils in schools. Nevertheless, it highlighted a gap in the statutory curriculum and something that I still believe needs to be addressed.

## Role of making – skills

Linked to the role of making, as part of being human, is the development of skills. One of the key features of any activity involved in making artefacts and products is the use of skills and knowledge related to materials and machine tools. Prior to the development of the Design and Technology National Curriculum the subjects of craft, design and technology and home economics were popular with pupils. These had a very strong focus on the development of fine and gross motor skills to make products in wood, metal, textiles and food. One of the key drivers in developing practical skills was to supply the manufacturing industry with young people able to use what they had learned for jobs. When the design and technology curriculum was developed (DES 1988), not everybody was destined for a job involving practical skills, but it was recognised that this had to be one of the features of the subject, and organisations, such as the Engineering Council, had a significant influence on the development of the curriculum at that time. A good description of the social-cultural influences on the subject at the time can be found in David Layton's (1992) published booklet on the shaping of the subject.

As the subject developed, it was necessary to broaden the range of skills so that pupils could use machine tools and machines used for computer-aided manufacturing. At this point, the range of materials was such that teachers were often expected to be able to move from one material to another and develop, in pupils, an essentially generic knowledge of how to work with tools and materials. In addition to the physical skills required to work with materials, being logical, being organised, working independently and working as a part of a team were all seen as important attributes for employment, and they still are.

Some 30 years later from the creation of the subject, it is necessary to ask the question whether the development of fine and gross motor skills is really necessary as a part of pupils' general education given that very few young people will be involved directly in the production of products by hand, with hand tools or indeed with machine tools or CAD/CAM (Computer Aided Design/Computer Aided Manufacture). Given the fact that much of what we used is produced by computer-aided manufacturing systems, with incredible precision and repeatability, it is difficult to see how pupils might make anything of the quality that is demanded by themselves, and other users, in the current context.

It is also the case that there are other demands on curriculum time for design and technology and, consequently, limited scope for hands-on experience with the materials which contemporary products are made from. Nevertheless, we do actually live and work in the material world on a day-to-day basis and come across the need to use our skills at home and in the workplace. As Ingold argues, the development of new technology does not signal the end of skill. The question therefore arises about which fundamental skills, and with which materials, it might be useful to develop with pupils in classrooms of the future.

## Role of making – knowledge

Whilst direct physical contact with materials and developing fine and gross motor skills for pupils may not be as important as they used to be, it is important that students develop some fundamental knowledge about materials and processes. For those involved in using the latest three-dimensional (3D) printing technology, for example some basic understanding of thermoplastics is useful to have. Even more important is knowledge about structures and, when we are manufacturing complex pieces, an understanding of stress concentration and the forces that may act on products that are made. For example in making a wall mount for a Bluetooth speaker at home, I made sure to use rounded corners rather than sharp corners to avoid splitting – not uncommon with 3D-printed products where layers of material are bonded to each other. One of the best ways of gaining a 'good working knowledge' of materials is, of course, by making things by hand. For example, developing an understanding of grain in wood or bias in textiles is easily done in a practical way and enables us to be able to make informed decisions about how to proceed when making (McCormick 1997) or indeed understand how things have been made.

Another area of knowledge that pupils should understand is in relation to the sources of materials and how they are be disposed of after use. Being aware, for example, that the aluminium foil on a chocolate egg has taken a good deal of energy to produce from bauxite and will have involved considerable amounts of transport across different countries is useful to be aware of when considering making something in aluminium. It is also helpful to know that the foil may be recycled and used again to make more foil or other products out of aluminium. Taking this into account and designing for disassembly would then enable the materials from the product to have a 'second life'.

This kind of basic knowledge about the sources and process involved in manufacturing the raw elements used in products is I believe important for young people to know. As well as being helpful when designing, it can inform their choices about what to use and consume in the future whilst being aware of the consequences of material sourcing, production, use and disposal.

## Role of making – design

Next, we can consider the role of making when designing and the links between making and designing. One of the key aspects of much design and technology activity as recognised by the Nuffield Design and Technology Project (Nuffield 1995) in the early years of the National Curriculum was the bond between designing and making. A key statement that I remember at the time often quoted in relation to the project was that pupils should be able to design something that they can make and be able to make what they have designed. This symbiotic relationship, between making and designing, has always been important within the subject and part of any design process will surely be a consideration of how something is to be made. Even with contemporary 3D printing technology, this is still the case as the machines that are used work in specific ways that mean not everything that you could design can actually be manufactured. Having created a 3D model for example, it is necessary to check it with another piece of software such as Cura (Ultimaker.com) in order to determine whether it is feasible to make with the machine being used.

Even when designing relatively simple things such as felt puppets it is often useful to make a paper or card model in order to see how to proceed. It may also be useful to join materials together in order to see how a product might hold together or indeed be taken apart. Such model making involves the application of fine and gross motor skills along with an understanding of modelling materials such as card, calico and modelling clay. Interestingly, with food technology, any prototyping needs to be done with the real ingredients being used, and in this sense, modelling is making.

The skills and knowledge gained through making activities can help with decision-making which is a key part of designing (Woodward 2021). Consider for example the design of a wall-mounted key holder. This is something that could be made in a number of different ways with different materials and when designing, pupils would need to consider the impact that their design decision might have on the making skills and processes that would be involved. At its simplest, we could make a key holder from a single piece of thin steel welding rod and a pair of pliers. The end result is very dependent on hand skills, and making this would certainly draw on our understanding of steel as a resistant material. Alternatively, we could create hand-sewn pockets in textiles to store the keys which would require us to use our knowledge of materials and sewing machines to make something that was fit for purpose. A third option would be to shape the key holder from wood using a jigsaw and use a battery-powered hand drill to make holes for dowel pegs. This would draw on our knowledge of those tools and our understanding of grain in wood to ensure that the thin sections would not break. With a focus on CAD/CAM, we could use a 2D design program and CNC router to cut out a shape from an acrylic sheet and bend it into a holder with a strip heater. This could only be done by pupils who are familiar with both the software and the hardware. Finally, we could draw a model from scratch using an online 3D modelling website and print it out using recyclable plastic. Functionally, all of these might be fit for the purpose of holding the keys so they are readily available. As we can see, however, a good-quality end product will be dependent on the designer's experience, skills and knowledge about materials and processes – something that can really only be gained through making.

## Role of making – well being

One of the other roles that making has is developing our ability to think and act at the same time, which is good for cognitive development. Realising our own ideas, in three dimensions, is both rewarding and self-affirming. Anyone that has engaged in making something that is very detailed will know that it is an absorbing activity and one that can be a good distraction from worrying about other things. This role of making, which engages us in physical activity, cannot be underestimated as a positive contribution to our well-being. With the ever-increasing amount of time spent interacting with communication devices in an essentially passive way, there is a need to maintain kinaesthetic psychomotor skills to avoid us losing them altogether. Making something, we can say, therefore, is essentially good for us and usually a lot of fun! Enabling pupils to understand this and see the value of being active in the world should surely be an important part of any curriculum in any country.

## Role of making – curriculum

After considering the role of making in relation to skills, knowledge, design and well-being discussed earlier, we can now consider the place of making activities within a contemporary design and technology curriculum in schools. Since the subject became part of the National Curriculum some 30 years ago, we have, as users of technology, become somewhat distanced from the means of production. Large-scale manufacturing facilities, often in other countries, produce much of what we use on a daily basis, and we often have little say in the way that things are designed and made. This raises a number of questions about the role of making and the degree of agency we have in shaping the world around us. Should there be, for example, activities that are purely about pupils developing their fine and gross motor skills through making without necessarily being involved in designing? These could be focused on developing their coordination and accuracy as well as appreciating the physical and working properties of materials. Such activity might be short in time and very focused in terms of skills but still an important part of the subject (McLain 2021).

## Making in practice

So far, the discussion has been relatively theoretical, looking at the rationale for undertaking making activities and their value as part of people's general education. For practising teachers working in busy schools, however, there are several important practical considerations. The first one of these to consider is the resources that are available in terms of the materials, tools, machine tools and CADCAM that pupils are able to use. Anyone who has used a machine tool will be aware that there are limitations in terms of the size of what can be done and the accuracy that can be achieved. As a consequence, the technology effectively mediates what can be made (Verbeek 2005). This alone will mean that different things can be made in different schools and that making activities are context-dependent.

In addition to the availability of resources and materials (often dictated by school budgets), the influence of health and safety policies is another practical consideration. Take a moment to reflect on the context in which you are working and what tools pupils can use. What access do they have to knives for marking out and cutting? Do they have total access to the laser cutter like some schools I have been in? Or is it kept under close control by a technician like others I have seen? You might also consider the influence of school senior management and policies in determining what can and cannot be done in a school workshop. When I first started teaching, casting with aluminium was always a highlight of the practical sessions undertaken with GCSE pupils. Now it's rare to see even on a small scale.

The subject knowledge of teachers is another factor that can have a significant effect on the opportunities that pupils have for making. Enabling pupils to work with tools and resources requires a level of confidence by the teacher themselves and an understanding of appropriate pedagogical strategies (Ellis 2007). For many teachers of design and technology, they will have come to the subject with skills and knowledge in a particular area which might be linked to working with a specific set of materials. So a specialist in food technology might be employed as a teacher within the design and technology department and anticipate using their subject knowledge about food to support pupils learning. This might be the case for a time, and then as a result of stuff changes or timetabling, they may be asked to teach in a different material area such as textiles. For those involved in other subjects across the school this expectation to teach completely different content may appear odd, but in reality, such teaching across material areas is not uncommon.

Linked to this is the increasing range of materials and processes that products are made with outside school environments. Since design and technology became a subject in the national curriculum, there's been an increased use of plastics, developments in computer-aided manufacturing and 2D and 3D computer-aided design, all of which have gradually found their way into classroom and workshop environments. For busy teachers, keeping up with the ever-changing skills and knowledge required is difficult. With some of the most specialist resources, there may only be one person in the school who actually knows to use it properly. If they are off ill or leave the school, then that resource may become redundant and the opportunities for pupils to make things with it will be lost.

Making things well takes not only skills and knowledge but time. With the current version of the National Curriculum (DfE 2013) there is much to be covered and time for making may be at a premium. Overcoming this is sometimes a matter of considering scale and asking pupils to make something that is small but with precision. It may vary according to age but is important in enabling pupils to understand that quality products take time to make and for them to value the results of their own physical activity. This links very well with another factor that induces learning experiences for pupils, namely motivation. Providing opportunities for pupils to engage in authentic making activities will help keep them motivated and at the same time engaged in practical activity, making class management easier for teachers. From personal experience, I remember pupils coming to the workshop and the first thing they would ask was whether it was a practical or a theory session. My response to this question usually had significant effects on their engagement and behaviour as well as my stress levels during the lesson!

## Conclusion

In 1992, the charity Intermediate Technology produced a book titled *Make the Future Work* (Budgett-Meakin 1992). The aim was to raise discussion with teachers about the nature of technology and consider appropriate technology for our future and the implications that would have for classroom practice. Some 30 years later, there is an even stronger need than ever for an authentic education about technology that enables young people to value the awe and wonder of what we can achieve as human beings as well as develop a critical attitude towards technology practice that shapes our way of living and the nature of what it is to be human. So now really is a good time to take stock of current practice and find answers to the various questions raised earlier about making activities in design and technology. What should be the focus in terms of skills knowledge values and attitudes?

On a very real level, the future will be dictated by technology and our relationship with it. In the current context, we appear to have little say, or agency, about the ways in which technology develops. This is in part because of our distance from the means of production, and there is a danger that we've become so far removed from the process of making that we are unable to see the effects that this all has on the made and natural world. To have the capacity to make informed decisions for the future, we need to have a very real understanding of how materials are transformed into technology and what happens to them over time. It is surely only through hands-on activity with materials that we are able to see the relationships that technology has with the world. It is this argument that makes in-depth making activity a central part of general education for all. This need not take a great deal of time, but an experience of additive and subtractive processes involved in working with materials, that is joining and shaping, should be an essential part of education.

## Questions

As we have seen in this chapter, making can help to develop skills, acquire in-depth knowledge, support designing activities and be good for our wellbeing (Banks and Owen-Jackson 2007).

1 What emphasis is given to making skills in your school's design and technology curriculum? Is it enough?
2 What materials do you think pupils should be working with in a future beyond petrochemical plastics?

3 What could you do to increase your own level of confidence when making things in different materials?
4 What could you do to further develop pupils making skills in design and technology lessons?

## References

Banks F and Owen-Jackson G (2007) The Role of Making in Design and Technology. In D Barlex (Ed), *D&T for the Next Generation*. Whitchurch: Cliffeco Communications. Available online at: https://dandtfordandt.wordpress.com/resources/dt-for-the-next-generation/
Budgett-Meakin C (1992) *Make the Future Work*. London: Longman.
Chapman and Pearce (1998) *GCSE Design and Realisation*. London: Collins.
DES (1988) *National Curriculum Design and Technology Working Group: Interim Report*. London: HMSO.
DfE (2013) *National curriculum in England: framework for key stages 1 to 4*. London: Department for Education. Retrieved from https://www.gov.uk/government/publications/national-curriculum-in-england-framework-for-key-stages-1-to-4
Ellis V (2007) *Subject Knowledge and Teacher Education*. London: Continuum.
Feenberg A (2017) *Technosystem; The Social Life of Reason*. Cambridge, MA: Harvard University Press.
Hardy A (2013) Email to Alan Duncan, MP for Rutland and Melton. Available online at: https://ntudte.blogspot.com/2013/03/letter-to-mp.html
Kelly A et al. (1987) *Design and Technological Activity; A Framework for Assessment*. London: Assessment of Performance Unit, Department of Education and Science.
Layton D (1992) *Values and Design and Technology*. Design Curriculum Matters: Occasional Paper No. 2. Loughborough: Loughborough University.
Lury C (2011) *Consumer Culture*. Cambridge: Polity Press.
McLain M (2021) Key Pedagogies in Design and Technology. In Hardy A (Ed), *Learning to Teach Design and Technology in the Secondary School*. London: Routledge.
McCormick R (1997) Conceptual and Procedural Knowledge. *International Journal of Technology & Design Education*, 7(1/2), 141–159.
Nuffield (1995) *Nuffield Design and Technology: Study Guide*. Harlow: Longman.
Pavlova M and Pitt J (2007) The Place of Sustainability in Design and Technology. In Barlex (Ed), *D&T for the Next Generation*. Whitchurch: Cliffeco Communications. Available online at: https://dandtfordandt.wordpress.com/resources/dt-for-the-next-generation/
Penfold J (1988) *Craft, Design and Technology: Past, Present and Future*. Stoke on Trent: Trentham Books.
Verbeek P (2005) *What Things Do: Philosophical Reflections on Technologye, Agency and Design*. Pennsylvania, USA: Pennsylvania State Press.
Von Mengersen B (2013) *Sustainability + Needlecraft = Textiles Technology: Could a Return to 'Needlecraft' Skills Enhance Sustainable Practice in Textiles?* PATT27: Technology Education for the Future, A play on Sustainability. pp. 335–362. Christchurch: University of Canterbury, New Zealand.
Woodward P (2021) Designing in Design and Technology. In Hardy A (Ed), *Learning to Teach Design and Technology in the Secondary School*. London: Routledge.

# 8 Entrepreneurship in technology education

*Adri Du Toit*

## Background

The preparation of pupils with the diverse knowledge and skills they will need for the world of work is a growing global concern. For technology education to effectually contribute to achieving this purpose, pupils have to be provided with insights into how they could use the knowledge and skills embedded in these subjects in the world of work, including how it could be developed into opportunities to create their own employment. This is especially significant as unemployment levels keep on increasing globally, with some countries – such as South Africa – reporting that a shocking 74.7% of their young people were unemployed at the start of 2021 (Solidariteit, 2021). As a result, several countries have started to include entrepreneurship education in their school curricula as part of their attempts to address youth unemployment. Embedding cross-cutting themes or content such as entrepreneurship or employability into existing subject curricula helps teachers to understand the totality of what pupils must learn (Stabback, 2016). Entrepreneurship education is frequently embedded in existing subjects and in a few instances, in design and technology. However, considering the purpose and focus of technology subjects in different countries, two debates endure: (1) Why entrepreneurship should be taught in technology education? and (2) If it should be, then how can it be embedded in technology education? This chapter analyses why and how entrepreneurship education can be embedded in technology education and explores a few cases where it has been successfully included in technology subjects. Recommendations for including entrepreneurship in your teaching and learning of technology are also suggested should you choose to embrace it.

## Concept clarification and outline of chapter

Before delving into entrepreneurship education and how it is or could be embedded in technology subjects, it is important to clarify a few concepts as they are used or referred to in this chapter.

*Entrepreneurship* encompasses more than the narrow business or economic role it is often associated with. Although entrepreneurship – as an undertaking or process of implementation of knowledge and skills and competencies – is generally linked to self-employment and venture creation, it contributes many more benefits than only these (Chaker & Jarraya, 2021). Highlighting the social role of entrepreneurship, Blenker et al. (2012:421) state that 'the energy which is present in entrepreneurial processes' contributes to solving social problems and can 'enrich life in general'. Entrepreneurship is therefore viewed as a process that has the potential to contribute economic and social value when entrepreneurs apply entrepreneurial knowledge, skills, and competencies (such as critical thinking, effective communication, or innovation) to solve problems to address the needs of individuals and communities. These skills and competencies are discussed in more detail further on in the chapter.

*Entrepreneurship education* can be explained in various ways and scholars tend to disagree on what to include and exclude in its definition (Sirelkhatim & Gangi, 2015). This chapter was written from the viewpoint that the knowledge, skills, and competencies which entrepreneurs require for successful entrepreneurship, can be taught. Therefore, building on the previously mentioned definition of *entrepreneurship* as a process, the definition of *entrepreneurship education* provided by the European Commission (2011:2) as 'a process through which learners acquire a broad set of competencies [that] can bring greater individual, social and economic benefits since the competences acquired lend themselves to application in every aspect of people's lives' is adopted here.

*Technology education* in this chapter refers to teaching and learning in distinct school subjects focused on developing technological knowledge and skills, usually scaffolded around the design process. Different countries use different names for these subjects: for example, Botswana, Singapore, England, and Wales use the name 'design and technology', whereas Canada and South Africa refer to similar subjects simply as 'technology education' even though these subjects also include significant design components. Although the same term is often used in relation to information technology, digital technologies, or electronic devices, for the current discussion the focus is on the much broader descriptions of teaching particular content in distinct school subjects.

Having clarified how each of these terms is viewed, we can now move on to the questions of why, how, and if entrepreneurship should be included in technology education. The discussion leads with an overview of the skills pupils are expected to develop in preparation for the world of work (irrespective if they will be working for an employer or creating their own employment), followed by a broad analysis of the skills which technology education can contribute in this regard. These skills are then compared to entrepreneurship skills, contributing some answers to the 'why' question. The subsequent section explains how entrepreneurship education could be approached or embedded into existing technology education, providing more information on the 'how' and 'if' questions. To provide you with the bigger picture, this is followed by some reasons why some authors are opposed to the idea of pertinently linking entrepreneurship to technology education subjects. The final section compares and explains how different countries have embedded entrepreneurship education within technology education. Informed thus, you should be able to draw your own conclusions about the debate for or against including entrepreneurship in technology education, notwithstanding the conclusion of the author of the current chapter. You can therefore develop your own thoughts on 'if' entrepreneurship education should be embedded in technology education.

## Preparing pupils with skills required for the world of work

There is an enduring but growing need to prepare pupils with skills that they will need in the world of work. This need is based on the perceived and reported gaps between school learning and the needs of employers or workplaces (Goss, 2018). Focused development of skills will not only bridge this gap to better prepare pupils for employment but will also support lifelong learning and improved citizenship (Nichols, 2020) by preparing pupils for everyday life and the demands presented by the fast-developing and ever-changing world in the 21st century. In other words, these skills are needed to prepare pupils for their futures (Kaufman, 2013). Countless skills could be listed as necessary to attain these goals, but a few skills recurrently appear in research and discussions on this topic; therefore, the following are listed in alphabetical order:

- agility, adaptability, and flexibility (planning skills, self-directedness, perseverance)
- collaboration within and across different groups and networks (including teamwork)
- critical thinking (reasoning, systems thinking, making informed judgements and decisions)
- effective communication using various platforms (oral, digital, written, design)
- innovation and creativity (thinking in different and new ways)
- lifelong and contextual learning (continuous learning)
- problem-solving skills (identification, clarification, analysis, application of processes, developing solutions)
- research skills
    (accessing and analysing information; information and media literacy; Care, Kim & Sahin, 2020; Germaine et al., 2016; Glossary of Education Reform, 2016; Kaufman, 2013; Noss, 2012; Saavedra & Opfer, 2012; Shaw, 2009; Shaw, 2014)

The list is self-explanatory, containing skills which individual pupils should develop as part of their educational journey in preparation for their future lives and employment. In addition to these, Shaw (2009:12) adds 'citizenship – taking on civil and global issues' as another skill that pupils will need to enable them to function optimally in, and contribute meaningfully to, their communities. Adding this particular skill will contribute to developing pupils not only as individuals but also as global citizens and support them in implementing their knowledge and skills to make a difference in the world around them, contributing to positive change.

The skills listed here are often referred to as 21st-century skills, which are increasingly in demand from employers and for individuals to adapt to and cope in changing times. The list of skills is not static and is continuously changing, in line with changes in the world of work, technological advances, and social and global changes. In the same vein, some scholars – such as Ankiewicz (2020) – argue that technology subjects were initially developed as part of efforts for education to keep up with similar changes in the world of work, technological development, as well as societal and global issues. Also, since its inception technology education has evolved, in keeping with the requirements of the changing world, as Ankiewicz (2020:n.p.) explains: 'Changes in different countries suggest that educational goals in technology education have moved beyond the achievement of factual knowledge and skilled performance and have become more concerned with the development of transferable skills and knowledge.' This statement underscores that technology education includes knowledge and skills development as a pertinent goal, not only for individual learning but also to be transferable to other situations (for example, to the world of work). It contributes reasoning towards the debate about why entrepreneurship education should be included in technology education. The next section therefore broadly outlines the knowledge and skills that are associated with school subjects for technology education.

## *Technology education contributing to skills needed in the world of work*

The contribution of technology education to developing 21st-century skills has been continuously noted in published research in this field (De Vries, 2018). It is often claimed that technology as a subject is ideally suited to develop these broad or general skills (De Vries, 2018) which are needed for everyday life, as well as being preferred by employers. For example, Fox-Turnbull (2018:563) explains that technology education's 'emphasis on design, innovation, creativity, entrepreneurialism, cooperation, and societal integration', together with practical skills development, makes it ideal to 'facilitate learning for the future across all walks of life'. Skills development is closely linked to the design process (also sometimes referred to as the 'technological process'), which serves as the 'backbone' for learning in technology education (Du Toit, 2020:6). The design process is scaffolded around various steps or phases in either a linear or a cyclical approach. Although various terms might be used in different countries for the steps in the design process, they generally involve problem identification and analysis; designing and evaluating potential solutions; executing or making a product; evaluation of the choice of materials, the design used, and the effectiveness of the solution; and communicating results to interested parties. These steps require pupils to utilise and apply skills such as problem-solving, innovation, creative and critical thinking, conducting research, teamwork, evaluating information, communication of findings, and considering their way of thinking or level of learning (metacognition) throughout the process. When these skills are applied in the design process to produce a product or artefact to address a human (or a 'customer's') need or problem, it not only makes the technology 'learning experience more authentic and practical but will also contribute additional motivation for learners to meet the needs and wants of their customers' (Du Toit, 2020:9), reinforcing the value of the learning for pupils themselves. Hence, the product or artefact being developed in the design process should be viewed as a potential entrepreneurial opportunity (Du Toit, 2020). In this way, utilisation of the design process reinforces the potential of technology education for developing these valuable skills.

Technology education can therefore contribute significantly to developing the skills that pupils are expected to develop for their everyday lives, as well as in preparation for the world of work irrespective of whether they will be working for an employer or creating their own employment. Employers tend to be prescriptive about the skills they require from their employees and which therefore need to be developed as part of education. What often seems to be missing, however, is the potential value of these same skills for pupils to create or contribute to self-employment opportunities – something that is crucial considering the high levels of unemployment experienced globally.

In many countries, entrepreneurship is seen as one of the strategies that can be used to develop skills in pupils that will contribute to self-directed employment or income generation, which in turn can reduce unemployment (Mbanefo & Eboka, 2017). It is believed that entrepreneurship education contributes 'entrepreneurial skill acquisition that will make them [pupils] employers rather than employees of labor' (Mbanefo & Eboka, 2017:212) in future, which in turn will contribute to efforts to reduce unemployment. Entrepreneurship education is furthermore toted as contributing 21st-century skills for everyday life that are not only useful for pupils to create their own employment or income opportunities but that also align well with the skills which employers require (Dahlstedt & Fejes, 2017; Mbanefo & Eboka, 2017) and therefore requires deeper examination.

### *Entrepreneurship skills to prepare pupils for life and (self-)employment*

The skills associated with entrepreneurship that are taught in entrepreneurship education align closely to the 21st-century skills listed earlier, as well as the skills developed in technology education. For example, the European Commission (2011:23) mentions that entrepreneurship requires skills 'such as teamwork, sense of initiative, decision making, problem solving, leadership, risk-taking and creativity'. Furthermore, Mbanefo and Eboka (2017:208) explain that 'entrepreneurship could be seen as the act of identifying, initiating, organizing, and bringing an idea or vision to life, be it a new product, service, process, strategy, or market'. The close alignment of the skill sets for life in the 21st century, the world of work, those developed in technology education, and required in entrepreneurship education, indicate that pupils should be taught not just to utilise these skills in their everyday lives but to prepare them for employment or self-employment. To ensure that this broad goal is attained, education should be planned well. For this reason, and to unambiguously inform pupils of the potential that exists in technology education for them to develop their own employment or income opportunities, using the knowledge and skills taught in the subject, entrepreneurship education is often embedded into technology subjects. Combining entrepreneurship with technology education has to be carefully constructed if such learning is required, including suitable training for teachers to enable its effective implementation (Du Toit & Gaotlhobogwe, 2018). A few of the challenges associated with embedding entrepreneurship into existing subjects are therefore discussed next.

In curricula that are already content-heavy, it might be difficult to find time to fit in additional learning content on entrepreneurship (Mbanefo & Eboka, 2017). The extended training required of teachers to support effective entrepreneurship education in existing subjects (such as technology) creates the impression of adding to their existing heavy workload (Du Toit & Gaotlhobogwe, 2018) is another reason why teachers are sometimes opposed to embedding entrepreneurship into existing subjects. Effective entrepreneurship education requires collaboration between schools and entrepreneurs who serve as mentors or advisors, which poses administrative challenges (Chikasanda et al., 2015; Mbanefo & Eboka, 2017). Furthermore, support or 'buy-in' is needed from teachers, school management, and parents, which, when lacking, may result in pupils having a reduced perception of the value of entrepreneurship education (Chikasanda et al., 2015; Mbanefo & Eboka, 2017). In instances in which technology teachers believe the purpose of technology education to be (only) to develop pupils' technological literacy, it would be important to change their conceptions of this purpose and to convince them of the value that entrepreneurship education can contribute to pupils' learning in the subject.

This section contributed some insights into 'why' (or perhaps why not) entrepreneurship should be included in technology education. If we continue with the assumption that such an inclusion will contribute value to technology as a subject, the next step is to explore how this inclusion can be scaffolded in your teaching to contribute to meaningful learning, as discussed in the subsequent section.

## Education *about*, *for*, and *through* entrepreneurship

Approaches to teaching entrepreneurship generally involve education *about*, *for*, or *through* entrepreneurship (Chaker & Jarraya, 2021). Each of these approaches has a different purpose and is structured according to its qualities. This section sheds some light on the second debate addressed in this chapter, which asked, "If entrepreneurship education should be included, then, how can it be embedded in technology education?"

Education *about* entrepreneurship has a theoretical and informative purpose, to increase pupils' awareness of what entrepreneurship is and how it could contribute to self-directed employment generation (Chaker & Jarraya, 2021). Content tends to be generic, that is learning about a business plan, the qualities of entrepreneurs, or the entrepreneurs who have been successful in a certain country. This approach to entrepreneurship education informs pupils about the options available to them for becoming entrepreneurs themselves in future but will only serve a motivating role if the teaching is enthusiastic and relevant. If, for example, the teacher refers to a local entrepreneur who successfully applied technology knowledge or skills to solve a problem, pupils might make the connection between the usefulness and entrepreneurial potential of the learning in technology education and become more entrepreneurially inclined as a result.

Education *for* entrepreneurship is more practical and utilises active, real-life, and learner-centred learning strategies to bring entrepreneurship education closer to entrepreneurial experiences that pupils might encounter in the real world (Du Toit, 2020; Sirelkhatim & Gangi, 2015). Teachers utilise the techniques mentioned earlier to encourage entrepreneurship practice, such as generating ideas, team building, business planning, opportunity recognition, adapting to change, and expecting and embracing failure (Chaker & Jarraya, 2021; Sirelkhatim & Gangi, 2015). This approach develops pupils' entrepreneurial knowledge, skills and competencies when they apply knowledge and skills to scenarios, based on real-world cases, 'as entrepreneurs' – in other words, their entrepreneurship education develops when they pretend (or learn) to think or act like an entrepreneur (Chaker & Jarraya, 2021; Du Toit, 2020). If this approach is to be utilised in technology education, pupils have to be explicitly informed of their 'role as entrepreneurs' in the subject. This implies that, for example, the product or artefact that is developed in technology education in the design process should be profitable, should adhere to 'customer' requirements, and should offer opportunities for development and refinement to increase its potential 'saleability'. To this effect, it might be useful if technology teachers and pupils approach the design process with a particular 'consumer' in mind (Du Toit, 2020), which will bring the learning closer to what entrepreneurs may experience in real life, without adding much additional content to the curriculum. Taking it further, pupils can compete or 'tender' for addressing the consumer's needs or problems, which will contribute to developing additional skills such as collaboration, evaluation, and communication. Interactive learning from peers will also be supported when pupils assess and compare their own solutions to those of their peers.

Education *through* entrepreneurship is the closest that pupils can get to 'being' entrepreneurs as part of their school education. This type of education supports pupils to become entrepreneurs rather than merely pretending to be entrepreneurs (as is the case in education for entrepreneurship). The approach uses experiential learning to develop entrepreneurial competencies and is mostly business orientated, with venture-creation and advancement of entrepreneurs as the main purpose (Chaker & Jarraya, 2021; Sirelkhatim & Gangi, 2015). To afford pupils a real taste of being an entrepreneur, education through entrepreneurship requires collaboration with real-life entrepreneurs, as well as investors and shareholders, making it a complex undertaking. It becomes especially daunting when one considers regulations such as pupil protection laws, privacy issues, schools' requirements before allowing pupils to leave the school premises for learning, or the paperwork involved in screening visitors (such as entrepreneurs) to schools, which will add much administration to the workload of teachers. It is therefore understandable that programmes that develop education *through* entrepreneurship are often run by organisations outside schools, which usually have more resources and time at their disposal than teachers might have.

Based on this broad overview of education *about*, *for* and *through* entrepreneurship, an approach that provides education *for* entrepreneurship seems to have the most potential to add valuable entrepreneurship education without taxing teachers too much, and without adding excessively to existing teaching content.

The debate whether (or 'if') entrepreneurship education should be included in technology education is an ongoing one. That entrepreneurship education will add more value to the subject is indisputable. Education for entrepreneurship will contribute to the development of pupils' 21st-century skills for application in their own lives, but also in real-world scenarios. And, when teachers point this out – for example when pupils apply the design process to develop artefacts for consumers – it will help pupils realise the potential that learning in this subject has for developing their own employment opportunities in future.

Although research on the inclusion of entrepreneurship in technology education is not as extensive as one might expect, several countries have already purposefully included entrepreneurship education in their technology curricula and, considering how they approached it, may provide you with insights into how you could embed entrepreneurship education in your own technology classroom.

## Entrepreneurship education in technology subjects across the globe

Several countries have succeeded in embedding entrepreneurship education into their technology curricula, many with the specific purpose to contribute to reducing unemployment in those countries (Du Toit & Gaotlhobogwe, 2018; Stabback, 2016). A few examples from across the globe are discussed next to provide some insights into how and why different countries chose to include entrepreneurship education in their technology subjects.

In **Botswana**, one of the aims for Junior Secondary design and technology is that the subject should enable pupils to 'develop entrepreneurial skills that they can apply in their day-to-day business transactions and to market their products effectively' (Botswana MoESD, 2008:ii). This aim affirms the potential of interlinking entrepreneurship education with product development in technology education. The aim furthermore clarifies the intention of that curriculum that pupils should learn how to market their products effectively as part of technology education. The Botswana design and technology curriculum therefore aligns with research that recommends the use of real-life learning – in other words, in technology education, pupils can design, develop and produce a product with a particular consumer need or want in mind, and subsequently, they should also be able to think about how the product will be marketed to that same target audience.

In the **Caribbean**, the need to research and develop small-scale production, based on indigenous technologies, was established some time ago (Prime, 1992:50). The purpose of entrepreneurship education in the Caribbean is to develop pupils' entrepreneurial thinking, behaviour, and skill sets (Pounder, 2016). When combining this purpose with indigenous knowledge and technology education, it opened up opportunities for pupils to use their knowledge and skills to develop 'new products and to improve the quality and quantity of traditional products, making themselves financially self-sufficient and generating employment' (Prime, 1992:50). Using existing learning in technology with a focus on product development for small-scale production, in combination with indigenous knowledge, thus contributed to more meaningful learning that could be utilised to help reduce the high levels of unemployment in the Caribbean (Pounder, 2016).

Similarly, in efforts to reduce youth unemployment and eradicate poverty, **Malawi** identified the need to empower its youth with technological literacy and entrepreneurship. To attain this purpose, the Malawian Ministry of Education, Science and Technology elected to reintroduce technical and vocational education into their upper primary school level (Chikasanda et al., 2015). After its implementation, an analysis of this programme found that Malawian teachers believe that this interlinked education would provide pupils with 'skills for their survival after school' (Chikasanda et al., 2015:457), as well as 'knowledge, creativity and skills . . . vital for students to embark on income generation activities for personal and family needs' (ibid., p. 458), indicating that it was viewed as useful, life-relevant, and context-driven. Based on these findings, it was recommended that, in Malawi, 'curriculum development of technology studies should incorporate learning for entrepreneurship development to instil entrepreneurial attitudes' in pupils (ibid., p. 459). The recommendation highlights the need identified in several studies to explicitly address pupils' and teachers' attitudes (their 'buy-in' or a positive mindset) toward entrepreneurship as a valuable part of school education.

One example of such a positive view of the value that entrepreneurship education can contribute, was reported for technology education in **Estonia**. In this country, entrepreneurship is described as a fundamental component of conducting a technology lesson (Soobik, 2016). The combination of several fundamental components contributes to a more holistic approach to technology education in Estonia, which aims to develop a 'broad vision of interplay between technology, society and culture' in that country's pupils (Soobik, 2016:441). This cross-cutting interlinking of different themes or topics aligns well with literature describing the need to provide teachers and pupils, with a broader picture that all that pupils have to learn in preparation for their futures.

A broader picture of the potential value of entrepreneurship education in technology education is described in the upper secondary curriculum of **Sweden**. Svärd, Schönborn, and Hallström (2016:454) propose that 'the subject of technology should allow students to develop entrepreneurial skills, defined as supporting curiosity, confidence, creativity and courage, resulting in the ability to act, in innovation and problem solving'. This expanded description of skills associated with entrepreneurship education emphasises the potential of such learning to contribute to developing these skills in technology education. In turn, these skills will contribute value to pupils' everyday lives, as well as for their future careers – whether they are employed or create their own employment opportunities. The same authors describe the need for authentic learning, including risk-taking (which is a key aspect of learning in entrepreneurship too), as part of endeavours to make learning more meaningful *and* useful for pupils (ibid., p. 455).

When learning can be applied in real life, pupils view it as more meaningful and useful. One of the core subject foci within the Learning Outcomes Framework for the subject design and technology in **Malta**, is 'design, entrepreneurship and innovation' (Pule, 2019). The same curriculum continues to explain the importance of 'entrepreneurship in the development and progress of society' (Pule, 2019:465), supporting the view that entrepreneurship education contributes valuable learning not only in the lives of pupils but also to the benefit of the greater society. These broad application opportunities contribute to making learning more meaningful for pupils.

As a final example, despite **Jordan** having a well-educated workforce and high technological uptake (Yale Jackson Institute, 2018), they also resolved to combine vocational subjects, like technology, with entrepreneurship education. Their reasons for this inclusion echo several of those listed earlier for other countries. In particular, the Jordanian government wanted to (1) create awareness of entrepreneurship and self-employment as an alternative career option; (2) develop positive attitudes or mindsets toward entrepreneurship and self-employment; (3) develop knowledge, competencies, and skills required in entrepreneurship; and (4) prepare pupils with the skills needed to work productively in small-scale businesses (Yale Jackson Institute, 2018). The approach used in Jordan therefore adheres to the general requirements for the effective embedding of entrepreneurship education into other subjects described in literature.

Developing plans and programmes to embed entrepreneurship education into technology subjects is an ongoing endeavour. For instance, in South Africa, which has one of the highest levels of youth unemployment in the world and where technology education is compulsory for six years of their school system, plans are only now being developed and rolled out by that country's Department of Basic Education to pertinently include entrepreneurship education into the existing curriculum. For this purpose, a consumer approach toward product development, aligned with the design process in technology education, was recommended (Du Toit, 2020). In addition, targeted training of teachers to support the implementation of effective entrepreneurship education is also being planned, which should support this endeavour. As more countries implement this interlinked approach, more insights can be developed into how entrepreneurship education can be embedded into technology education to the benefit of pupils.

From these examples, you can derive that there are various ways to meaningfully include or embed entrepreneurship education into technology education. The reasons for such inclusion vary, but skills development is always a key outcome. And the value that these skills will contribute to the lives of pupils, and the societies in which they reside, is undeniable.

## Conclusion

The potential to include entrepreneurship education to add value to technology education is overwhelmingly positive. Highlighting the value of the skills taught in technology for self- or other employment, together with entrepreneurship education, will increase pupils' cognizance of this subject's potential to provide them with useful and meaningful learning. Support for the debate on 'why' entrepreneurship education should be included in technology education, is therefore strong. The suggestions made in this chapter for embedding education *for* and *through* entrepreneurship in technology subjects can be used to address the debate on how this can be done effectively. Such learning and its associated skills development will not only be useful in pupils' own lives – now and in their future careers – but it can also open up more opportunities for them to utilise technology knowledge and skills to create their own employment. In turn, when pupils utilise entrepreneurship and technology skills to address problems and develop products, they will make the world a better place – by reducing unemployment as well as contributing positively to the societies they live in.

## Questions

1 Do you think that entrepreneurship education should form part of the technology curriculum? Justify your answer.
2 What value will be added to technology as a subject, by including entrepreneurship as part of the learning content?
3 How could embedding entrepreneurship content into the technology curriculum contribute to preparing learners for life in general, as well as for future employment (including self-employment)?

4 Which approaches can be used to effectively teach entrepreneurship content together with the existing technology curriculum content in your school?
5 Can entrepreneurship with a 'not-for-profit' purpose also contribute value to technology education?

## References

Ankiewicz, P. 2020. Technology education in South Africa since the new dispensation in 1994: An analysis of curriculum documents and a meta-synthesis of scholarly work. *International Journal of Technology and Design Education.* doi:10.1007/s10798-020-09589-8 Date of access 4 February 2021.

Blenker, P., Frederiksen, S.H., Korsgaard, S., Muller, S., Neergaard, H. & Thrane, C. 2012. Entrepreneurship as everyday practice: Towards a personalized pedagogy of enterprise education. *Industry and Higher Education*, 26:417–430.

Botswana Ministry of Education and Skills Development [MoESD]. 2008. *Junior Secondary Syllabus: Design and technology.* Ministry of Education and Skills Development, Republic of Botswana. Gaborone: Government Printers.

Care, E., Kim, H. & Sahin, A.G. 2020. *Optimizing Assessment for All. Developing 21st Century Skills-embedded Curriculum Tasks.* Washington, DC: Brookings Institution.

Chaker, H. & Jarraya, H. 2021. Combining teaching "about" and "through" entrepreneurship: A practice to develop students' entrepreneurial competencies. *Industry and Higher Education*, 1–11. DOI:10.1177/0950422221991005

Chikasanda, V.K., Mgawi, R.K., Mtemang'ombe, D. & Alide, Y. 2015. Introducing technology studies in Malawi's model primary schools: Towards building a technologically literate society. *International Journal of Technology and Design Education*, 25:453–466.

Dahlstedt, M. & Fejes, A. 2017. Shaping entrepreneurial citizens: A genealogy of entrepreneurship education in Sweden. *Critical Studies in Education*, 1–15. DOI: 10.1080/17508487.2017.1303525

De Vries, M.J. 2018. Technology education: An international history. In M. De Vries (Ed.), *Handbook of Technology Education*, pp. 73–84. Delft: Springer.

Du Toit, A. 2020. Threading entrepreneurship through the design process in technology education. *African Journal of Research in Mathematics, Science and Technology Education*, 24(2):180–191.

Du Toit, A. & Gaotlhobogwe, M. 2018. A neglected opportunity: Entrepreneurship education in the lower high school curricula for technology in South Africa and Botswana. *African Journal of Research in Mathematics, Science and Technology Education*, 22(1):37–47. DOI:10.1080/18117295.2017.1420007

European Commission. 2011. *Entrepreneurship Education: Enabling Teachers as a Critical Success Factor.* Brussels: Entrepreneurship Unit.

Fox-Turnbull, W. 2018. Classroom interaction in technology education. In M. De Vries (Ed.), *Handbook of Technology Education*, pp. 551–566. Delft: Springer.

Germaine, R., Richards, J., Koeller, M. & Schubert-Irastorza, C. 2016. Purposeful use of 21st century skills in higher education. *Journal of Research in Innovative Teaching*, 9(1):19–29.

Glossary of Education Reform. 21st Century Skills. 2016. https://www.edglossary. org/21st-century-skills/#:~:text=Critical%20thinking%2C%20problem%20solving% 2C%20reasoning,self%2Ddiscipline%2C%20adaptability%2C%20initiative Date of access 2 February 2021.

Goss, D.L. 2018. *Contemporary Approaches to Bridging Classroom and Experiential Education – A Phenomenological Study*. DEd Dissertation, Department of Educational Studies, The Patton College of Education of Ohio University.

Kaufman, K.J. 2013. 21 Ways to 21st century skills: Why students need them and ideas for practical implementation. *Delta Pi Record*, 49(2):78–83. DOI:10.1080/ 00228958.2013.786594

Mbanefo, M.C. & Eboka, O. 2017. Acquisition of innovative and entrepreneurial skills in basic science education for job creation in Nigeria. *Science Education International*, 28(3):207–213.

Nichols, J.R. 2020. 7 Skills students will always need. https://www.teachthought. com/the-future-of-learning/how-to-prepare-student-for-21st-centurysurvival/ Date of access 1 February 2021.

Noss, R. 2012. 21st century learning for 21st century skills: What does it mean, and how do we do it? In A. Ravenscroft, S. Lindstaedt, C. Delgado Kloos and D. Hernandez-Leo (Eds.), *21$^{st}$ Century Learning for 21$^{st}$ Century Skills*, pp. 3–5. 7th European Conference on technology Enhanced Learning, Saarbrucken, Germany, September 2012. Heidelberg: Springer.

Prime, G.M. 1992. Technology education in the Caribbean – Needs and directions. *International Journal of Technology and Design Education*, 2(3):48–57.

Pounder, P. 2016. Entrepreneurship education in the Caribbean: Learning and teaching tools. *Brock Education Journal*, 26(1):83–101.

Pule, S. 2019. Curriculum components of technology education within the Maltese National minimum curriculum from year 1999 to 2016. *International Journal of technology and Design Education*, 29:441–472. doi:10.1007/s10798-018-9455-2

Saavedra, A.R. & Opfer, V.D. 2012. Learning 21st-century skills requires 21st-century teaching. *Phi Delta Kappan*, 94(2):8–13.

Shaw, A. 2009. Education in the 21st century. *Ethos: Social Education Victoria*, 17(1):11–17.

Shaw, A. 2014. 3 Compasses to guide you to 21$^{st}$ century schools. https:// www.21stcenturyschools.com/uploads/2/1/5/4/21542794/3_compasses_to_ 21st_century_education.pdf Date of access: 2 February 2021.

Sirelkhatim, F. & Gangi, Y. 2015. Entrepreneurship education: A systematic literature review of curricula contents and teaching methods. *Cogent Business & Management*, 2:1–11.

Solidariteit. 2021. Youth unemployment: Government looks on as disaster unfolds. Media press release, Thursday, June 3. https://solidariteit.co.za/en/youth-unemployment-government-looks-on-as-disasterunfolds/ Date of access: 23 August 2022.

Soobik, M. 2016. A theoretical model of technology education. In M.J. De Vries, A. Bekker-Holtland & G. Van Dijk (Eds.), *Technology Education for 21st Century Skills. Proceedings PATT-32 conference* (pp. 437–443).

Stabback, P. 2016. What makes a quality curriculum? UNESCO International Bureau of Education. In-Progress Reflection No.2 on Current and Critical Issues in Curriculum and Learning, March, 2016, No.2 IBE/2016/WP/CD/02

Svärd, J., Schönborn, K. & Hallström, J. 2016. Designing a module for authentic learning in upper secondary technology education. In M.J. De Vries, A. Bekker-Holtland & G. Van Dijk (Eds.), *Technology Education for 21st Century Skills. Proceedings PATT-32 conference* (pp. 454–462).

Yale Jackson Institute for Global Affairs. 2018. Meeting the Challenge of Youth Unemployment: Analysis and Lessons from Jordan, Liberia, and South Africa. Capstone Project: Solutions for youth employment & The World Bank Group. December 2018. Available from https://www.s4ye.org/s4ye-publications Date of access: 23 August 2022.

# 9 Gendering the curriculum

*Ulrika Sultan*

## Introduction

That there is a gender difference in enrolment in design and technology education across the world is evident. Often this difference means more boys than girls enrol in the subject fields – at least in the global North and the Western world. The reasons for this gender gap are multifaceted and not to be explained easily, but what is known is that design and technology is an inspiring and practical subject. In the EU and UK (Eurostat, 2020), the percentage of women among higher education students was slightly higher than men, but fewer women than men choose to study STEM subjects. This choice is also notable in secondary school education, and even though many different interventions have been made, the gender–STEM gap remains. This gap is a loss for our common future. In design and technology, pupils learn and practise how to become resourceful, innovative, and active citizens. It is the subject for developing an understanding of the created world's impact on the individual, society, and the environment, a subject for all pupils, no matter gender, so with a gender differential, not only are girls missing out on learning and contributing to society, but society is also missing out on their contribution to enhancing the transformation of and innovation of it.

But let us dig deeper into this gap with a focus on design and technology education (Table 9.1).

## Are boys better at STEM subjects?

One general and recurrent claim for boys' higher enrolment in design and technology is that boys are better at spatial tasks and logic whilst girls are better at verbal and emotional tasks (Lauer et al., 2019). But when studying these claims, research on cognitive development fails to support them (Spelke, 2005). Instead, research provides evidence that (for example) logic reasoning develops from a set of biologically based cognitive capacities that males and females share (Lauer et al., 2019). This means that women and men can develop equal talent for mathematics and science, for example, thus showing that girls and boys are more similar than they are different.

DOI: 10.4324/9781003166689-12

*Table 9.1* Summary: glossary of key terms

| Glossary of key terms | |
|---|---|
| Gender | Gender in this context means the social and cultural gender. Not the biological sexes. Social and cultural gender is the perceptions and notions that exist in our society about what is feminine and masculine. Gender is constantly being constructed, it is created based on our values, attitudes, and experiences (e.g. Butler, 1990/1999; Lindsey, 2015). |
| Gender contract | Gender contract describes the order in society that distinguishes and sorts women and men. It is invisible and often unconscious. It illustrates how we associate some colours, behaviours, characteristics, workplaces and more, with female or male (e.g. European Commission, 1998). |
| A gender-conscious pedagogy | To be gender-conscious means to be aware of one's own and one's professional perceptions of women and men, and to see how it affects teaching (e.g. Warin & Adriany, 2017) |
| Gender neutrality | The idea that policies, language, and other social institutions e.g. social structures, gender roles, or gender identity should avoid distinguishing roles according to people's sex or gender (e.g. European Commission, 1998) |

The problem with seeing some abilities being better than others might hinder how we allow and train pupils to use creativity and imagination to solve problems within a variety of contexts. We want the pupils to apply a repertoire of knowledge, understanding and skills. An aim calling for a range of abilities.

Like this position that there are favoured abilities, how we measure knowledge seems to affect the outcomes for pupils' performances. Girls have been proven to do as well as or outperform boys in STEM classwork but do worse on tests according to the Programme for International Student Assessment (PISA; 2015, 2018). We should bear in mind that PISA is designed to give estimates at a population level rather than at an individual level. PISA results from pupils across 40 countries who had taken identical tests suggested that girls were more anxious about tests than boys were, and this seems to have affected their scores. This anxiety seems to have roots in a stereotype that labels girls as not interested in subjects such as design and technology. This stereotyping is likely to interfere with girls' self-confidence, academic efficacy, and sense of belonging. Yet when looking into mathematics, researchers found that in more gender-neutral countries such as Norway and Sweden, the gender gap in test results disappeared (Guiso et al., 2008). Why this happens is not clear and easily explained. A range of explanations for the lack of a gender gap seen in the test results are such as an educational system and pupils' study culture is favouring girls has been given.

The Relevance of Science Education (ROSE) research project addressed how 15-year-old pupils related to science and technology (S&T). The purpose of ROSE was to gather and analyse information from the pupils about several factors that potentially have a bearing on their attitudes to S&T and their motivation to learn S&T (Sjøberg & Schreiner, 2010). It is an interesting study since it researched 40 countries and, by doing so, different cultures of technology education. The study's researchers wanted to inform discussions on how to make science education more relevant and meaningful for pupils in ways that respect gender differences and cultural diversity. According to the ROSE study (Sjøberg & Schreiner, 2010), there has been a growing gender difference in the richest countries, such as Northern Europe and Japan, with girls being more negative towards technology than boys. This is a result repeated in other more recent studies too (Jidesjö et al., 2021; Sun et al., 2019). But we should remember attitudes to technology among young people are mainly positive, attitudes such as future work within fields of technology, especially among pupils outside Europe and North America (cf. Jidesjö et al. 2021; Sjøberg & Schreiner, 2010; UNESCO, 2017). The ROSE study identified that boys' interests in technology were mainly in the technical, mechanical, and electrical realms. Whilst girls' interests tended to be in the fields of health and medicine, beauty, ethics, and aesthetics. This points to girls' and boys' interest being context-dependent. Context-dependent, instead of thinking about technology as a whole, pupils show interest in themes or parts of technology. Both boys' and girls' interests are within technology and fall into the stereotypes of what boys and girls should be interested in. We will soon return to this thought.

## Designing and making for a more sustainable world

In 2015, the 2030 Agenda was adopted by all United Nations member states, providing us with 17 Sustainable Development Goals (SDGs; United Nations, 2022). The SDGs are a call for global strategies to improve health and education, reduce inequality, spur economic growth, and tackle climate change. Sustainable and environmental issues are shown to be important for all pupils but mainly for girls. Research, such as that by Sjøberg and Schreiner (2019), shows that girls, more than boys, think people should care more about protecting the environment. Boys, on the other hand, think environmental problems are exaggerated (e.g. Sjøberg & Schreiner, 2010, 2019), a result the researcher network Centre for Studies of Climate Change Denialism confirms (Hultman et al., forthcoming). It points to boys and men being influenced by the notion of being a man equals having success, a career, and considering himself to be somewhat separated from the natural world, making it more difficult to have a strong environmental engagement. But boys in the ROSE study, more than girls, think that science and technology can solve environmental problems. Girls tend to more believe that individual choices make a difference; this is often seen as being aware of the impact of food on sustainability and choosing to become vegetarians more often than boys, giving them a possible understanding of where and how a variety of food is grown and processed (Sjøberg & Schreiner, 2019).

In design and technology, these insights about girls' and boys' different perspectives can be useful. When designing a product, one or more design criteria(s) can beneficially be more focused on sustainability; this benefits the pupils as it lets them practice and engage in environmental issues affecting themselves and other users. It also broadens their preconceptions and encourages them to challenge their personal beliefs by exploring and evaluating a range of existing products and ideas against environmental design criteria. By doing so, they recognise that technology is socially shaped and that gender is crucial in its development, production, and use.

## A socially constructed gender gap?

'Being technical' is a phrase more associated with boys and men than with girls and women. Gender research stresses that the construction of an interest in technology is expressed in and reflected in a social continuity (e.g. Berner, 2004). This means that if we are met in recurring situations and with the same expectation from the surrounding society of how we should be, behave, or what we should be able to do, it will shape our gender identity and our interests. By having the knowledge that pupils begin to construct their self-identities through observation of others, participating in society, we can challenge notions of technological interest, of masculinity and femininity.

To create an understanding of why girls, seem to have a more negative attitude to the subject of technology, we need to start from the child's first encounter with education. In Swedish preschool's activities, Hallström et al. (2015) examined children's technical activities. When the children played indoors, the researchers saw a difference between how girls and boys played. Construction play involved both boys and girls, but boys played to a greater extent with toys such as excavators and cars. After studying girls' and boys' free play with technology, the researchers were able to conclude that girls were more interested in technology as an object, that is they were users of technology, while boys used technology as an activity; in other words, they were makers of technology. A notable conclusion was that children generally had an equally positive attitude towards technology, at this young age, a child does not see themselves as technical or non-technical. Some factors that could be the reason girls lose their interest in technology as they get older follow:

- A lack of identification (who gets to be technical?)
- Low self-confidence regarding technical skills (who have gotten the chance to train these skills?)
- External influences and expectations (parents, peers, teachers, society)
- A lack of subject competence in the teacher (a lack of qualified teachers is a problem)

To challenge notions of what is masculine and feminine, teaching design and technology can highlight views, behaviours, characteristics, products, professions, and knowledge that are considered suitable for women and/or men:

- How are boys affected by the fact that they are expected to be interested in technology and, for example, be able to manage computers and repair cars?
- What does it mean for girls that boys are expected to be interested in technology and, for example, be able to manage computers and repair cars?

As a teacher, I can problematize the subject content I choose to teach about and the practical examples the pupils encounter by screening the teaching material I choose to use so that it does not reinforce general gender stereotypes about women and men. For example, schools are largely still focusing on men's history of technology, while women's inventions seldom are mentioned. These are factors that can easily be changed.

About 50% of boys responded positively to the statement 'I would like to get a job in technology' (Sjøberg & Schreiner, 2010), whereas only a few girls expressed an interest. It is a gender difference seen before and after the ROSE study, but it points to something interesting. There seems to be something about the perception of 'technology' that disengages girls' interest in a way that seems to exist in all well-developed countries, especially Western. Since more gender-neutral counties had a narrower gender gap when testing for STEM, a gender gap in STEM education and careers should be non-existent. Yet, in Sweden for example, which ranked first in the EU on the Gender Equality Index, there is still a higher proportion of men in STEM-related careers and education than women. But that depends on how we define STEM or technology.

In Sweden, the gender ratio among those applying for higher education has been more or less the same for a long time: 60% women and 40% men:

> Health care and nursing has continued to be the most female-dominated subject area with 84 per cent women, while engineering continued to be the most male-dominated area with 66 per cent men. The gender distribution is most even within the natural sciences, 45 per cent women and 55 per cent men.
> (Swedish Higher Education Authority, 2015/2019)

What happens if we think outside the gender stereotype of feminine and masculine coded STEM and define health care and nursing as working in science and technology? Because in truth, that is what it is, as well as working closely with humans. This closeness to humans often hinders the general person to see beyond it being female-dominated and therefore seen as 'soft'.

If revising what skills and knowledges are hidden in the acronym STEM a range of educations and careers will fit in the descriptions of having a STEM career. We should also question the meaning of referring to the gender gap as being about girls or boys. We should instead recognize that within groups there may be variation, and between groups intersections. This may be even more clearly visible in single-sex educational settings.

## Gender stereotypes affect us all

First, what do we mean by 'gender'? Gender is a key concept for understanding how inequality and equality arise. It highlights the values, attitudes and experiences of women and men existing in society (Butler, 1990/1999). We create gender constantly, every day, every minute. Describing pink as a girl's colour and blue as a boy's colour is an example of how we create gender. Gender expressions are different in various cultures, eras, and parts of the world. How we act, are, and are expected to be as a woman or a man expresses itself differently in the global South, North, East, or West. For example, one way of being a girl in a suburb of Stockholm does not mean it is the same as being a girl in the suburbs of Johannesburg in the 2020s. Gender becomes an identity. I like to think of creating gender as a kit, where the kit contains a set of skills, manner, and behaviour that you, as a boy or a girl, are expected to perform. Holmegaard et al. (2014) summarise it nicely in their identity research by saying the kit (again, my expression) influences the ways pupils understand and think about themselves. It shapes the ways in which the pupils perceive their possibilities and limitations. To generalise: as a boy you are expected to be noisy and interested in sports – have a favourite team and keep track of the scores; as a girl, you are expected to be soft-spoken, pretty, and interested in humanities.

Even young children can absorb and be influenced by gender stereotypes, and these can be as negative for boys as they are for girls but in different ways. One of the stereotypes associated with design and technology and STEM is that it is for smart people. When researching stereotypes, results reveal that girls of 5 years old are just as likely as boys to associate being smart with their own gender (Archer et al., 2013; Bian et al., 2017). However, for those aged 6 and 7, girls were less likely than boys to make the association (Bian et al., 2017). These findings suggest gendered notions of intelligence are picked up early and start influencing the sorts of interests that girls pursue. Remember, as discussed earlier, there is little to no difference in boys' and girls' ability to learn and succeed in design and technology. We need to instead tackle the stereotypes they are exposed to, and we need to do this early. The division into female and male is a strong categorisation, as we all do, often without being aware of it. We create gender in preschool and school; children, pupils, and educators do this together. We need to be aware because the question is whether it results in an unequal or equal activity.

## Getting inspiration from gender studies – The 'what can we do?'

### How can we attract pupils to a future in design and technology?

Gender studies is an interdisciplinary academic field, a field using different theories that describe how gender is created but mainly psychology, sociology, and theories from philosophy have and are influencing the study of gender (Lindsey, 2015). Therefore, depending on what lens, we look through when studying gender, the results of what we see will somewhat differ. This chapter has chosen to put forth theories with their foundation in sociology. This is because of its closeness to pedagogy. The following are two different theories, the three levels of gender and the gender contract. These are ways of highlighting and thinking which can be used as help in analyses of how gender and gender patterns are created in teaching design and technology.

Sandra Harding (1986/1995) describes how gender affects how we think and reason. Gender is constantly present and affects our way of interpreting life. She describes it as a process that takes place simultaneously on three different levels:

(1) symbolic (norms and beliefs)
(2) structurally (how work is organized and divided)
(3) individually (individual gender identity)

#### SYMBOLIC

An example of how symbolic gender is manifested is here presented by a girl in primary school year 1 (ages 6–7). The class assignment was to draw pictures presenting the concept of family. The girl in her portrayal of the concept of grandmother, showed a woman with long skirts and a headscarf, supporting herself on a cane. When her teacher asked if it was her own grandmother she was showing, the girl replied: 'No, my grandmother does not have a cane; she builds motorbikes. But when you think of a grandmother, it's like this'. Although the girl on an individual level has her own experience of the concept of grandmother, she has a different conception on the symbolic level and reproduces the traditional image of the concept of grandmother.

#### STRUCTURAL

A classroom example of structural gender (how activities are organized) showed in research is that boys receive more time and more attention from educators than girls do (Bassi et al., 2018). Often in a classroom, the teacher would repeat a question or a comment by a boy for the class, but if a girl answered, they wouldn't repeat the question or comment. Critics of this argue that boys act out more and therefore need to be controlled and addressed by name, but it is still giving significance to the boys – even their disobedience is more interesting than the girls' participation. When researching design and technology differences in teaching practices between boys' and girls' classrooms, Ivinson and Murphy (2007) saw how also a single-sex teaching can create settings which limit pupils' learning and engagement in the subject.

A way to gain knowledge of the kinds of structures manifesting in your classroom you can do an exercise to practice gender consciousness. Take a moment and be attentive to what kinds of gender roles are rehearsed, challenged, or repeated during your lessons. These statements can function as guidance:

(1) Girls are often celebrated for being quiet.
(2) The kind and quiet girls get their work done—and on some levels, it's working.
(3) 'Being tough' is an important trait for boys.
(4) Boys are often asked for help by the girls to solve problems during computing and electronical components.
(5) Girls are often asked for help by the boys to solve problems during food and textile sessions.

These statements are chosen because of their stereotypical nature. The first statement is a tool to see if I, as a teacher, am making a difference in my expectations of the pupils in my classroom. If I answer yes on the first statement – am I celebrating the boy's quietness as often? If not, why? The Organisation for Economic Co-operation and Development (OECD, 2015) showed teachers are likely to give girls higher marks than boys of a similar ability. Girls seen as likely to be better behaved in class, and those expectations may result in their work begin given higher marks. Making my expectations visible to myself is a first step in understanding and changing structural issues.

The second statement is more intricately connected to the progress and products as the pupils create. A lack of self-confidence in one's own ability may be responsible for the observed underachievement among girls in STEM subjects (OECD, 2015). One of the hinders is the idea of wanting to achieve perfection. Boys tend to be better at applying a 'try and try again' mentality when problem-solving, depending on the type of task involved, whereas girls aim for something to be 'right the first time'. So it can be valuable for you to think of the kind of tasks given and how the pupils work solving them, creating tasks in which girls and boys get to practice and become better at seeing mistakes as learning, thus taking the edge off perfection.

The third statement is connected to the roles our pupils perform. If performing gender stereotypes research call that behaviour as being a stereotype threat. For boys, this performance threats boys' notion of belonging in academic work as well affecting their school performance (Spencer et al., 2016).

The fourth statement is about the gender roles on display in the classroom. In Sultan et al. (2020) we learned that girls (age 11–12), during lessons in technology education, expressed not being given enough space by the boys to try things for themselves and that they did not like it when the boys told them what to do. Yet at the same time, they asked the boys for help, even when they could have solved the issue themselves. This indicated that the girls were living up to the stereotype of girls as not being good at technology, and asking the boys for help strengthened that notion whilst enhancing the idea of boys being good at technology.

The fifth statement is used to see how gender roles may play out in a setting traditionally seen as a more feminine one. There is an expectation from girls that boys are better at certain design and technology content and vice versa. These expectations come from surrounding views of how boys and girls should perform their gender, making up the 'how to be a girl' and 'how to be a boy' kit. Are the boys in your classroom living up to the stereotype of boys not being good at the content provided? Are the girls living up to the expectation of being a good cook or tailor? By seeing how girls and boys interact within the subject, we can identify what gender kits are in play and challenge our pupils to develop confidence and be creative outside their comfort zone, expand their skills and understanding. Food and textiles as design and technology provide subject knowledge important for a sustainable future. By making changes in the structures of our teaching and planning we can decolonize the curriculum, scaffold our pupils to successfully participate in, and create and change the technological world.

INDIVIDUAL

On the individual level, our pupils' self-image or view of identity in relation to technology can be revealed. It can help us go beyond the homogenous groups of 'boys' and 'girls' and see the individual doing and learning in design and technology. If the pupils express a negative self-image, it may be linked to a view of what technology and being technical means to them. This reminds us as educators that gender is interlocked with class, ethnicity, and social relations in society's institutions and practices (e.g. Harding, 1986/1995). If wanting to strengthen the individual's engagement in technology, we need to understand how they perceive the content taught and how they themselves relate to that content.

Harding's (1986) theory of gender also shows that it is possible to work with gender equality at several levels. For example, as an educator, I can collaborate with my pupils' ideas about women and men (symbolic level), and I can change my teaching activities so that it becomes equal (structural level), without equality at home (individual level), reaching for gender neutrality within my classroom.

## Second theory – the gender contract

The gender contract theory explains how we create invisible rules, norms, customs, and expectations about masculinity and femininity in our society (Hirdman, 1988). The theory is characterized by three basic principles:

(1) Women and men are separate. Male and female are completely different and often also opposites of each other, so-called dichotomies. We talk about 'boys will be boys' and 'quiet girls', girl toys and boy toys, and so on.
(2) Male is valued higher than female. Male is norm. What counts as male has a higher status than what counts as female. For example, it is valued higher for a girl to be called 'boyish' or 'tomboy' than it is for a boy to be called 'girlish'. What men do tends to be attributed higher value.
(3) Everyone participates in creating the gender order. Both women and men (+ nonbinary), participate in creating this gender order, often unconsciously. It is perceived as 'normal' for us that this should be the case. The gender contract is created at the group level and as structures in society.

How can the gender contract be implicated in our teaching and planning of design and technology education?

### First principle: Women and men are separated

If wanting to explore this principle, you, as department staff, could discuss questions like What expectations do we have of our pupils? Are we assuming the boys to be engaged in certain activities and the girls in other? If so, why? How can I as a teacher challenge my students to go beyond their own assumptions of potential? Later in the chapter, some possible answers are given.

### Second principle: Male is valued higher than the female

Giving certain kinds of technology more status than others can be an issue. We traditionally have divided technology into hard and soft. For example, knitting needles are described as soft technology – they need people to be of any use. Hard technologies are described as functioning without being enacted on by people, for example a freezer. Soft technologies are often seen as promoting flexibility and creativity. Hard technologies are often seen as brittle and stifle creativity. Neither is good or bad. Yet it is still there, influencing how our pupils feel about their future within technology. Do our pupils feel like they belong in design and technology?

### Third principle: Everyone creates the gender order

Listen to how your pupils talk. This links to the individual level of gender. Which pupils are more uncomfortable around the woodworking areas and which pupils appear uneasy in the textile area? The gender contract is a tool to recognise patterns and help pupils to push the boundaries of technology, what it means to be technical, and their own abilities as individuals, not as a boy or a girl. However, gender roles are not pre-established, they are constantly re-interpreted and socially constructed. Even traditionally male dominant work environments and activities are affected by social gender.

## Using a gender lens – implications for design and technology

So, what can be the potential gender pitfalls and stereotypical responses to subject content? How can they be avoided?

One of the challenges of teaching technology is the broadness of the subject and that it contains so many areas of knowledge. The curricula can be interpreted in diverse ways and therefore the teachers' preferences, how they interpret the subject, and what knowledge they possess are decisive for what the pupils meet. Since design and technology are interdisciplinary, neither the boundaries of the subject nor the gender aspects are apparent. How to develop the knowledge our pupils need to perform everyday tasks participating in a technological world even though the subject content excludes boys and girls from fully engaging is a challenge. Or does the subject really exclude? Are food and textiles for girls and mechanical systems for boys? No, the subject has no gender – we, humans, are gendering it.

The question of making design and technology education more inclusive lies in the possibilities of developing activities engaging both sexes. However, this does not mean the content has to become more 'girly' or 'boyish'. The choices of content are not solely key to creating gender-conscious teaching. Providing our pupils with views valuing both technology process and product is necessary for creating a more gender-inclusive, broadminded, and open atmosphere in technology education. A good and functioning group where trust, confidence and fair treatment are an obvious foundation for inclusiveness. The tasks and the learning surroundings should allow the pupils to use diverse ways of solving the assignments.

A gender-conscious pedagogy assumes that gender is important for learning, knowledge, and teaching. As a teacher being gender conscious, you should reflect on gender, critically explore what gender means in your subject, and question what ideas we have about gender and its consequences for teaching. Gender-conscious teaching can mean becoming aware that the students are treated differently depending on, for example, gender and dependence on different perceptions of and expectations of girls and boys.

Gender inclusiveness can include methods that allow pupils to solve a problem in diverse ways. It can include tinkering, solving open-ended problems, and choosing assignments valuing process and product, context-related technology, and tasks connected to solving problems regarding sustainability. By giving examples relating to both girls and boys and methods highlighting process instead of focusing on the finished product (for example) you can create a more engaging classroom, for both sexes.

Sometimes our pupils work together in pairs. Boys with boys, girls with boys, and girls with girls. Be observant on how the gender roles play out when they work – is one in the pair more dominant? As a teacher, pay attention to the division of work during project work. For example, are tasks and responsibilities rotated or is the same person always taking on certain tasks? This is not unusual, but it can be of importance to know if it is a manifestation of traditional gender roles in play. By creating opportunities for other kinds of collaboration during class, traditions are challenged, perspectives broaden.

According to researcher Wendy Faulkner (2003), girls are more motivated to understand the background of a task and its connection to everyday perspective. They identify with the user and judge products and systems in terms of what is user-friendly. Human-centred design and/or service design can therefore be a way forward in engaging the girls. Boys, on the other hand, more often approach technical tasks in an isolated manner and see the context as irrelevant. Working contextually is not in bad for the boys but can scaffold girls' engagement in solving different tasks. Yet not every child fits neatly into this way of teaching. It should be remembered that trial and error and discussing and planning are both great ways to tackle a technical problem. These are skills pupils can be equally helped by and would benefit practising, regardless of gender. We should be careful not to gender the curriculum in a contradictory way. Adding a gender perspective can broaden a pupil's perceptions of their own possibilities regarding future education and work and so strengthening their self-identity as technical.

## Conclusion

This chapter's ambition was to shed light on the opportunities that work from a gender perspective in technology education can create. Challenge yourself and make changes in your teaching methods when you notice that there is a pattern of pupils or pupils of a certain gender performing their roles according to the 'kit', in a negative way. Remember that you and your actions are what create the group. As a teacher, relying on studies on, among other things, discussing how gender identities are created and shaped during learning technology means more pupils can have a chance to sustain their interests in technology. The technical knowledge and skills that technology education provides have an important role in giving learners the opportunities to improve their ability to interact with everyday technology and to be critical of it. Technical education means taking part in human culture and having the opportunity to shape the future of society. Technical knowledge is therefore a matter of democracy.

## Questions

1 What do you see as possible within teaching design and technology to counteract restrictive gender norms so that students can develop their abilities and interests without being limited by them?
2 What kinds of teaching materials do you use, and what norms are conveyed through these representations?
3 Across the world, there are different approaches to engaging girls and boys in the classroom. Some advocate for single-sex classrooms, others not. If you were free to decide how you wanted to organise your teaching – what are your thoughts on this, and why?
4 What would you say is a good way to counteract differences between pupils from a gender perspective in terms of results, expectations, treatment, participation, and influence in school?
5 What potential has design and technology in creating reflective conversations on issues related to gender equality?

## References

Archer, L., DeWitt, J., Osborne, J., Dillon, J., Willis, B. and Wong, B. (2013). 'Not girly, not sexy, not glamorous': Primary school girls' and parents' constructions of science aspirations. *Pedagogy, Culture & Society*, 21(1), 171–194. doi:10.1080/14681366.2012.748676

Bassi, M., Mateo Díaz, M., Blumberg, R. L. and Reynoso, A. (2018). Failing to notice? Uneven teachers' attention to boys and girls in the classroom. *IZA Journal of Labor Economics*, 7(1). doi:10.1186/s40172-018-0069-4

Berner, B. (2004). *Ifrågasättanden: forskning om genus, teknik och naturvetenskap*. Linköping: Tema Teknik och social förändring, Linköpings universitet.

Bian, L., Leslie, S. and Cimpian, A. (2017). Gender stereotypes about intellectual ability emerge early and influence children's interests. *Science*, 355(6323), 389–391. doi:10.1126/science.aah6524

Butler, J. (1990/1999). *Gender Trouble: Feminism and the Subversion of Identity*. New York: Routledge.

European Commission (1998). Directorate-general for employment, social affairs and inclusion. In *One Hundred Words for Equality: A Glossary of Terms on Equality between Women and Men*. Publications Office.

Eurostat (2020). *Tertiary education statistics*, data extracted in September 2020. Retrieved https://ec.europa.eu/eurostat/statistics-explained/index.php?title=Archive:Europe_2020_indicators_-_education&oldid=451570

Faulkner, W. (2003). Teknikfrågan i feminismen. In: Berner, B (Ed.) *Vem tillhör tekniken?* Lund, Arkiv förlag.

Guiso, L., Monte, F., Sapienza, P. and Zingales, L. (2008). Culture, gender, and math. *Science*, 320(5880), 1164–1165. doi:10.1126/science.1154094

Hallström, J., Elvstrand, H. and Hellberg, K. (2015). Gender and technology in free play in Swedish early childhood education. *International Journal of Technology and Design Education*, 25(2), 137–149 DOI: 10.1007/s10798-014-9274-z

Harding, S. (1986). *The Science Question in Feminism*. Ithaca, NY: Cornell University Press.

Harding, S. (1986/1995). Just add women and stir? In Gender Working Group of UN Commission on Science and Technology for Development (Ed.), *Missing Links: Gender Equity in Science and Technology for Development*. Ottawa, ON: IDRC.

Hirdman, Y. (1988). Gensussystemet - reflexioner kring kvinnors sociala underordning. *Tidskrift för Genusvetenskap*, 3, 49–63.

Holmegaard, H., Madsen, L. and Ulriksen, L. (2014). To choose or not to choose science: Constructions of desirable identities among young people considering a STEM higher education programme. *International Journal of Science Education*, 36, 186–215. doi: 10.1080/09500693.2012.749362

Hultman, Martin, Forchtner, Bernhard, Jylhä, Kirsti and Ekberg, Kristoffer (forthcoming). *Denial – Obstruction – Inertia: Explaining Inaction on Climate Science*. London: Routledge.

Ivinson, G. and Murphy, P. (2007). *Rethinking Single Sex Teaching*. Buckingham, UK: Open University Press. http://mcgraw-hill.co.uk/html/0335220401.html

Jidesjö, A., Westman A.-K. and Oscarsson, M. (2021). Trends and developments in student's interest in Science and technology: Results from the Relevance of science education second (ROSES) study in Sweden. In Søren W. Clausen, Peer Daugbjerg, Birgitte L. Nielsen, Martin K. Sillasen & Simon O. Rebsdorf (Eds.), *Science Education in the Light of Global Sustainable Development: Trends and Possibilities*, Science education in the light of Global Sustainable Development: Trends and Possibilities. Paper presented at *Proceedings of the 13th Nordic Research Symposium on Science Education*, pp. 148–156.

Lauer, J. E., Yhang, E., and Lourenco, S. F. (2019). The development of gender differences in spatial reasoning: A meta-analytic review. *Psychological Bulletin*, 145(6), 537–565. doi:10.1037/bul0000191

Lindsey, L. L. (2015). *Gender Roles: A Sociological Perspective*. Boston, MA: Pearson. doi:10.4324/9781315664095

OECD (2015). Girls' lack of self-confidence. In: *The ABC of Gender Equality in Education: Aptitude, Behaviour, Confidence*, OECD Publishing, Paris, doi:10.1787/9789264229945-6-en

Sjøberg, S. and Schreiner, C. (2010). The ROSE project. An overview and key findings. http://roseproject.no/network/countries/norway/eng/nor-Sjoberg-Schreiner-overview-2010.pdf

Sjøberg, S. and Schreiner, C (2019). ROSE (The Relevance of Science Education) The development, key findings and impacts of an international low cost comparative project. ROSE Final Report, Part 1. University of Oslo.

Spelke, E. S. (2005) Sex differences in intrinsic aptitude for mathematics and science?: A critical review. *American Psychologist*, 60(9), 950–958.

Spencer, S. J., Logel, C., and Davies, P. G. (2016). Stereotype threat. *Annual Review of Psychology* 67, 415–437. doi:10.1146/annurev-psych-073115-103235

Sultan, U., Axell, C. and Hallström, J. (2020). Technical or not? Investigating the self-image of girls aged 9 to 12 when participating in primary technology education. *Design And Technology Education: An International Journal*, 25(2), 175–191. Retrieved from https://ojs.lboro.ac.uk/DATE/article/view/2762

Sun, Y., Jidesjo, A. and Rundgren, S. C. (2019). Examining gender differences in students' entrance into and persistence in STEM programs in Swedish higher education. *The European Journal of Educational Sciences*, 06(01). doi: 10.19044/ejes.v6no1a5

Swedish Higher Education Authority (2015/2019). Gender equality in higher education. https://english.uka.se/statistics/gender-equality-in-higher-education.html

United Nations. (2022). *Transforming our world: The 2030 agenda for sustainable development | Department of Economic and Social Affairs.* Sustainable Development. https://sdgs.un.org/2030agenda

UNESCO (2017). *Cracking the Code: Girls' and Women's Education in Science, Technology, Engineering and Mathematics (STEM).* Paris.

Warin, J. and Adriany, V. (2017). Gender flexible pedagogy in early childhood education. *Journal of Gender Studies,* 26:4, 375–386, DOI: 10.1080/09589236.2015.1105738

# 10 Managing curriculum change

*Sarah Davies*

There has been a growing debate across many countries about how the design and technology (D&T) curriculum should evolve and teachers' role in making this happen. This chapter initially considers the different reasons that drive curriculum change in D&T and how change is dealt with. By looking at both the drivers of curriculum change and D&T teachers' responses to those changes, this chapter offers different perspectives on the evolution of the D&T curriculum and subject teachers' role in managing the process. Next, the chapter explores the different ways that D&T teachers cope with the challenge of curriculum change through three case studies, which describe D&T teachers' experiences of managing the process. Finally, the chapter draws on the case studies to discuss the role of D&T teachers in curriculum change and the challenge this process poses for established viewpoints and practice.

## Why does a curriculum change happen?

In his book *The New Meaning of Educational Change* (2015), Michael Fullan insists that successful change is only possible if those responsible for making it happen are helped to understand why the change is needed. Therefore, an excellent place to start is by asking, Why does a curriculum change happen? Fullan suggests that curriculum changes can be classified into three categories – natural events, policy reforms and voluntary reasons.

The first driver of curriculum change relates to natural events. Natural events are unpredictable and bring about unplanned changes to the curriculum. Flooding, hurricanes and snowstorms are examples of natural events that are extreme. When these unforeseen natural events happen, teachers are forced to react to temporary or permanent school closures that lead to changes in curriculum and teaching methods. The global pandemic in 2020–21 is an example of a natural event that brought about unplanned changes to how the curriculum was delivered. During the pandemic, a move to online lessons offered the solution to school closures and social distancing. Tony Ryan, the D&T Association chief executive officer, recognised this situation's challenges for D&T teachers and advised a staggered introduction of practical working once social distancing rules subsided (D&T Association,

2020). The unpredictable nature of these natural events drives teachers to react and innovate in challenging ways.

The second category relates to policy reform. A policy is written and agreed on by a group of people, a business organisation or the government for the purpose of improving a particular situation. In the case of education, policy reform is usually designed by the government to improve education for young people. Improvements might result in a policy reform that changes an existing curriculum design, learning intentions, teaching materials and assessment processes. Reasons for policy reform that affect education are best explained in this quote from the Department for International Development (2018):

> Education has the power to change lives. It opens doors to better employment, more active citizenship and well-informed health choices which benefit future generations. At its best, it transforms the prospects of poor and marginalised children and builds more meritocratic societies.

The quote emphasises the importance of education in pupils' lives because education has the power to change lives for the better. However, Ball (2017) reminds us that although good reasons are behind policy design, the implementation can cause issues for those asked to make the change a reality. The teachers asked to make the change reality are not always the same group of people who designed the reform. Therefore, policy reform can make teachers feel insecure about the level of change required and what knowledge and expertise they will consequently need to implement the change. For example, in England, the government-designed policy reforms to improve economic productivity, competitiveness and international standards (Department for Education, 2010). The government redesigned curriculum content, intentions and assessments towards a knowledge-centred model. The knowledge-centred model emphasised facts and discipline expertise, as explored by Ellis (2014). This shift toward a knowledge-centred model that improves education for young people also has the potential to cause issues for D&T teachers' ideas about what, how and why they teach the subject (Davies, 2022).

Fullan observes that the first two categories can be viewed as impositions on teachers because the drive for change comes from external forces outside the school, in contrast to the third category, which relates to voluntary reasons for curriculum change. Fullan suggests that dissatisfaction, inconsistency and intolerability with the current situation drive voluntary reasons for change. Consequently, because these changes are voluntary, teachers control the curriculum change and drive curriculum based on their individual or collective intentions, often context-dependent. Voluntary reasons for change relate to what teachers and members of the D&T community identify as a problem and set out to change intentionally. For example, a voluntary reason for a curriculum change could be linked to D&T reports on pupil performance data. One such report by Diana Choulerton, the then D&T subject lead for the Office for Standards in Education, Children's Services and Skills (OFSTED) in England, reported that

- typically, students make less progress from starting points in D&T than most other subjects.
- boys typically make significantly less progress than girls except in systems and control.
- disadvantaged students typically make much less progress than non-disadvantaged students.

(Choulerton, 2015)

This report was significant for D&T teachers. In addition, it led to considerable debate at a D&T consultants meeting I attended in 2016 about the changes needed to address these issues.

In conclusion, we can see that change happens for various reasons. Reasons for a curriculum change can be imposed on teachers through natural or policy events or welcomed through voluntary intentions. Teachers need to understand how they can cope with a curriculum change, whether imposed or voluntary. I look at this in the next section.

## How do teachers deal with change?

Fullan (2015) offers a model of change that can help understand how D&T teachers might deal with curriculum change. The model involves three steps: an initial sense of loss for the teacher, the alignment of the teachers' values with the change and a symbolic fight between what must change and the actions required to achieve them. I discuss each in turn. First, the teachers must go through a sense of loss in recognising what has been removed or altered concerning change. For example, some D&T teachers in England were affected by the removal of food from General Certificate of Secondary Education (GCSE) D&T. Second, the teacher needs to align their subject values with the values of the change. This means finding a way to settle any clashes between the ideas and beliefs of the teacher with the those of the proposed change. An example of this might be the collision of different ideas about the place of vocational learning in D&T and whether schools are the place for this type of knowledge and skill development. Finally, the teacher must learn and adopt new practices that make the change happen. Adopting new practices sounds easy when written down, but Fullan describes this as a symbolic fight for the teacher – a fight between what they used to do (past practice) and what they need to do now (new practice). A new practice that might require additional professional knowledge and skills. For example, some D&T teachers in England struggled to initially develop new practices that emphasised the teaching of electronics within textiles topics. Research by Davies and Rutland (2013) found that the issue for the teachers was linked to distinctions in the department that presented a symbolic barrier between electronics and textiles resources and knowledge. Fullan's model of change offers a way to think about the issues and problems that teachers face during the process.

Another theory that might help us think about the complexity of change is English sociologist Anthony Giddens (1994). Gidden's offers a view of people and modern society, which can help us think about teachers' role in change. For example, suppose we apply his idea and assume that the outcome of a curriculum change relies on a combination of capability (people) and opportunities afforded by the situation (modern society). In that case, we see that both a teacher's agency (their intended action) and school structures (the context within which they work) play a role in change. To examine this further, I have explained the concepts Gidden uses within his theory below because these concepts can help us interrogate how D&T teachers might respond to change. The concepts fall into two categories. The first category – enabling responses – includes the embedding of tradition and professional discourse or dialogue. The second category, restrictive responses – includes the concepts of professional disengagement and coercion or threat.

## Enabling responses

The embedding of tradition conceptualises any new practice or process ingrained in resources and practice from the past. The resources and practices act as a starting point for what happens in the present and potentially the future. In England, teachers have been encouraged by professional development organisations to map their old curriculum against the new policy reforms. Mapping activities help teachers reflect on similarities and differences between the old and the new curriculum. The process often leads to identifying curriculum gaps, which can be filled with alternative resources and practices. Nicholl et al. (2013) offer a strategy for developing a new tradition through their Designing our Tomorrows project. The project describes combining past skills-based embedded traditions with knowledge-based activities that are sometimes missing from the taught D&T curriculum. The project advocates authentic 'situated' learning experiences and offers pupils problem-solving activities rooted in real-world problems. The Designing our Tomorrows project provides a set of traditions that teachers can embed to enable a positive response to change.

Professional discourse or dialogue conceptualises the interchange of ideas between groups of teachers. For example, when teachers talk about curriculum, they reflect on possible solutions to imposed or voluntary curriculum change. Opportunities for conversations about curriculum within a teacher's school or via subject-specific networks can generate the space for this type of subject-specific professional dialogue. However, in England, these opportunities have been eroded over the years due to a combination of reduced local authority intervention and the deregulation of teacher education (see Chapter 6). When opportunities for professional dialogue are limited, access to social media and support from a subject association (e.g. the D&T Association in the UK) become essential. Two examples of social media that support professional dialogue and the interchange of ideas outside of local opportunities are the Talking D&T Podcast (Hardy, 2021) and the website David and Torben for D&T (Barlex and Steeg, 2021). In addition, listening in and conversing with other members of the D&T community can enable the change process to be better understood and valued.

## Restrictive responses

Professional disengagement conceptualises the action or process of withdrawing engagement in a curriculum change. When we feel alienated by a curriculum change and struggle to connect our established practices with those required of the curriculum change, we can feel restricted in what we can do (or not do) because of the change. In a worst-case scenario, this can mean D&T teachers are choosing to leave the profession altogether. For example, during the 1990s, when D&T entered the National Curriculum in England, Paetcher (1995) interviewed secondary teachers working in London. Paechter found that teachers professionally disengaged from curriculum change by sustaining practices from before or retreating to other subjects within the curriculum.

Coercion conceptualises the practice of persuading someone to do something by using force or threat. Policy reforms and school inspection processes are examples of threats to teachers' practice. Not attaining a good examination or inspection grade can force teachers to change a curriculum. The conforming action is often restrictive and likely to lead to a short-term effect on the curriculum change process. Research conducted by Doyle et al. (2019) found that D&T teachers' working with a new curriculum in Ireland taught something very different to what they identified the curriculum to be. The new curriculum highlighted a misalignment between teachers' perceptions of a subject change and the actual practice of change in the classroom. The policy reform coerced the teachers to visualise the subject in a way they did not fully understand. In turn, a false perception led to a continuation of traditional practices that created a barrier to change. Feelings of coercion can also lead to a shallow understanding of the change that threatens any new practice's sustainability.

Giddens's concepts offer an alternative way of thinking about how teachers navigate curriculum change and how resolutions can be made. The change process can result in various outcomes that might be viewed as more successful than others. Teachers' management of a curriculum change depends on their role and the opportunities afforded by their situation to enable or restrict the change process.

## A set of case studies

In this section, I share three case studies from my doctoral research interviews with a range of D&T teachers involved in a curriculum change in England. Each case study has been chosen to exemplify a different context and perspective. Fullan's ideas about change categorisation and Giddens's ideas about capability (people) and opportunities afforded by the situation (modern society) have been used to analyse the various case studies.

The case studies use pseudonyms to protect the identity of the individual participants.

### Case study 1: Kerry

When the research interview was conducted, Kerry worked as a department head at a large multi-academy trust (MAT) school in England. He had taught in three different schools during 11 years of teaching. Kerry was keen to promote a collective culture within his department and encouraged his teachers to innovate and take risks with their teaching and curriculum content. However, he was dissatisfied with his team's current D&T experiences. For example, Kerry wanted to improve the teaching of textiles specialist knowledge within the curriculum. He felt that once he could fill this gap in his team's expertise, he would offer all pupils in the school a diverse range of D&T experiences.

The subject department was understaffed, and they did not have enough D&T teachers to deliver all the lessons on the timetable. However, due to overstaffing in other school areas, teachers who usually teach different curriculum areas were timetabled to teach design and technology. This meant Kerry needed to plan a curriculum that specialist and non-specialist D&T teachers could teach.

At first, Kerry felt powerless in improving textiles specialist knowledge within the curriculum. He wanted to develop a community amongst the teachers, but the non-specialist teachers could not join team meetings during which discussions about teaching and curriculum occur. Moreover, the non-specialist teachers had other commitments, and the temporary nature of the arrangement limited their desire to develop new knowledge and skills. Besides this fact, they were not ready to innovate and take risks because they did not yet have the confidence to teach basic design and technology.

Kerry was concerned about the arrangement, but after talking to the non-specialist teachers, he started seeing different ways to support non-specialist teachers temporarily. He adapted curriculum materials and paired experienced specialist teachers with non-specialists. The workshop and desk-based lessons were split up so specialist teachers could teach that specialist (workshop) content, and non-specialist teachers could teach the more straightforward (desk-based) lessons. The desk-based lessons included quizzes and knowledge organisers to teach content knowledge, whilst the specialist D&T teachers taught the practical process knowledge.

The problem of not offering textile lessons within the curriculum was still unresolved, but Kerry had an idea. The food technician within the department told him they had previous experience in textile technology and was willing to share their expertise with him and support in-class teaching. As a result, small-group teaching activities introduced textile aspects into the curriculum. The process built Kerry's confidence around teaching outside his specialism.

Finally, Kerry reflected on the reason behind understaffing and connected this to a timetabling complexity: because the department used a rotation system for teaching 11- to 14-year-old pupils, they needed extra flexibility in covering all D&T lessons. As a result, the team required a bigger teaching team at specific points in the week, which was not a variable that Kerry could control. However, it could be solved if he could timetable an equal number of teachers and lessons through a linear delivery pattern. This meant removing the rotation system and implementing one where the teacher remained with a group for the whole year.

In breaking down Kerry's account of managing a curriculum change, the case study reveals two reasons for the change: first, a natural event – working with non-specialist teachers forced Kerry to map the curriculum to non-specialist teachers' knowledge and skills – and second, a personal dissatisfaction – Kerry is dissatisfied with his pupil's current curriculum experience. These two changes contrast in that one is external and the other is voluntary. Nevertheless, Kerry resolves the situation by adapting curriculum and delivery methods and developing his textile knowledge and skills.

The change process that Kerry goes through involves a shift in viewpoint about design and technology. After focusing on the loss of specialist expertise in his teaching team and the gap in the textile curriculum, he fights his way through the challenge ahead in two ways:

- A new tradition of splitting workshop and desk-based activities is evolved into a new practice. Kerry uses the traditional plans to design alternative curriculum delivery models. The redesigned curriculum matches the expertise of the teaching team.
- Kerry uses his professional dialogue with colleagues to identify additional knowledge and skills within the team. For example, in conversation with his technician, he learns that they have an unutilised talent.

As a result, a new tradition is established. Every D&T lesson no longer needs to be taught by a teacher with practical expertise. In addition, the shift supports Kerry in his goal to extend textile experiences for pupils.

This example shows us that change is not one thing or another and that natural events, which cause change, can be temporary. The tension between losing specialist expertise in the teaching team, designing alternative curriculum delivery models and spotting hidden talents within the existing team is paramount. Kerry resolves the situation through a combination of creating a new tradition and professional dialogue. Adapting curriculum traditions is challenging and can lead to loss, but this example shows that professional conversation can resolve the problem. Understanding what we can and cannot do and how others can support us in the journey takes time and opportunity. Time and opportunities that not all teachers have.

### Case study 2: Judith

Judith worked in a high-performing 11–18 school in England when I conducted the research interview. She had been teaching for ten years, and this was her second school since she completed her initial teacher education. Before teaching, Judith had worked in the textile and fashion industry. The school she worked in now comprises a small team of five teachers who shared her passion for design and technology. Judith was keen to use her industrial experience to promote engineering knowledge and skills and make her teaching relevant to her pupils. She wanted to do this because she felt her own school experience of the subject had been traditional; the gendered aspects of design and technology, like textiles and food for girls, had been the only specialism available to her.

In 2017 the English government introduced new subject content and assessment for GCSE qualifications for teaching to 14- to 16-year-olds. The redesigned qualifications aimed to ensure economic productivity and competitiveness to raise academic standards. The redesign meant a shift from coursework activity towards examinations for design and technology. The new qualifications also involved repositioning D&T as a single subject, no longer offering specialist 14–16 studies in graphics (paper and cardboard), resistant materials (metal, plastic, wood) and textiles. This merging of material areas also meant teachers were now required to teach core technical knowledge and skills. Judith and her colleagues needed to develop pupils' knowledge and skills and decided to adopt the 'single subject' earlier when the pupils are aged 11 to 14 because they felt that this would help them build their expertise and prepare pupils for the new examination.

At first, Judith worried that she did not have sufficient competency in the new subject content, and she identified that she would need to develop her expertise. Her desire to help her pupils learn the new content drove her to build her knowledge to stay one step ahead of the pupils. Judith recognised that this would take much work on her part, and she rose to the challenge because she believed the new content better suited her goal for a relevant and non-gendered curriculum.

Next, she needed to work with her colleagues to develop the whole team's expertise, not just hers, across material areas. They employed two strategies to overcome the problem. First, they divided the 11–14 curriculum so that each team member took responsibility for planning and resourcing a learning unit. Then, they used a weekly meeting session to teach each other the new knowledge and skills needed to teach each learning unit. For example, Judith planned a unit covering knowledge and skills related to food contexts. The learning unit was in an area she had been teaching for several years.

Along with another colleague, Judith identified 'flashpoints' within the learning unit that might prove tricky for the non-food specialists to teach. So, Judith and her colleague teamed up to teach their colleagues the new content during the weekly meeting sessions. The approach was formal and informal as the training sessions often led to lunchtime conversations about teaching the new content and which methods would support pupil learning best. In return, Judith learned how to teach about pewter and timber from her colleagues. Once she read the unit of learning prepared by her colleagues, she practised new practical skills in the workshop during the weekly sessions. The process was ongoing, and the team devised units of learning and training sessions as the year progressed rather than trying to frontload everything. The timetabling of the training sessions ensured that the team stayed at least one step ahead of the pupils.

Finally, in the summer term, Judith and her colleagues were able to teach a learning unit that prepared pupils for the single-subject version of the curriculum. In addition, the team designed an open design brief. The design brief tested pupils' answers to a multi-material design context. The design brief required teachers to adopt new teaching methods that they felt were modern and no longer encouraged gendered decisions about specialist material areas.

Judith's account of managing a curriculum change offers an insight into how policy reform can drive D&T curriculum and assessment changes. Judith and her colleagues had to recognise that they lacked specific knowledge and skills and develop this for teaching the new single subject. Even though Judith and her colleagues had the change imposed on them, they resolved to plan the curriculum collectively and supported each other in developing single subject expertise across the team.

The change process that Judith went through involved a shift in curriculum and teaching methods. After focusing on the need to stay ahead of her pupils, Judith soon started to think about sharing her expertise in food and textiles with other team members. In return for this, she also gained professional development. Judith embraced the challenge of change and moved away from her previous specialist identity. A textile teacher with specialist knowledge and expertise in one subject area, as explored by Paechter (1995), to a teacher of D&T with knowledge and expertise across the different subject areas. Although the policy change is an example of Gidden's theory of coercion, Judith aligned her desire to support pupils with the aims of the curriculum change. Judith made the change meaningful by connecting her desire to promote relevant and non-gender teaching with a rejection of the persisting tradition of material specialist isolation. For example, female teachers (like Judith) are often associated with planning and teaching design and technology's food and textile aspects. Although the female teacher continues to take responsibility for planning the food aspect of the curriculum, she is redesigning the units of learning to be taught by all her colleagues (both male and female). Judith is supported through the change process by opportunities for professional dialogue with her colleagues. These opportunities counteract the hardship of giving up free time to learn new content with the reward of formal and informal conversations focused on teaching and learning. By adopting new teaching methods, Judith expands her curriculum knowledge and teaching skills whilst fulfilling her personal goal to make the subject suitable for all pupils, regardless of gender.

Judith's example shows us that even though policy reform is an imposed change, the change can be meaningful when linked to personal desires for the subject. The tension between coercion and free will loosened through professional dialogue. The challenge for many teachers is professional dialogue opportunities, and this example presents an argument for those opportunities being available to all teachers working in schools today.

## Case study 3: Mary

When the research interview was conducted, Mary worked in a large secondary school in England with a high intake of pupils with English as an additional language (EAL). She had been teaching as a D&T teacher for three years. Mary worked in her second since completing her initial teacher education. Like Judith, Mary had a career in the textile and fashion industry before teaching. She worked with a small team of four D&T teachers within a creative arts faculty. In addition, Mary was a member of a cross-school assessment group; she thought it was essential to work with colleagues within and outside her D&T department. Mary believed this because she valued opportunities to share ideas and solve problems as a collective.

Over the previous three years, Mary had encountered substantial curriculum change. Each year, her faculty had devised alternatives to the traditional rotation system of teaching D&T lessons. In the traditional rotation system, pupils experienced short units of learning in various material areas annually. The system allowed pupils to experience all the different material areas but for a short period of 10 weeks. The faculty was concerned that pupils made less progress in D&T than other school subjects. The faculty felt this was partly due to the nature of rotation systems and learning, thinking that short learning units lead to repetitive and shallow understanding. Therefore, the team decided to extend each rotation from 10 to 30 weeks, resulting in one material area learning unit across the pupils' first three years of secondary school. In other words, the pupils would only experience a different material area once. So, for example, pupils might experience a textiles unit of learning in their first year of secondary school or their third year but not both.

At first, Mary questioned the shift to teaching her textile unit of learning only once in three years; she worried that pupils might forget what they had understood. Then she researched pupils' progress in textiles and identified that most pupils had made no progress over the three years when taught using the rotation system of 10 weeks per material area. So, Mary revised her curriculum materials to adapt to the more extended, single experience with this new insight. She enjoyed this process and felt this pushed her to develop her teaching by considering the different needs of her pupils, which benefitted her professional development.

As a result, Mary designed a flexible learning unit that could be adapted to meet her pupils' stretch and challenge needs depending on when and what age they were. She adopted strategies discussed in the cross-school assessment group. The process helped Mary better understand her learners' different needs and plans for tailoring teaching methods and content to a wide range of abilities. The process gave her confidence in her ability to differentiate teaching and learning. Mary also used her learning from the cross-school assessment group to adapt assessment materials and generate pupil-friendly learning outcomes. She reviewed the change in pupils' progress due to the more extended learning units and found that pupils had made significant progress compared to the previous year.

Analysis of Mary's account of managing a curriculum change shows the primary reason for the change is the faculty's dissatisfaction with pupil progress, echoing views from the OFSTED report (Choulerton, 2015). The change is voluntary, and the team adapts their embedded traditional rotation delivery system.

The change process that Mary went through involved a shift in her viewpoint about teaching design and technology. After focusing on the possibility of pupils' forgetting their experience and understanding of textiles, she started to think about the changes more positively, realising pupils would have time for more depth of learning experience. Professional dialogue with members of the department faculty and her research into the situation helped Mary conclude that the change was better for her pupils. The significant change that Mary undertook was an adaptation of her teaching plans. The new tradition of a short learning unit focused on one material area (textiles) created the springboard for a new teaching plan. Mary adapted her teaching materials to meet the needs of her pupils at different stages in their development. This action boosted her confidence and ability to differentiate teaching plans.

Mary's example offers evidence that voluntary reasons for change brought about by dissatisfaction with the norm can still lead to feelings of loss. The tension between what she used to do and what she does now is real. Change challenges teachers to reject established practices they once believed to be correct. So, it is no surprise that the process can lead to anxiety. Nevertheless, we see again that professional dialogue is a solution to change, and Mary talked to her cross-school assessment group to help her think through her situation. The classification of professional dialogue, which relates to the discussion about practice with colleagues, can also be expanded to include individual (internal) dialogue used to reflect on practice either written down or thought about in one's head.

In summary, these case studies have shown three different experiences of change. Kerry dealt with a natural event that impacted the curriculum in his department. Judith implemented a new curriculum imposed by policy reform, resulting in her knowledge and skill development. Furthermore, Mary chose to change the curriculum based on dissatisfaction with the current teaching situation, which led to a change in teaching plans and methods. The case studies demonstrate the point made earlier that when we or others (policy reformers) question what we teach, it is likely to lead to slight or significant changes in our teaching and curriculum. The teachers' accounts exemplify the process of change and how a loss that leads to anxiety and struggle can develop into a positive experience that generates new knowledge, skills and relationships.

## Conclusion

We need to live with change as D&T teachers and view change as a positive experience that moves the subject forward. D&T teachers need to find ways to positively deal with the loss, anxiety and struggle that change brings about. By considering the different reasons that drive change, we can start to accept that change can be voluntary or imposed and begin questioning ways to make the imposed meaningful and aligned to voluntary reasons for change. In accepting change, a process can begin in which teachers ask themselves whether actions are rooted in traditional practices and, if so, is this for the best. Accepting change and finding opportunities to establish a professional dialogue around the change counteracts restrictive responses like professional disengagement and the threat of coercion.

Considering (1) why curriculum change happens and (2) D&T teachers' capacity for responding to curriculum change, we can see the challenges, tensions and opportunities that change brings. Awareness of these issues enables us to look at problems in new ways, question the drivers associated with curriculum change and cope. Of course, curriculum change will always play a role in the work of a D&T teacher, and D&T teachers will always play a role in the success or failure of that change. However, by accepting that we have a role to play, we might be better prepared for the next iteration and better positioned to react quickly and respond to support the development and progress of the subject.

## Questions

1 What natural or policy drivers of change and/or voluntary drivers have you or your D&T colleagues experienced?
2 How did you set out to develop new D&T teaching traditions within your own practice and that of colleagues because of the changes identified in the first question?
3 How might you use this chapter to think about why these new D&T teaching traditions did (or did not) embed into your own and others' practice?
4 Do you have examples of how you have dealt with the feelings of loss that change brings and how you dealt with these feelings?
5 Can you think of alternative solutions to the ones that each case study teacher adopted? What benefits would these alternative solutions offer?

## References

Ball, S.J., 2017. *The education debate*. 3rd Edition. Bristol: Policy Press.
Barlex, D. and Steeg, T., 2021, David and Torben for D&T. [online] Available at: https://dandtfordandt.wordpress.com/ [Accessed: Jul 1, 2021].
Choulerton, D., 2015. Design and Technology Association (DATA) summer school keynote 2015. [on-line] Available at: https://www.slideshare.net/Ofstednews/design-and-technology-association-data-summer-school-keynote-2015 [Accessed: Jul 6, 2017].

Davies, S., 2022, Teaching outside a subject specialism: strategies design and technology teachers use to manage change. PATT39: PATT on the Edge Technology, Innovation and Education, June 21-24, 2022, St. John's, Newfoundland & Labrador, Canada

Davies, S. and Rutland, M., 2013, Did the UK Digital Design and Technology (DD&T) Programme Lead to Innovative Curriculum Change within Secondary Schools? In: P.J. Williams, and D.S.P. Gedera, eds., Technology Education for the Future: A Play on Sustainability. New Zealand: The Technology Environmental Science and Mathematics Education Research Centre, University of Waikato, 2013, pp. 115–121.

D&T Association, 2020, Planning a return to school-based practise in design and technology. [on-line] Available at: https://www.data.org.uk/news/planning-a-return-to-school-based-practise-in-design-and-technology/ [Accessed: Jun 26, 2021].

Department for Education, 2010, *The importance of teaching: The case for change*. London: Crown Publishing.

Department for International Development, 2018, Education Policy. [on-line] Available at: https://www.gov.uk/government/publications/dfid-education-policy-2018-get-children-learning/dfid-education-policy [Accessed: Jun 26, 2021].

Doyle, A., Seery, N., Canty, D. and Buckley, J., 2019, Agendas, influences, and capability: Perspectives on practice in design and technology education. *International Journal of Technology and Design Education*, 29, pp. 143–159.

Ellis, A.K., 2014, *Exemplars of curriculum theory*. Abingdon, Oxon: Routledge.

Fullan, M., 2015. *The new meaning of educational change*. New York: Teachers College Press.

Giddens, A., 1994, Living in a post-traditional society. In Beck, U., Giddens, A. and Lash, S., eds. *Reflexive modernisation: Politics, tradition and aesthetics in the modern social order*. Cambridge: Polity Press, p. 100.

Hardy, A., 2021, Podcast. [on-line] Available at: https://dralisonhardy.com/podcast/ [Accessed: Jul 1, 2021].

Nicholl, B., Flutter, J., Hosking, I.M. and Clarkson, P.J., 2013, Transforming practice in Design and Technology: Evidence from a classroom-based research study of students' responses to an intervention on inclusive design. *Curriculum Journal*, 24 (1), pp. 86–102.

Paechter, C., 1995, Subcultural retreat: Negotiating the design and technology curriculum. *British Educational Research Journal*, 21 (1), pp. 75–87.

Part III
# Teaching design and technology

# 11 Influence of teachers' perceptions of subject knowledge on pedagogical approaches

*Dawne Irving-Bell*

## Introduction

According to Shulman (1986), pedagogical content knowledge, commonly known as PCK, is a special type of knowledge that only teachers have. In his work, Schulman describes PCK as the process where teachers transform specialist knowledge of their subject discipline into content suitable for effective pedagogical dissemination (Shulman, 1986, 1987). That is to say how teachers relate their pedagogical knowledge (what they know about teaching) to their subject disciplinary or content knowledge (what they plan to teach).

While completing my PhD, which explored the emergent identities of pre-service STEM teachers, it struck me that what if a teacher believes their subject knowledge is limited and they have insufficient specialist knowledge to transform? Developed from my research, this chapter considers the effect teachers' perceptions of their subject knowledge have on the pedagogical approaches they select to use in their classrooms. This is of particular importance in design and technology because of the challenges facing the subject, such as curriculum marginalisation and difficulties in the recruitment and retention of specialist teachers. These challenges are compounded because increasingly more teachers are required to deliver lessons beyond their immediate areas of expertise. An issue further complicated by limited opportunities to access subject-specific continued professional development.

As such, within the context of the longer term for implications for design and technology education, this chapter discusses the potential consequences of teachers' subject knowledge perceptions on their efficacy and explores the practical impact on practice in relation to the breadth and quality of the curriculum delivered. Also, the implications for the subject are discussed regarding the quality of teaching and the potential impact on pupil learning, engagement, progress and attainment. For reference, within the context of this chapter, *attrition* is the term used to refer to teachers who leave or are considering leaving the teaching profession.

## Defining key terminology

For context and to support consistency of understanding, I begin this chapter by defining key terminology and the main concepts referred to:

- PCK
- Self-sabotaging behaviour and identify drift
- Efficacy

### PCK

In his work, Shulman (1986, 1987) established the concept of PCK as being the integration of a teacher's pedagogical knowledge (PK), combined with their subject or content knowledge (CK). According to Shulman, PCK is a special type of knowledge that only teachers have and describes how teachers relate their PK (what they know about teaching) to their subject disciplinary or CK (what they plan to teach). Hence, PCK is the knowledge that emerges from the fusion of a teacher's specialist subject, disciplinary knowledge or CK and the selection of the most appropriate pedagogy (Figure 11.1). What is unique about the process here is the teacher's ability to transform their subject knowledge into material for teaching, making it comprehensible for pupils to understand. This transformation occurs as the teacher critically reflects on their knowledge and finds ways to represent the information to the pupil, often on many levels, tailoring the material to ensure equity of access for all. Hence, drawing predominantly on the work of Shulman (ibid), within the context of this chapter, *PCK* is used to refer to the process whereby the teacher transforms their specialist disciplinary content subject knowledge for effective dissemination.

It is worth noting that PCK is highly specific to the concepts being taught and is much more than just the transference of subject knowledge. For example, within the context of science teaching, Buchmann (1984) discusses the importance of maintaining a flexible understanding of the subject knowledge in order to see a specific set of concepts from a variety of viewpoints depending on pupils' needs and abilities. This is echoed by Gudmundsdottir

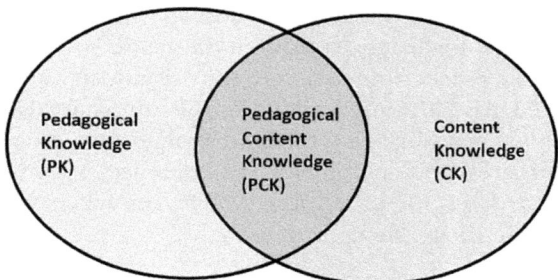

*Figure 11.1* A representation of the intersections between pedagogical knowledge and content knowledge.

and Shulman (1987), who note that this transformation is a process of the continual restructuring of subject matter knowledge for teaching. It was these and similar observations that led me to this question: If a teacher believes their subject knowledge to be in deficit how can they restructure something they do not have? Unable to find any literature to address my thoughts I turned my attention to an exploration of the tensions that lie within the notion of subject knowledge, because if a teacher's subject knowledge is deficient then their ability to adapt that matter for the purpose of teaching will likely be compromised. My research revealed the idea of a pedagogical subject knowledge gap, which is the gap in a teacher's specialist disciplinary subject knowledge, specifically the liminal moment at which subject matter should become PCK. It is this gap and the potential challenges, consequences and repercussions arising from it that are discussed within this chapter.

*Self-sabotaging Behaviour and Identity Drift*

*Self-sabotaging behaviour,* an original outcome from my PhD, is defined as the instance when a teacher sabotages themselves unintentionally through their actions, attitudes, or behaviour. The result being they unintentionally incapacitate their development, their own progress, or both. Research shows that deep-rooted personal philosophies, unrealistic ideologies, or naïve expectations are likely to be a significant contributory factor in self-sabotaging behaviour and this state manifests as feelings of anxiety that are likely to lower self-esteem (Irving-Bell, 2018). In another outcome of my research, identity drift is when an individual's ideological values and the reality of their classroom practice become unaligned and the individual is unable to reconcile their internalised identity with their external one.

Both outcomes, self-sabotage and identity drift have the potential impact over time to lead to teacher attrition (Irving-Bell, 2018).

*Efficacy*

Within this chapter, *efficacy* refers to a teacher's personal perception of their effectiveness in the classroom. On occasions when I refer to self-efficacy, I am describing how a teacher perceives themselves, specifically in relation to their self-confidence, value and worth as a teacher.

## The focus of this chapter

Having defined these key terms and concepts, I now move to explore the chapter's focus: to debate the impact of a teacher's confidence in their subject knowledge on their pedagogical choices. I will do this through the lens of

- curriculum: content, design, development and delivery. The pedagogical approaches and choices made and how the curriculum is taught.

- teacher efficacy: including identity, confidence and well-being.
- pupil outcomes: motivation, engagement, learner experience and attainment.

Before moving on, for clarity where conversation around a teacher's disciplinary subject knowledge occurs, no external judgement or assessment of or about the teacher's actual subject knowledge was or has ever been made. When referring to subject knowledge – be that strong, weak, insufficient or otherwise – this refers to the teacher's own views, be those perceived or real, of their own knowledge. In other words, it is how they see themselves.

### *Curriculum*

Research shows that a teacher's subject knowledge beliefs have the potential to influence not only what is taught, but how content is delivered (Irving-Bell, 2018). Under the sub-heading of curriculum in this section, I explore the impact of subject knowledge perceptions on

- the curriculum: content, design and development and what is taught and
- curriculum delivery: the pedagogical approaches and choices made relating to how the curriculum is taught.

Let us begin with what is taught. In my research when asked, 'What impact do you think weak subject knowledge has on a teacher's ability to teach?' without exception, participants believed that having weak or limited subject knowledge was more likely to impact negatively on the breadth and quality of the curriculum delivered. Within design and technology, this is invariably likely to result in an extremely restricted curriculum, with limited coverage of the full range of material areas, as this quotation from one research participant illustrates:

> If I'm not sure of what I'm doing I am more fearful of letting the children go off and explore take a risk or experiment. I tend to stick to a simple activity and the lesson is teacher-led board and textbook work, whereas when I'm confident we do all kinds of practical things.
> (Student Teacher/Research Participant)

When a teacher believes they lack knowledge or skill in a particular area, they either avoid having to teach those areas or, if forced, have the likely outcome of poor teaching. Where a teacher is required or instructed to deliver material areas that are out of their comfort zone the likely consequence is poor-quality lessons delivered by teachers using ineffective teaching approaches. Within design and technology this is likely to manifest as a distorted curriculum, weighted heavily toward the delivery of only one or two material areas, probably those preferred by the teacher where they feel more confident. The likely outcome here is two-fold: (1) pupils are restricted access to a full design and technology experience; (2) teachers potentially slide into self-sabotaging behaviours. We must also be mindful of the potential longer-term impact of a restricted curriculum on the department itself, in terms of limiting growth, staffing and potentially job security.

So far, I have discussed the potential downside of weak subject knowledge from a deficit viewpoint; before moving on, I explore the potential upside.

A handful of participants interviewed during my study held the belief that a good teacher can teach anything. So, while it would likely take a significant amount of preparation there is the possibility that a self-assured and experienced teacher, who despite not holding strong disciplinary subject knowledge, can deliver a good lesson. While perhaps not advisable for examination classes and the like, under these circumstances there is potential for a confident teacher to work and learn alongside their pupils. This engages the pupils in the co-construction of knowledge and encourages their participation in risky, exciting and extraordinary learning activities. Additionally, teacher may also find the adoption of such approaches are conducive in building effective learning communities, and effective in fostering strong working relationships with those they are teaching. However, while there maybe potential benefits to a confident teacher delivering unfamiliar content, within my study participants' perceptions of weak subject knowledge were overwhelmingly associated with poor teaching, plus limits the curriculum and the range of teaching styles used. This leads to the next section – a discussion of pedagogical approaches, that is to say how curriculum is delivered.

*Curriculum delivery*

As noted, teachers can feel anxious when they have significant concerns about their subject knowledge. These teachers struggle to transform and adapt curriculum content in such a way that makes what they teach easier for their pupils to understand. This is partly because where there is a perceived lack of adequate subject knowledge, the teacher is more likely to concentrate their attention on how to fill time, rather than focusing on effective ways to deliver curriculum knowledge. In my research, participants believed that that poor subject knowledge leads to narrow and shallow teaching, adopting approaches that inhibit the development of conceptual understanding. Teachers who deemed themselves to have poor or inadequate PCK were more inclined to deliver lessons that were procedural, depended on factual and simple recall questions and were reliant on pupils following rules: in other words, the pedagogical approaches were restrictive rather than expansive (see Chapter 13). My research found that teachers were more likely to deliver lessons that were teacher-led using the white board and textbooks. Specific to practical work, particularly within resistant material, participants expressed concerns about pupil behaviour and teachers with weak subject knowledge were hesitant to undertake practical work primarily because of the potential for increased health and safety issues:

> If the teacher hasn't planned the lesson properly because they lack that subject knowledge it is more likely for children to be off task and messing about. Behaviour is an issue but more importantly there is more chance of an accident occurring and someone getting seriously hurt!
> (Student Teacher/Research Participant)

This suggests that weak subject knowledge led to teachers planning less practical activity than those who were confident in their subject knowledge. However, in a small number of instances, practical work was increased, notably within food technology. There is a possible reason for this but because of the small number of responses this reason is offered under caution and in no way appertains to an exact claim. Analysis of my research data suggested that the increase of practical work undertaken in Food Technology was used as a mechanism by teachers to keep pupils occupied. This was because of the 'one-off bake it and take it home' nature of the work provided a safety net: a practical lesson being considered easier to teach than a food-related theory lesson. Keeping the pupils 'busy' helped to maintain behaviour, but in practice, pupils' learning was only at a surface level (see Chapter 13), with little or no real learning, understanding of concepts or consolidation of learning took place. While this surface approach to teaching undoubtably helped the teacher get through the lesson, this approach has the potential to be extremely damaging to the value and reputation of the subject. Also, surface approaches do little for pupil learning:

- Teaching piecemeal: no genuine attempt to bring to the fore the intrinsic structure of the topic or subject.
- Providing pupils with insufficient time to engage in tasks: emphasis on blanket coverage, at the expense of in-depth exploration.
- Assessing knowledge against a recall of facts: for example, utilising only summative assessment mechanisms to test pupils' knowledge, for example short-answer responses to questions or multiple-choice tests.
- Creating undue anxiety or setting low expectations of success.

Adapted from Biggs and Tang (2007:25)

The unintentional teaching of misconceptions was also cited as an area of concern by participants, as were issues around planning and preparation, accurate assessment and the ability to provide meaningful feedback:

> Planning is more time consuming as the teacher is themselves learning. Poor subject knowledge means that teachers are unable to assess with confidence and marking takes longer as there is uncertainty as to the correct answers and often further reading on the part of the teacher is necessary to be confident in their assessments of pupils' work.
> (Student Teacher/Research Participant)

Participants also alluded to the additional work created, it was not lost on them that this would affect those teachers who may already be experiencing feelings of anxiety or vulnerability. Hence, the potential detrimental impact of weak subject knowledge on mental health and well-being was also brought to the fore:

> Weak subject knowledge undermines you, erodes your confidence and can really have a detrimental impact on your own self-esteem.
> (Student Teacher/Research Participant)

Confidence in the classroom is essential and having explored the impact of subject knowledge perceptions on the curriculum, teacher efficacy, identity and well-being will be the focus of the next section.

However, before moving on, first let's conclude this section by examining the positive impact on pedagogy in the design and technology classroom when a teacher considers themselves to have strong subject knowledge.

Where subject knowledge was perceived to be strong, participants reported feeling more able to offer in-depth help and support to pupils. They felt reported feeling considerably less worried and hence much more confident in the classroom when they fully understood the topic they were teaching. From the pupils' perspective, good teaching correlated with strong, confident teachers in command of their subject knowledge:

> [T]eachers with stronger subject knowledge are more motivated and confident. If a pupil is getting it wrong, they can strip the problem down to its basics to explain it several different ways until the pupil understands.
> (Student Teacher/Research Participant)

Teachers with strong subject knowledge are more likely to be adventurous in their teaching, offering more varied and stimulating lessons. With the best lessons being those involving approaches that engaged pupils in activities where theoretical knowledge could be applied in a practical way. Confident teachers are more likely to adopt styles that facilitate pupils to question their learning and engage in experiential risk-taking experiences, leading to the facilitation of deep learning and ultimately a better grasp of the subject.

### *Teacher efficacy: impact on identity, confidence and well-being*

In this section, I focus on how a teachers' perceptions of their subject knowledge impacts on the development of their identity, efficacy and, in the longer-term, their general health and well-being.

When asked about the impact of subject knowledge on one's own development, participants in my study thought that where confidence is high a teacher is more open to the implementation of new practices. Participants believed that a deeper knowledge of their subject allowed for a more flexible and relaxed teaching style, which in turn helps to create a relaxed atmosphere conducive to learning, giving pupils confidence in their teacher's abilities. Consequently, teachers are more likely to be more confident, resilient and emotionally stronger. According to Pyhältö *et al.* (2015), these attributes generate a strong sense of professional agency which in turn reduces stress. Conversely, where a teacher believes they have deficient subject knowledge, their feelings of limited agency, professional inadequacy and vulnerability are more likely to thrive, which will probably lead to increased stress and anxiety. When a teacher is unsure of their own subject knowledge, they are more likely to keep using safe pedagogies. As already mentioned, this is likely to manifest as teacher-led and formulaic lessons, comprising worksheets and pointless practical lessons and the adoption of strict, traditional styles of teaching (Tschannen-Moran *et al.*, 2007) and conservative approaches, with the teacher performing perfunctorily, automaton like classroom duties (Zimmerman, 2011). Without a strong knowledge base, the teacher is less likely to innovative, to push professional boundaries or to take risks, which results in pedagogical decisions based not on the learning needs of pupil but on the teachers need to maintain control and manage classroom behaviour.

*What effect does this have on the teacher?*

Clearly things are less than satisfactory from multiple perspectives when subject knowledge concerns limit curriculum and result in poor quality lessons. However, when this manifests as anxiety and feels of being unable to cope, emergent issues relating to safeguarding, teacher mental health and wellbeing must be addressed.

An additional complication here is the growing number of design and technology teachers who are asked to teach disciplines outside of their specialist knowledge. This is a common occurrence within the secondary-age phase schools in England and given the deepening of teacher shortages (Lynch *et al.*, 2016; McIvor, 2017) is a practice likely to increase. Even the most experienced, confident teacher may find a request to deliver teaching beyond their immediate of expertise challenging. Hence, without careful consideration, preparation or planning time, enacting such requests has the potential to undermine confidence and lead to poor pedagogical choices even in the most experienced of teachers. My research established that over a relatively short period, when required to undertake these types of requests without proper support, there is a risk of feelings generated leading to a drift in the teacher's professional identity where the ultimate consequence is likely to be attrition (Irving-Bell, 2018), that is to say teachers leaving the profession. At this juncture, it is worth noting that other external forces, such as the working environment, school policy and class size also have the potential to impact adversely an individual teacher's agency and can either enhance motivation or exacerbate internal struggles and feelings of discomfort. Although these are not discussed here, it is worth being cognisant of these significant factors.

## Impact on pupil outcomes

In this section, I explore the implications of a teacher's subject knowledge perceptions on pupils' motivation, engagement, experience and outcomes.

Where teachers are confident, they have the capacity to design and deliver learning activities that lead to the co-creation of knowledge. Here pupils are more likely to adopt deeper approaches to learning. Teaching is perceived by pupils as being of a higher quality, which in turn leads to better learning outcomes (Prosser & Trigwell, 1999). Aligning with outcomes from my research, findings from other studies such as Marton and Säljö (1997) show that when a teacher is confident pupil engagement and enjoyment is increased. In design and technology, this means that pupils are more likely to experience active learning and undertake work in a wider range of material areas.

But what is the impact of weak subject knowledge on pupils? In their study Rockland et al. (2010) found that where a teacher's subject knowledge and understanding are deficient, the potential for learning is limited, resulting potentially in poor teaching were. According to Barber and Mourshed (2007), the impact of this on pupil progress may be severe. This is because where the teacher adopts a surface approach to teaching, the likelihood is that pupils assume a surface approach to learning, where learning focuses on memorising facts or recalling knowledge (Virtanen & Lindblom-Ylänne, 2010; Marton and Säljö, 1997). The characteristics of surface-level learning include

- the adoption of rote approaches to learning;
- concentration on the memorisation of facts, giving the impression that understanding has occurred;
- assimilation of information, recalling chunks of knowledge; and
- remembering, or finding the right answers.
           (Adapted from Savin-Baden [2000] and Gibbs [1992])

My research also revealed that surface approaches to teaching are frequently perceived by pupils as bad teaching, undertaken by 'poor' or 'lazy' teachers. At times it was quite difficult to listen to my participants recollections of the damage poor teaching had on both their motivation and confidence when they were pupils. In one account a participant described being 'assaulted by knowledge' while describing an occasion where subject knowledge has been delivered to the class with little or no consideration to adapt or modify the content to account for pupils' individual needs. This example can be interpreted as an example of the teacher not being able, or willing to, use their PCK in such a way that pupils' can appropriately access the content. Hence, knowledge was delivered in an unyielding and relentless way. Where content-centred, teacher-focused teaching approaches are employed, teaching is presented as the transmission of information and pupil motivation is reduced. Unsurprisingly, pupil engagement is lower, and the quality of teaching is perceived to be poor (Prosser & Trigwell, 1999; Trigwell & Prosser, 2004).

A further consequence of weak subject knowledge that surfaced was around behaviour management – the belief that poor-quality teaching was more likely to result in the teacher's inability to effectively manage pupils' conduct. Recalling their experiences as pupils, participants reported experiencing feeling anxious and trapped in a classroom when the teacher had no control. As teachers in training, participants explained how these anxieties are particularly amplified within design and technology because of access to potentially dangerous tools and equipment.

## Conclusion

At the liminal moment when subject matter should become PCK, if a teacher perceives their knowledge to be deficient then their ability to adapt that matter for the purpose of teaching is compromised. This creates a gap that has the potential to negatively impact the development and delivery of curriculum, limiting personal growth and development that ultimately may restrict the formation of the teacher's professional identity. Conversely, when the teacher's subject knowledge is perceived to be or is strong confidence, autonomy and self-efficacy is increased. Under these conditions, teachers are more likely to be open to innovation (Bandura, 1997). It is no surprise to learn that when a teacher does not have subject CK to draw on, they have difficulty in making knowledge accessible to pupils; plus, they struggle to explain why they are teaching it, either to themselves or their pupils. This is significant within design and technology teachers are expected to have a strong working and practical knowledge of a diverse range of material areas.

Within the context of design and technology, the impact of subject knowledge on all aspects of the curriculum is significant. When a teacher believes they have strong subject knowledge they will be more comfortable teaching a broader range of curriculum material areas. Also, because they are confident teachers, they are more likely to say when they do not know something and become willing to co-construct knowledge with their pupils. Plus, their passion for teaching and the subject shines through, and approaches that facilitate deep learning are more likely to be used. In these instances, practical lessons have a clear purpose and are well balanced with theory; pupils are engaged and managing pupil behaviour is less of a concern; these teachers are motivated and are less likely to suffer anxiety or leave teaching within a few short years of qualifying. Conversely, teachers who believe they have poor or inadequate subject knowledge are more likely to teach a restricted curriculum; their classroom practice often depends on textbooks and worksheet-based activities, giving less time for practical activities or too much 'low-value' practical work. When this happens, pupils are often unable to articulate what they have learnt about the purpose of the activity. Poor or inadequate subject knowledge also has the potential to impact pupil behaviour and help maintain control of their classroom pedagogy is more likely to be teacher-led, with rote learning pedagogies being employed. As a result, content is restricted to the teacher's own knowledge and surface approaches to learning are adopted, presenting limited opportunities for pupils to experience an activity that would lead to deep learning. For pupils, teaching is likely to be thought of as being of low quality, and over time, pupils are more likely to disengage. In this situation, teachers may feel vulnerable and their well-being may be affected, leading to their confidence being further eroded, potentially leading to them leaving the profession. Hence, it is desirable, if not essential, for teachers to be confident and hold a strong sense of self. In helping teachers be pedagogically competent and confident, they develop resilience and, as such, become better prepared to cope with the constant challenges and changes a career in teaching inevitably brings. Within England and Wales, the study of design and technology is not mandatory beyond Key Stage 3; therefore, if the subject is to survive and thrive by encouraging more pupils to study the subject in upper secondary school the pupil experience needs to be exceptional. But the solution is not simply to make the subject more fun or easy in an attempt to seduce pupils because these approaches would devalue the subject.

As this debate draws to a close, reflecting on the topics explored, I offer some final thoughts that I hope those reading this chapter will find useful in developing their practice and supporting the emergent practice of others. What I am advocating for is everything that a confident teacher already does, which is to use a breadth of approaches, including those that encourage pupils to take ownership of their work and instil a passion for the subject. Incorporating pupil-focused approaches that encourage stretch and challenge, within a scaffold of support, to enable personal development and growth in confidence. Design and technology teachers are always seeking solutions, endeavouring to find new ways to solve problems, but there is no single or simple solution to address weak CK. Personal views of subject knowledge and its impact on pedagogy raise a series of complex, interlinked issues. Here perhaps the first step in addressing these issues is to be mindful of them. Through debate and discourse, keeping the issues firmly on the table, working to create an environment where teachers feel comfortable airing the limitations of their subject knowledge, reaching out to colleagues for support and guidance, the simple act of awareness raising could be a catalyst for change.

By working openly to discuss the challenges in this way, we can help support the guardians of our subject, those teachers who are working at the chalk face and are charged with making, taking and facing the difficult daily decisions around curriculum design, delivery and implementation. Decisions that help safeguard teacher well-being and, in doing so, help ensure that design and technology remains a vibrant and engaging subject for all.

## Questions

1 What strategies do you use to ensure you continue to develop your subject knowledge?
2 Within your context, what is the impact of insufficient or weak subject knowledge?
3 Within your setting, how do you support your colleagues to develop their subject knowledge?

## References

Bandura, A. (1997). *Self-efficacy: The exercise of control.* New York: W. H. Freeman.
Barber, M., & Mourshed, M. (2007). How the world's best performing systems come out on top.
Biggs, J., & Tang, C. (2007). *Teaching for quality learning at university Maidenhead.* Berkshire, UK: McGraw-Hill Education.
Buchmann, M. (1984). The priority of knowledge and understanding in teaching. In J. Raths & L. Katz (Eds.), *Advances in teacher education* (Vol. 1, pp. 29–48). Norwood, NJ: Ablex.
Gibbs, G. (1992). *Improving the quality of student learning: Based on the Improving Student Learning Project funded by the Council for National Academic Awards.* Technical and Education Services.
Gudmundsdottir, S., & Shulman, L. (1987). Pedagogical content knowledge in social studies. *Scandinavian Journal of Educational Research, 31*(2), 59–70.
Irving-Bell, D. (2018). *The formation of science, technology, engineering and mathematics teacher identities: Pre-service teacher's perceptions.* Lancaster, UK: Lancaster University.
Lynch, S., Worth, J., Bamford, S., & Wespieser, K. (2016). Engaging Teachers: NFER Analysis of Teacher Retention, September 2016. *National Foundation for Educational Research (NFER).* https://www.nfer.ac.uk/publications/LFSB01/
Marton, F. & Säljö, R. (1997). Approaches to learning. In F. Marton, D. Hounsell, & N. Entwistle (Eds.), *The experience of learning* (pp. 39–58). Edinburgh: Scottish Academic Press.
McIvor, J. (2017). Warning over STEM teacher recruitment. *BBC News.* 30th August 2017. http://www.bbc.co.uk/news/uk-scotland-41083438
Prosser, M., & Trigwell, K. (1999). *Understanding learning and teaching. The experience in higher education.* Buckingham: Open University Press.
Pyhältö, K., Pietarinen, K., & Soini, T. (2015). Teachers' professional agency and learning – From adaption to active modification in the teacher community. *Teachers and Teaching: Theory and Practice, 21*(7), 811–830. doi:10.1080/13540602.2014.995483
Rockland, R., Bloom, D.S., Carpinelli, J., Burr-Alexander, L., Hirsch, L.S., & Kimmel, H. (2010). Advancing the "E" in K-12 STEM education. *Journal of Technology Studies, 36*(1), 53.
Savin-Baden, M. (2000). *Problem-based learning in higher education: Untold stories: Untold stories.* London, UK: McGraw-Hill Education.
Shulman, L. S. (1986). Those who understand: Knowledge growth in teaching. *Educational Researcher, 15,* 4–14.

Shulman, L. S. (1987). Knowledge and teaching: Foundations of the new reform. *Harvard Educational Review, 57*, 1–22.
Trigwell, K., & Prosser, M. (2004). Development and use of the approaches to teaching inventory. *Educational Psychology Review, 16*(4), 409–424.
Tschannen-Moran, M., Hoy, A.W., & Hoy, W.K. (2007). The differential antecedents of self-efficacy beliefs of novice and experienced teachers. *Teaching and Teacher Education, 23*(2007), 944–956.
Virtanen, V., & Lindblom-Ylänne, S. (2010). University students' and teachers' conceptions of teaching and learning in the biosciences. *Instructional Science, 38*(4), 355–370.
Zimmerman, B. J. (2011). Motivational sources and outcomes of self-regulated learning and performance: Graduate center of city University of New York. In Barry J. Zimmerman, & Dale H. Schunk (Eds.), *Handbook of self-regulation of learning and performance* (pp. 63–78). Routledge.

# 12 Transition between primary and secondary school

*Cathy Growney*

## Introduction

Pupils make transitions from one year to the next throughout their education. The transition between primary and secondary school is significantly more complex than the transitions that take place annually within schools (Bagnall, 2020; Mahmud, 2020). First, this chapter provides an overview of primary to secondary transition complexities and implications in general and, second, the transition in the context of design and technology. It discusses strategies used to smooth transition and difficulties that arise. Teachers' thoughts on these strategies were obtained through interviews.

## The context

It is important to set the context of 'transition'. In England, children start primary education in Reception (R), the September following their fourth birthday. The school years are broadly divided in line with child development set out in Table 12.1. In most of the country, primary and secondary form the two main stages of school; the move from primary into secondary school is known as Key Stage (KS) 2–3 transition.

KS2–3 transition has been in the spotlight for many years as a long-standing problem in the education system (see Jindal-Snape et al., 2020, systematic review and Galton & McLellan, . tracking of issues from the 1970s onwards). A concern identified by many, including Evans, Borriello and Field (2018), is a regression in the performance of pupils at the early stages of secondary school. The Government Office for Standards in Education, Children's Services and Skills (OFSTED) has continued to find problems with transition, for example inadequate building on from KS2, evidence suggesting that many Year 7 pupils were revisiting KS2 work and secondary baseline assessments lacking enough accuracy to make them useful, all of which it reports to 'have a detrimental effect on the rate at which [pupils] make progress during the first years of their secondary education' (OFSTED, 2015:28). This report referred to all areas of the curriculum. Schools use a range of strategies to smooth transition; mostly they concern social and pastoral issues rather than academic and curricular aspects. In this chapter,

DOI: 10.4324/9781003166689-16

Table 12.1 English school stratification

|  |  | Age | Year group | Key stage (KS) |
|---|---|---|---|---|
| School | Primary | 4/5 | Reception | Foundation |
|  |  | 5/6 | 1 | KS1 |
|  |  | 6/7 | 2 |  |
|  |  | 7/8 | 3 | KS2 |
|  |  | 8/9 | 4 |  |
|  |  | 9/10 | 5 |  |
|  |  | 10/11 | 6 |  |
|  | Secondary | 11/12 | 7 | KS3 |
|  |  | 12/13 | 8 |  |
|  |  | 13/14 | 9 |  |
|  |  | 14/15 | 10 | KS4 |
|  |  | 15/16 | 11 |  |

I focus on these latter aspects as these relate to design and technology rather than on pupils' well-being.

Design and technology research has contributed to debates about the primary–secondary divide. Kimbell and Stables's (2008) found experiential differences between Year 6 and Year 7, such as the environments in which teaching and learning took place, the 'negotiated' learning tasks in Year 6 and the 'controlled' tasks in Year 7, and Year 6 designing being carried out through modelling whereas Year 7 being carried out in advance of making and routinely on paper (2008:147). They said that 'far from progressively stretching the autonomous decision-making of learners, our practices actually demanded far greater dependency in Year 7 than in Year 6' (2008:225), indicating regression. Whilst Dakers and Dow (2004) do not comment on pupil regression at the secondary level, they do note that on the whole secondary teachers were content to have a 'fresh start' approach (2004:121) without regard for or value of pupils' prior experiences or attainment, with little evidence of continuity of learning. Benson explains, 'few secondary teachers . . . had a good understanding of . . . primary design and technology' (2009:61). Ascertaining whether there is underachievement in Year 7 is problematic since records for Year 6 pupils in design and technology are not always passed on to secondary schools making regression difficult to substantiate. With the advantages of purpose-built learning spaces equipped with sophisticated resources and subject specialist staff (teachers, assistants, technicians) found in secondary schools, one might expect to see pupils' progress escalate rather than dip. Although these authors were writing a while ago, little has been done since to address the issue of pupils' progress in design and technology. Therefore this chapter debates how Year 6 and Year 7 teachers can collaborate in order to ameliorate primary–secondary design and technology. What transition strategies are available? Can they be realistically instigated? Should strategies favour the pastoral concerns of pupils or academic concerns?

## Primary and secondary characteristics

As stated, few researchers have compared the similarities and differences in design and technology across the primary–secondary age phases, most comparisons are more than 10 years old, although significant reforms have taken place since then. Gone are the days when the normal experience of Year 7 design and technology was taught through a carousel system of between three and six projects rigidly timetabled over the course of a year, each project led by a different teacher in a different workspace. The learning was largely directed by teachers focusing on pupils' explicit understanding of concepts unlike the more flexible, pupil-led projects experienced at primary school in which pupils had the same teacher, all year, for all subjects; at the heart of the primary design and technology focus was the user and teachers capitalised on pupils' tacit knowledge (Kimbell, Stables &Green, 1996).

The latest National Curriculum reform has led to a more familiar pedagogy across the Year6/7 transition, but there are still considerable differences. In Table 12.2, I have summarised the differences already identified using early research (Benson, 2009; Growney, 2013; Stables, 1994) and then added the more up-to-date picture. I have separated the differences under the headings of culture, curriculum and environment, which I explain further in the following sections.

### *Primary culture*

Primary schools provide a reassuring culture that encourages pupils' socio-emotional well-being alongside their cognitive development. Typically, pupils enjoy the security of a single teacher almost all day throughout an academic year. Primary pedagogy is built on pupils feeling cared for by a teacher who knows them as individuals (Alexander, 2010; Mellor & Delamont, 2011; van Rens et al., 2018). Primary teaching and learning styles are predominantly collaborative using whole- or small-group class discussions, alongside small-group activities and investigations (Black, 2019; Stables, 1994). Learning is largely a flexible and holistic interactivity between teachers and pupils.

### *Primary curriculum*

Primary teachers are required to be proficient across all subjects in the primary curriculum. This is quite a challenge; since the curriculum emphasis in teacher training is in numeracy and literacy (DfE, 2011), other curriculum areas have less time allocated, so few primary teachers feel sufficiently expert in subjects such as design and technology. In their enquiry of Scottish primary teachers' confidence in teaching technology education, Dakers and Dow found that 'the vast majority of primary teachers had had no experience of technology whatsoever, either in their initial teacher education or

Table 12.2 Design and technology characteristics

| | Year 6 | Year 7 |
|---|---|---|
| Culture | Teacher by non-specialists<br>Teachers rarely have D&T CPD<br><br>Teaching Assistants and other adult helpers have little if any specialist D&T training<br>Flexibility in timetabling – concentrated in intensive periods e.g., consecutive days of afternoons | Taught by specialists<br>Teachers update their specialisms annually<br>Teaching Assistants, technicians and other adult helpers have access to D&T training time tables – allocated sessions at dedicated times each week |
| Curriculum | Projects are more likely to be corss-curricular<br><br><br><br><br><br>Projects are pupil-centred (pupil needs are at the core).<br><br>Projects experiential and open-ended; often negotiated through collaborative activity with pupils and the teacher; pupil autonomy; pupil led (pupils determine the direction)<br>Pupils are facilitated and supported in their decision-making process for selecting appropriate activities; the teacher's role is progress chaser<br>Designing and making activities are integrated, most designing is modelling rather than drawing<br>Pupils typically work in pairs or small groups to encourage scaffolding of learning through talk | Only tenuous cross-curricular links are made; there is little collaboration with subject specialist from other curriculum areas<br>Projects are curriculum-centred (the curriculum is at the core)<br>Projects are curriculum-centred (the curriculum is at the core)<br>Projects are directed by the teacher, lessons are task-specific with clearly defined learning objectives and assessment of progress; prescriptive<br><br>Pupils are instructed to do predetermined activities, including homework, monitoring pupils is important; the teacher's role is facilitator<br>Strong focus on modelling to develop pupils' ideas. The iterative process is recorded through sketches, models and photographs<br>Pupils typically work on their own individual projects with reflective small group activities; whole-class discussion/listening is common |
| Environment | Multi-purpose classrooms with basic specialist equipment; celebratory, highly personalised | specialist rooms with high-tech facilities; little personalisation; more hazardous |

subsequent CPD [continuing professional development]' (2004:121); other researchers had similar findings in England (Benson, 2012). English and mathematics dominate the morning timetables, so all other curriculum areas are fitted into afternoons. Many primary schools opt to take a cross-curricular approach to fulfil the statutory curriculum, consequently design and technology is often integrated into a topic or theme. The thematic approaches provide real and relevant contexts that the latest programmes of study for design and technology require (DfE, 2013). Although in cross-curricular work Barlex, Given and Steeg caution 'in any themed work we would argue that the contribution of each collaborating subject should be made explicit' (2017:15) to ensure that one subject does not overshadow others and the distinct integrity of each area is not compromised.

## Primary learning environments

Generally, almost all lessons (with the exception of physical education and music) are taught in generalist classrooms allocated to each primary class. The pupils enjoy a secure, stable and nurturing environment over the whole year. Primary classrooms are all-purpose spaces in which pupils have familiarity and ownership of classroom spaces and with that, roles and responsibilities. Notice boards reflect recent and ongoing work; they are informative and celebratory. Design and technology resources and equipment are usually stored centrally in the school and moved to classrooms as required; due to curricular demands, this may only be for a few time periods each year.

## Secondary culture

Contrastingly, secondary teachers tend to specialise in a single subject. Many have pastoral responsibilities as a form tutor: pupils spend a small part of the day with a form tutor, and the rest of it is spent with different teachers in different specialist areas. Design and technology teachers teach many classes across the age range (Years 7–13); the subject has its own singular identity; it has its own timetabled lessons alongside other curriculum areas. Typically, a Year 7 pupil will have at least one hour of design and technology lessons each week. As a result, it takes time for teachers and their pupils to get to know each other well.

## Secondary curriculum

The secondary approach simultaneously aims to engage pupils' creativity and fulfil the National Curriculum requirements for which they are scrutinised by school senior leaders and OFSTED. Teachers ensure pupils have a broad experience with incremental progressive steps working towards the first public examinations at Year 11. To that end, schemes of work inevitably have some prescription. Teachers monitor pupils to ensure there is progress; again, there are explicit aims. Some activity is carried out in groups, but the monitoring of pupils individually means that pupils tend to work on their own. Tasks include solving problems in genuine contexts considering values and society. Designing, modelling and making take place within the breadth of the subject. Teachers aim to increase pupils' independence in project direction within the devised frameworks.

## *Secondary learning environments*

Primary and secondary learning environments differ remarkably. Secondary departments usually have different types of classrooms, mostly unlike those in primary schools; rooms have workbenches and stools rather than chairs and tables; they often have sophisticated specialist equipment and resources; alongside the resources are the need for hazard warnings and safety notices. The rooms are used by many classes so the space is less personalised. Typically, Year 7 pupils visit design and technology classrooms no more than twice a week. Given the infrequency of using the facilities, it takes time for new pupils to find the spaces comfortable and familiar.

## *Summarising the characteristics*

The differences between primary and secondary circumstances are glaring, primary teachers oversee the full breadth of the curriculum, and they have strong personal relationships with each pupil in their class. Whereas secondary teachers (and their support teams) are trained in one curriculum area, primary teachers have less time with each class they teach, so they take longer to develop the strong relationships that exist in the primary sector. Timetabling design and technology is fixed in secondary schools but flexible in primary. The status of design and technology in the secondary sector is indicated by its firm position on the timetable and suite of specialist rooms. Year 7 pupils have design and technology homework for the first time, and their progress is regularly monitored. This is quite unlike the primary case where monitoring is less regulated and the subject itself is not necessarily identified in thematic cross-curricular approaches. Concern for the approach was questioned by Aston and Jackson (2009:68), who asked if it 'will provide teachers with opportunities to raise the profile of D&T or only serve to lessen the value, status and importance of the subject, resulting in its disappearance into a 'muddy' curriculum'. That said, the holistic interactivity between teachers and pupils through authentic meaningful themes lends itself to pupil-centred, flexible learning and the iterative qualities of design and technology. The palpable differences between the phases can be ameliorated when teachers from both phases learn from each other. The more primary and secondary teachers know about each other's phases, 'the greater the degree of coherence, continuity and progression that can be achieved' (Dakers & Dow, 2004:118).

## Primary–secondary partnerships

The National Strategies (DfE, 2011) provided an effective drive for improving developmental progress across the Year 6/7 divide. The strategies included

1. fostering strong primary-secondary partnerships through joint Professional Development,
2. developing effective liaison, and
3. shared planning and assessment (Growney, 2013).

In the following section, I explain these three strategies and evaluate them drawing on first-hand experience of a sample of teachers. I interviewed five secondary subject specialists and six primary teachers between August 2020 and September 2021. I asked them open-ended questions about their experiences of primary–secondary transition strategies in design and technology. Whilst being a small-scale survey, the teacher voices provide interesting insights into transition practice.

### *Continuing Professional Development*

*Strategy*

The rationale for joint continuing professional development (CPD), whereby primary and secondary teachers attend the same training, is that it presents opportunities to convey the details of design and technology activity in both phases. Training topics could be on any aspect of design and technology, for example long-term planning, the iterative design process, designing or facilitating small-group discussions. The training exposes each phase to the other, revealing equivalent issues in different contexts; what work takes place and how it is facilitated. Primary and secondary teachers can initiate dialogue and share experiences. Teachers can develop a common vocabulary; they can carry out audits of their own strengths and gaps in experience. This can lead to further CPD, led and negotiated by the teachers themselves. Initiatives may evolve such as learning new teaching methods from lesson observations. Critically, over time teachers become more appreciative of primary–secondary differences to the benefit of transition pupils.

*Teachers' comments*

Establishing opportunities for teachers to visit each other's schools and observe design and technology seldom occurs, so few teachers have insight into the other's classrooms and practice. The most successful exchanges were initiated through CPD. Some teachers interviewed described the benefit of a biennial in-service training day based at the secondary school for all secondary and primary staff from partner schools. The connections made led to further contact between primary and secondary teachers.

The secondary teachers described observing primary design and technology taking place within a cross-curricular theme. This resulted in teachers from two of the secondary schools planning cross-curricular transition work, thus maintaining primary learning methods and continuity of practice. Inspired by the cross-curricular work in KS2, one secondary school teacher campaigned to the senior leadership team to be involved in a transition event that took place exclusively with the core[1] curriculum areas. Now the event continues with design and technology alongside the three core subjects. Another secondary teacher noted 'huge differences in primary cultures for learning'; she listed 'certificates and praise, open-ended questioning styles, territories of the classrooms, visual displays and wall spaces full of colour and wonder'. She attempted to replicate some of these in her own classrooms and intended to set up more staff visits between schools. For the benefit of the Year 7 pupils, she was also keen to enable primary staff to see former pupils in their Year 7 environments.

Much was made of the 'iterative design process' in the latest National Curriculum orders (DfE, 2013). The process of ideation followed by testing and reflecting on ideas, which trigger new ideas has long been in the concept of design and technology but having it spelt out in the orders forced a rethink on design and technology activity. A primary teacher said:

> The iterative process works very well for us; we aim to have breadth and balance that's also pupil led and real; we'd been working like this already. All our work is questions based, we ask the pupils open ended questions and see where it leads. We revisit the questions and ask the pupils how it's going? What needs doing next? How can it be done? We do something and then reflect. After the floods last year, we developed a project on floodwater technology, there was real creativity. We raise issues, like climate change. We linked the water consumption work with a school in Gambia in which the pupils learnt about the influences of technology.

If secondary teachers were able to observe such strong examples of primary work, reference could be made in Year 7 benefitting the continuity of learning. The experience of a secondary head of department revealed that these opportunities are likely to be missed, he said, 'Most planning for the secondary curriculum is done working backwards from KS4 public exams rather than building on from KS2'.

All the teachers interviewed spoke of reduced links in recent years with primary or secondary partners. The secondary teachers talked of the changed status of design and technology having an influence. One expanded, 'design and technology was left out of the English Baccalaureate, it became optional at KS4, few of the school's high-achieving pupils opted for design and technology. We now have fewer staff and a smaller budget'. This implies that there is less time to build relationships with other local schools.

The primary teachers indicated that they get little time to give design and technology its due attention and have little, if any, CPD. They indicated that previously there was considerable support from the local secondary school. One primary teacher conceded that it wasn't just the secondary school withdrawing that changed:

> It was great while it lasted but it couldn't be sustained. We would have made more progress if our staffing was more stable but the roles of the teachers kept changing. Either they moved to different schools or their role in our school changed, new teachers arrived, more CPD took place and then it all changed again. We were in a repetitive cycle and never took the work to the next level.

Another primary teacher said, 'there is no local authority support, no CPD with secondary schools and no design and technology conferences'.

The teachers from both primary and secondary phases indicated that finance has been a barrier to progress. A primary teacher stated,

> In the last ten years the school budgets have stayed the same but we've had more things to spend money on, like Educational Psychologists – 79% of the budget goes on staffing. That leaves little for anything else. Design and technology and music have been falling off the edge.

## Summary

Whilst all teachers acknowledged that linked CPD was beneficial and had been reasonably successful at some point. They all believed that they weren't doing as much as they could to the detriment of Year 6/7 pupils. In two cases, linked CPD had led to mutual observations and closer understanding; in turn, there had been positive changes in practice, for example secondary cross-curricular work and altered classrooms. Stretched budgets and lack of time inhibited moves to increase the amount of joint CPD.

### *Effective and meaningful liaison*

#### *Strategy*

Joint CPD is intended to train teachers using unfamiliar pedagogical styles and at the same time enable teachers to develop relationships. When the relationship works well it leads to further bespoke CPD. However, it is only possible if the liaison between the staff is effective and mutually beneficial. It enables staff to meaningfully share expertise, negotiate and collaborate, with the objective being a cohesive continuity for pupils through transition. Van Rens et al. (2018) go further, emphasising the importance of relationships between the primary and secondary schools as well as the pupils' parents, the three stakeholder groups supporting pupils' transition.

An effective strategy of the partnerships is developing bridging units of work. Bridging units (Jindal-Snape et al., 2020) are projects that link learning in primary schools to that in secondary. They are planned to be started with a portfolio of work in primary school that is taken to and continued in secondary school. They should have an intrinsic value in themselves and should have the clear objective of learning continuity. Collaboration should be mutually beneficial to primary and secondary staff. Teachers develop their design and technology expertise and become more informed about pupils' experiences and primary/secondary pedagogies. Teaching styles are harmonised through bridging units so that pupils' transition experience is less fraught and more familiar.

In the most ambitious scenario, collaboration takes place in three steps:

(1) conceiving the bridging unit
(2) developing and collating resources
(3) teaching and learning with Year 6

Year 6 is taught through a combination of teachers from both phases. Staff negotiate who leads the teaching and the role of the other teacher; they sometimes choose to team-teach. When the pupils enter Year 7, it is intended that the unit of work continues. The population of Year 7 pupils in a secondary school will have come from a range of different primary schools. Inevitably unit experiences vary, but there is scope for pupil-led dialogue, starting with what the units have in common. The pupils already have something to offer; they learn a lot about each other very quickly and become more at ease; teachers garner much about the pupils too.

*Teachers' comments*

When interviewing teachers, I found Year 6 teachers unable to devote much time to liaising with secondary partners as they prioritise preparation for end-of-Key-Stage SATs.[2] Once the tests are complete there is scope for collaborative work but time is pressured. All the secondary teachers identified the same problem of collaborative planning with Year 6 staff for transition bridging units. Some managed it regardless and others opted to work with Year 5 teachers and pupils instead, missing the crux of transition difficulties.

Secondary teachers made up for the loss of direct contact with classes by attending primary graduations, assemblies and exhibitions in which pupils' work was celebrated. In some cases, they exhibited primary work at the secondary school indicating to pupils that the work was valued. One secondary teacher talked about how she cultivated a partnership with her four primary partner schools. She began by clarifying a common language to improve consistency. Then, the schools created a cross-curricular bridging project to start with Years 5/6 and then continue with Year 7. Two difficulties occurred: first, the Year 6 teachers had little time to devote to the collaboration until the SATs were complete; they expected the secondary staff to lead the project. To overcome this issue, there was more participation from Year 5 teachers. The second issue arose between the four different primary schools, collaboration was problematic, so the bridging unit had to be adaptable to suit each of the four schools. The secondary teacher had to work hard to find commonalities when embarking with the Year 7 pupils. This teacher's problem would be exacerbated if there were more than four partner schools.

One primary teacher talked of the demise of the formal links with the secondary school. There had been a dedicated secondary specialist who worked almost every week developing schemes of work and collaborating with staff all the way through Years 1 through 6. The teacher recalled:

> The work was thorough, and we worked really effectively as a team for a few years. Her mantra was that you can only build on what was already laid down so she threaded progression from the youngest pupils to Year 6 ready for transition. The finance reduced and gradually it ground to a halt.

She continued about the demise:

> The staff change, the support change, there is a discomfort. They do a 'challenge' or 'taster day'; unbelievably the taster day includes a test for auditing purposes! They feel like a PR thing more than anything really, they invite two of our year 5 pupils, they have a good time, we don't really know what they do.
>
> On the subject specialisms, the secondary teachers know so much more than us. We're not embarrassed as such but we do sometimes feel inferior or patronised. It doesn't help that we're called 'feeder' schools, it's like we provide the fodder for secondary school.

Another primary teacher talked about the impossibilities of bridging units:

> It was easier in the old days when we had local authority advisors. Our Year 6s end up in three different secondaries. We can't liaise with all of them in all subjects! In the old days the advisor could get all the Year 6/7 coordinators from **all** the primary and secondary schools in a room for a day's training and plan an all-round bridging unit.

## Summary

Teachers indicated that ideal transition relied upon strong primary–secondary partnerships and they recalled successes in partnerships, well-intentioned plans became unworkable. A lack of time and finances became an obstacle to effective collaboration which virtually ceased. Teachers became less confident in their aspirations of partnerships.

There seemed to be a drift backwards to the situation I described in 2012: 'partnerships are not mutually negotiated but are led by the secondary school . . . in order to address the perceived weaknesses in primary teachers' subject proficiency' (Growney, 2013:54). This tendency was also revealed in the research of van Rens, Haelermans, Groot and van den Brink (2018) when they reported that there was little evidence in recent times of meaningful liaison and that secondary teachers often disregarded pupils' previous experience.

Liaison is difficult because there are seldom opportunities. It is even more problematic in densely populated communities where there are many primary schools and several secondary schools. Such scenarios mean it is extremely complicated to establish bridging units that work for all. Since cross-curricular work is common in the primary phase, it would make sense to develop cross-curricular bridging projects, such as those created by Winn (2020) when she collaborated with secondary teachers from different subject areas in her secondary school and primary teachers in partner schools; she explains her success was achieved through good communication.

## Planning and assessment

### Strategy

The final aspect of successful primary–secondary partnerships advocated by Dakers and Dow (2004), is planning with integral assessment procedures:

> There is a clear need for primary and secondary teachers to work closely together in the area of assessment to ensure that there is trust from both sides regarding the reliability of assessment procedures and the use to which assessment is put in determining continuity and progression in learning for individual pupils
>
> (2004:122)

Assessment in design and technology has been widely debated. National Curriculum (DfE, 2013) reforms require that schools develop their own in-house formative assessment processes for tracking progress. The problem with each school having a unique system is that records transferred between schools may be difficult to interpret. Primary–secondary partnerships can resolve this by establishing joint progression pathways with assessment criteria and glossaries of terms. This is time-consuming but the Design and Technology Association has published a helpful Progression Framework (DATA, 2014), ideal for partner schools to use when developing a common assessment system.

### Teachers' comments

The primary teachers interviewed recorded pupils' attainment in relation to their cross-curricular topics but not specifically on design and technology. One teacher said,

> With Art and D&T [design and technology] we don't keep records in our mark books; we always make a display of the pupils' work, when the display is complete we alert the subject lead who photographs the

display, the photo goes in [the] subject leader's file for evidence, for inspections; sometimes they ask for six samples of work, two from high achievers, two from middle and two from lower achievers; they keep photos of these too.

Secondary teachers did not expect to see any primary assessments and yet needed to know pupils' capabilities. On assessment, a secondary teacher stated,

> League tables motivate the school; progress is driven by measurable levels [of progress], the Year 7 pupils must have an attainment level [grade] to work from. The school obtain pupils' levels using a 'baseline assessment' at the beginning of Year 7; the KS2 programme of study is used to derive the baseline assessment activity

## Summary

In my sample, there is no evidence of primary assessments in design and technology being passed on to secondary schools, so there is no evidence of Year 7 regression. However, monitoring pupil progress in the secondary schools is essential so pupils are assessed soon after starting Year 7 and their progress trajectory is monitored thereafter. Experiencing baseline assessments in the initial stages of secondary school has been criticised as an unnecessarily disappointing and uninspiring start.

The lack of monitoring evidenced in Year 6 throws up two related concerns. The first is trust between primary and secondary teachers. Dakers and Dow indicated that secondary teachers lacked trust in data they received from primary schools and that primary teachers perceived that their work was not valued by secondary teachers. This concurred with some comments made by teachers in my sample. The second is that monitoring pupil progress is an indicator of the importance of the subject. Both factors indicate a mutual mistrust of teachers in the two phases. Unless the schools in the primary–secondary partnership reach consensus on assessment systems, tracking pupils across the primary–secondary divide is not feasible. If bridging units that included negotiated assessment criteria are widespread, testing at the outset of Year 7 is not necessary; instead, pupils can hit the ground running with positivity.

## Conclusion

From the position of the National Curriculum, the chances of improving transition in design and technology look promising. The pattern of carousel systems in Year 7 is not prevalent so pupils and teachers are more able to develop close relationships and progression is more coherent. Learning environments are not changing so frequently. Consequently, experience isn't as different as it might have been for pupils starting secondary design and technology. Additionally, the explicit emphasis on the iterative process has meant there is more small-group discussion and collaborative activity in design and technology; this again means that secondary learning styles have a closer resemblance to primary learning. However, in-house assessment methods mean that assessment pathways have deviated rather than converged across the primary–secondary divide. More issues persist, such as (1) the importance of KS2 SATs which deter Year 6 teachers from devoting time to building primary–secondary partnerships and (2) the lower budgets and status of design and technology in secondary schools.

Effective transition strategies all point to strong primary–secondary partnerships. Once established, the task of maintaining them is difficult; there seems to be a seesaw of progress and regression. In their case studies of four secondary schools over five decades, Galton and McLellan found that 'none of the four schools used bridging units. For the most part the "fresh start" approach was favoured' (2018:274). The teachers' voices from my interviews reveal collaborative partnerships have become a lower priority, progress is therefore jeopardised.

At the heart of the debate are the pupils themselves. Recent research suggests that focusing on well-being is more important than the structure of educational systems. For example, Jindal-Snape et al. (2020) recommend that not only should primary and secondary schools work together to improve continuity of pedagogical approaches, but they should also help pupils develop a sense of 'school belonging' by providing opportunities for pupils to develop peer networks and secure attachments to secondary teachers and other staff.

In the current climate widespread, linked CPD may be unrealistic, as is effective liaison between Year 6 and Year 7 teachers. Developing comprehensive assessment systems may be even more remote since the time dedicated to joint planning is substantial and ongoing, as shown by the comments from the teachers I interviewed. If the only transition strategies secondary design and technology teachers can employ are inviting pupils to enjoy taster days, then that, at least, will give pupils the chance to develop relationships with pupils and staff and become familiar in new surroundings; that, at least, is a beneficial starting point.

## Questions

1 How should primary and secondary schools distribute the responsibilities of pupils transitioning across the learning phases?
2 What strategies and opportunities already exist to ease the transition in your school? How can design and technology 'piggy-back' on these?
3 How can primary–secondary partnerships become strong, meaningful, and sustainable rather than superficial and short-lived?

## Notes

1 English, mathematics and science.
2 Standard Attainment Tests – these assessments take place in the May of Year 6, they test English (grammar, punctuation, spelling, reading) and mathematics. Results are collated and published by the UK government.

## References

Alexander, R. (ed) (2010) *Children, Their World, their Education Final report and recommendations of the Cambridge Primary Review*. London: Routledge.

Aston, S. and Jackson, D. (2009) Blurring the boundaries or muddying the waters? *Design and Technology Education: An International Journal* 14(1), 1360–1431 https://ojs.lboro.ac.uk/DATE/article/view/203 accessed: 25/09/2021.

Bagnall, C. (2020) Talking about School Transition (TaST): An emotional centred intervention to support children over primary-secondary school transition. *Pastoral Care in Education* 38(2), 116–137. https://www.tandfonline.com/doi/abs/10.1080/02643944.2020.1713870 accessed: 05/06/2021.

Barlex, David, Given, Nick and Steeg, Torben (2017) The curriculum; A design & technology perspective on the Ofsted curriculum survey; A Working Paper. D&TforD&T https://dandtfordandt.wordpress.com/working-papers/the-curriculum/ accessed: 28/10/2020.

Benson, C. (2009) Working together: primary and secondary teacher liaison. In Arien Bekker, Ilja Mottier, Marc J. de Vries (eds), *Strengthening the Position of Technology Education in the Curriculum, Proceedings PATT-22 Conference Delft, the Netherlands, August 24-28, 2009*.

Benson, C. (2012) The development of quality design and technology in English primary schools: Issues and solutions. In T. Ginner, J. Hallström & M. Hultén (Eds.), *Technology Education in the 21st Century, Proceedings PATT-26 Conference, Stockholm Sweden June 26–30, 81–88*.

Black, A. (2019) *Primary and secondary teaching: What's the difference?* TES https://www.tes.com/news/primary-and-secondary-teaching-whats-difference accessed: 22/02/2021.

Dakers, J. and Dow, W. (2004) The problem with transition in technology education: A Scottish perspective. *Journal of Design and Technology Education* 9(2), 116–124 https://ojs.lboro.ac.uk/JDTE/article/view/689 accessed: 22/02/2021.

DATA (2014) design and technology Progression Framework – Guidance KS 1-3 https://www.data.org.uk/shop-products/design-and-technology-progression-framework/ accessed: 22/02/2021.

DfE (2011) The national strategies 1997 to 2011 https://www.gov.uk/government/publications/the-national-strategies-1997-to-2011 accessed: 22/02/2021.

DfE (2013) The national curriculum in England July 2013 https://www.gov.uk/government/collections/national-curriculum accessed: 22/02/2021.

Evans, D., Borriello, G. and Field, A. (2018) A review of the academic and psychological impact of the transition to secondary education. *Frontiers in Psychology* 9, 1482 https://doi.org/10.3389/fpsyg.2018.01482 accessed: 05/06/2021.

Galton, M. and McLellan, D. (2018) A transition Odyssey: pupils' experiences of transfer to secondary school across five decades. *Research Papers in Education*, 255–277. doi:10.1080/02671522.2017.1302496 accessed: 05/06/2021.

Growney, C. (2013) Why is transition from primary to secondary school so difficult? In Owen-Jackson, G. (ed.), *Debates in design and technology education* (pp. 51–63). London: Routledge.

Jindal-Snape, D., Hannah, D., Cantali, D., Barlow, W. and MacGillivray, S. (2020) Systematic literature review of primary–secondary transitions: International research. *Review of Education* 8(2), 526–566. https://dera.ioe.ac.uk/32851/7/00546054.pdf accessed: 05/06/2021.

Kimbell, R., Stables, K. and Green, R. (1996) *Understanding practice in design and technology*. Buckingham, UK: Open University Press.

Kimbell, R. and Stables, K. (2008) *Researching Design Learning: Issues and findings from two decades of research and development*. New York: Springer.

Mahmud, A. (2020) The role of social and emotional learning during the transition to secondary school: An exploratory study. *Pastoral Care in Education* 38(1), 23–41. https://doi.org/10.1080/02643944.2019.1700546 accessed: 05/06/2021.

Mellor, D. and Delamont, S. (2011) Old anticipations, new anxieties? A contemporary perspective on primary to secondary transfer. *Cambridge Journal of Education* 41(3), 331–346. doi:10.1080/0305764X.2011.607154 accessed: 05/06/2021.

OFSTED (2015) *Key stage 3: The wasted years*. London: OFSTED [online]: www.gov.uk/government/publications/key-stage-3-the-wasted-years accessed 10/2020.

Stables, K. (1994) Discontinuity in transition: Pupils' experience of technology in year 6 and year 7. *International Journal of Technology and Design Education* 5(2), 157–169 doi:10.1007/BF00766814 accessed: 05/06/2021.

van Rens, M., Haelermans, C., Groot, W. et al. (2018) Facilitating a successful transition to secondary school: (How) does it work? A systematic literature review. *Adolescent Research Review* 3, 43–56 doi:10.1007/s40894-017-0063-2 accessed: 05/06/2021.

Winn, D. (2020) Developing links with other subjects. In Hardy, A. (Ed), *Learning to teach design and technology in the Secondary School: A companion to the school experience* (273–288). London: Routledge.

# 13 Teaching for technological justice
## Embracing indigenous designs

*Mishack Gumbo*

## Introduction

This chapter argues for technological justice for indigenous designs in design and technology education (design and technology education and technology education are used interchangeably in this chapter). In recent years, teaching for social justice in teacher education programmes has been spotlighted to prepare teachers to work with diverse learners (Gumbo, 2017; Kutay, 2020). From a decolonised perspective, there is a need to transform design and technology curriculum and teaching to achieve justice for indigenous learners. The need to transform design and technology is informed by the scientific approach and modern industrial conceptualisation of the subject (Gumbo, 2018; Williams, 2000) which favours Western culture at the expense of indigenous culture. As a result, there is no equal treatment of indigenous and non-indigenous learners in design and technology classrooms (Eggleston, 1992; Custer, 1995; Gumbo, 2017). Therefore, this chapter confronts the injustice that seems to dominate the subject by contributing a version of Heek's model that can be applied in both indigenous and non-indigenous contexts to ensure justice to indigenous learners. In the chapter, I describe technological justice as it refers to design and technology. I explore indigenous technology from indigenous contexts. This exercise is done by engaging four cases in India, Zimbabwe, South Africa and Australia. Next, Heek's model of per-indigenous, para-indigenous and pro-indigenous approaches is explained and used to frame the chapter. Heek's model is applied to give insight into how design and technology can be transformed or decolonised through the model. Two versions of the model are proposed to that effect, that is the Model for Teaching Technology in Indigenous Contexts (MTTIC) and the Model for Teaching Technology in Non-Indigenous Contexts (MTTNIC).

## Technological justice

Teaching for justice can be understood in the light of the statement made by Scheffler (1968):

Teachers cannot restrict their attention to the classroom alone, leaving the larger setting and the purposes of schooling to be determined by others. They must take active responsibility for the goals for which they are committed and for the social setting in which these goals may prosper. If they are not to be mere agents of others, of the state, of the military, of the media, of the experts and bureaucrats, they need to determine their own agency through a critical context of their calling.

(p. 11)

The statement expresses the crucial role that teachers should play, not only as receivers and implementers of curriculum or knowledge dispensers but also as critical engagers of curriculum and pedagogies especially for the sake of indigenous learners. Technological justice is mainly about promoting an ethos of social justice. In the external environment to the school, social justice is about equal participation in a democratic society and the distribution of resources to all (Naidoo, 2007; Fujiyoshi, 2015). To the technology teacher, technological justice would mean creating a design and technology classroom environment that facilitates awareness and appreciation for learners with diverse cultural backgrounds which is related to their racial or ethnic, language, socio-economic, gender and sexual orientation (Naidoo, 2007; Lee, 2011). Such a classroom environment is necessary for indigenous technology not to be underplayed.

As change agents, therefore, teachers should critique the larger socio-cultural and political dimensions of teaching and schooling (Naidoo, 2007) to equally value indigenous and non-indigenous learners in their classes (Bruchac, 2014; Jacob, Sabzalian, Jansen, Tobin, Vincent & LaChance, 2018). There are also children of indigenous descent in diaspora whom educational practices should serve properly (Haig-Brown, 2009). According to Papaioannou (2010), there is an unequal generation and diffusion of innovation and as such political principles of justice must be observed. This inequality is expressed in insufficient food, lack of or poor shelter, unsafe drinking water, diseases and so on, especially to indigenous people who have hitherto suffered colonisation.

Design and technology is one of the gateway subjects which aims to produce artists, designers, blacksmiths, metallurgists and others of the future. However, the achievement of this aim largely depends on the type or form of technology taught to learners and how it is taught. If ethno-technology is not taught to learners, no ethno-specialists in technology will be produced to design suitable solutions for indigenous communities. Design and technology curriculum should therefore not be biased towards indigenous learners (Department of Basic Education [DBE], 2011). Here I am citing the South African DBE because its Curriculum and Assessment Policy Statement (CAPS) Grades R–12 (learners aged 5–18 years old) is framed on seven principles which are social transformation; active and critical thinking; high knowledge and high skills; progression; human rights, inclusivity, environmental and social justice; valuing indigenous knowledge systems; and credibility, quality and efficiency. Specifically, the aims of technology education include biases and impacts of technology, as well as indigenous technology (DBE, 2011). However, the implementation of CAPS downplays indigenous technology as it is undervalued in teacher education and professional development training.

Indigenous populations form close to 400 million people of the world's population (World Bank, 2011; Sarivaara, Maatta & Uusiaitti, 2013). This number harbours more than 5000 different groups of distinct cultures, forms of social organisation, livelihood strategies, practices and others (International Labour Office [ILO], 2018). About two-thirds of indigenous people live in Asia (United Nations [UN], 2014), more than 14.2 million in Africa (United Nations Department of Economic and Social Affairs [UN-DESA], 2017) and 45 million in Latin America (Comision Economica Para America Latina [CEPAL], 2014). Yet, these populations are underrepresented and underserved educationally.

Sarivaara et al.'s (2013) definition of indigenous people helps address the challenge to define them. Unlike many other scholars who have defined indigenous people single-handedly, Sarivaara et al. (2013) consider a multi-pronged approach to the definition covering Hawai'i, First Nations, Métis and Inuit, Maori and Sámi. A common denominator in the definitions of these groups is that they have experienced colonisation:

> They have lived in the area before the settlement or the formation of the modern state borders and have maintained either wholly or partly their own social, economic, cultural, and political institutions.
> (Sarivaara et al., 2013, p. 370)

Sarivaara et al. (2013) state further that they still maintain a continuous historical connection with the societies preceding colonisation. Hence, discourses about indigenous people are not devoid of decolonial stories against the background of their experiences with colonisation.

In the light of the preceding definition, indigenous people are characterised by technological practices and designs, among other things, which are endowed in their culture. Scholars (e.g. Smith, 1999; Williams, 2000; Senanayake, 2006; Chilisa, 2012; Shizha, 2014; Chilisa, Major, Gaotlhobogwe & Mokgolodi, 2016; Kwaira & Gumbo; 2017; Gumbo; 2018) call for the indigenisation of curriculum as a response to the historical marginalisation of indigenous people and to ensure, in the context of this chapter, technological justice. This call suggests a decolonial approach to the design and technology curriculum for the recovery of indigenous people from colonial impact (Datta, 2018) and technologism (Jones, 2018), a form of colonisation that is driven by technological oppression. Prime (1993), Seemann (2000), Gumbo (2020), Nhemachena, Hlabangane and Matowanyika (2020) and others critique the colonial function (a driver of technological injustice through curriculum and teaching) of technology education.

# Indigenous technology: context-based cases

In the light of the earlier expressed need for technological justice, learners should be exposed to, and learn about, indigenous designs instead of conventional designs which are mainly influenced by Western culture. To this effect, there exists indigenous technology which can enrich the design and technology curriculum. I explore indigenous technology cases from three different contexts to support this point.

## *India: engineering technology in bridge design and others*

Watson (2019) reports on the rope bridge design of the Khasi tribe in India. The design is based on a tree concept in the sense that natural tree trunks are used to anchor the bridge that goes over massive rivers for people to cross during monsoon weather. The deeper the tree's roots grow into the ground, the more the bridge becomes durable and stable.

Indian designers have over the years attempted to free themselves from imported technology, especially from Britain. This is in line with Bang, Marin, Faber and Suzukovich III (2013), who claim that 'indigenous people are significantly underrepresented in the fields of science, technology, engineering and math' (p. 705). In the 1880s Indian technicians grew in number to replace the British experts, even though Indian technicians had succumbed to the British technology that had been forced into the country (Tripathi, 1996). The first cotton mill known as *gara-bo* spindle, produced commercially by the middle of the 1870s, used power from a waterwheel; it was, however, regarded as primitive by Western technicians (Tripathi, 1996). However, the mill captured a large domestic market because of its low cost (Tripathi, 1996). The issue of the cost attached to Western technology and indigenous technology has been debated by scholars such as Gaotlhobogwe (2017) and Mlambo (2016) based on indigenous wooden coasters and homestead construction, respectively.

Furthermore, Indian technicians feature in iron, chemical, agricultural, cement and sugar production industries. For example the sugar production industry has from time immemorial locally produced unrefined sugar through traditional methods (Tripathi, 1996) – I argue that this traditional processing of sugar would not pose danger to the people's health. Also, popular names behind the Indian technological development include Laxmanrao Kirloskar (agriculture), Walchnd Hirachand (shipping and agribusiness), J.N. Tata (Ring Mill, steel). However, names of indigenous experts such as these are not mentioned in design and technology and engineering curricula; this sends a wrong impression that indigenous people are antitechnological, that they cannot contribute to technological development and that technology is the phenomenon that exists among Westerners only. A transformed teaching of technology can diffuse this myth.

India could not further its indigenous technology due to the dominance of imported British technology into the country. The British monopoly was even visible in patenting – around 1930, out of 1099 applications filed in Indian patent offices, only 212 originated in India and the rest were from Europeans (Tripathi, 1996). To make matters worse, the European colonisation made indigenous peoples yearn for foreign technology (Lutz, 2005). The dependency syndrome goes deeper so much that in my context, parents are often heard reprimanding their children, 'O se ke wa tshwara, o tla senya dilo tsa makgowa' (Tswana; Don't touch, you will damage White people's things). This is a self-defeating statement which denies indigenous children venturing opportunities.

In India, technical education and training were so significantly downtrodden that only two technical colleges existed in the 1880s (Tripathi, 1996). The fact that technological dependence continued might well tell that even technical education offered in those colleges was foreign. Tripathi (1996) engages the concepts, the technological syndrome and technological myopia to express the depth of India's dependence on British technology. According to Tripathi (1996, p. 87), technological syndrome refers to the tendency of a subject people to emulate practices, behaviour and institutions of the ruling country, whereas technological myopia is about uncritical technological choices and a lack of experimentation to modify the imported technology to suit local conditions and needs. A transformative approach to design and technology is needed to confront the implied colonial expression in the curriculum and pedagogy of the subject (Gumbo, 2017). Indigenous learners can gain confidence in sharpening their critical skills and seeing themselves as the designers of the future by engaging in decolonial discourses as part of their learning.

There are Indians as natives of America, as well, who attempt to cling to their indigenous cultural practices. Bang et al. (2013) conducted a community-based design research study with the Chicago American Indian community over four years. The study involved community members who consisted of elders, parents, teachers, community content experts, degreed experts, other interested adults and youth. They involved indigenous methodologies in both participatory activities and data collection. The main findings covered indigenous conceptualisation and epistemologies surrounding the learning of technology by the youth in the contexts of fire technology, agriculture technology and natural resource mapping. The reporting concentrated on fire technologies through the four principles which emerged in each of the four years. Principle one was about engaging original and everyday technologies; principle two was about exploring the nature and uses of technologies; principle three involved situating technologies in cultural and socio-historic contexts; principle four was based on technological innovation and learning by engaging in community-driven goals and use of technology as a tool toward those goals. These principles yielded the ontological and epistemological aspects of technology to demystify the reification of Western technology above indigenous forms; show convergence of indigenous people's use of natural senses to quantify and qualify things in science and technology and test tubes and chemicals; and inject new pedagogical stances and teacher reasoning. This has crucial implications for design and technology as shown in the last section of this chapter through the application of Heek's model.

## Zimbabwe: tangible and non-tangible technology

Mapara (2009) gives an account of the Tangwena people regarding their experience with nature which guides their activities. The Tangwena can observe weather patterns in relation to bird behaviour for weather forecast. Mapara (2009) argues:

> Even though these people do not have the technology that is available today they can through observing their fowls and other birds tell whether the rains are going to stop or not. They have developed the skill of forecasting the weather by at least two days and at most three weeks.
>
> (p. 151)

This is technology because indigenously, there are tangible and non-tangible technologies which have ramifications on material, social and communication technologies. According to Ogunbure (in Gumbo, 2020), social technology includes methodologies, organisational and management skills, negotiation and counselling techniques and social institutions (e.g. patriarchy, women's league, songs, jokes). Communication technology covers language, signs and symbols, drumming and more. So, observation and forecasting fall under non-tangible technology.

To illustrate tangible technology, Kwaira and Gumbo (2017) conducted a developmental participatory study in Makonde Rural District of North-West Zimbabwe. The villagers are mainly rural farmers who have shown a need for equipment to process their crop products. The researchers used their knowledge and skills in design and technology to address this need. They teamed up with the villagers to build maize, oil and peanut butter processing machines. These machines were mainly built from thrown-away materials. The importance of these machines is that the farmers participated in their construction; as such, they maintained and fixed them.

## Australia: engineering technology of the boomerang and variable-ratio transmission

Two engineering excellences were documented by Kutay (2017). The first is by David Unaipon, who lived between 1872 and 1967. Unaipon designed a boomerang which influenced the helicopter's propeller system during World War II. Unaipon converted the rotation motion into a tangential reciprocal movement, a basis of the modern sheep shears. The second is by Eric Willmot, who worked as an engineer in the 1980s and 1990s. He 'developed a system for continuous variable-ratio transmission for use in gearing' (Kutay, 2017, p. 14). His work about the controllable variable-motion in mechanical engineering rigid body mechanisms was used in Australia's first hybrid car.

### South Africa: architectural technology of vernacular home

Architecture is characterised by the use of natural materials, such as quarry, glass, sticks and mud. The Zulu build grass-thatched domed dwellings which are laid out in circular homesteads around a central cattle kraal. In this case, the *umuzi* (homestead) has several huts with garden plots, cattle kraal and livestock, tools and equipment and agricultural storage huts (Mlambo, 2016). Choosing a building site is determined by one's connection with the ancestors, land and burial rights. As far as the family-to-clan arrangement are concerned, the man and his wife or wives, unmarried daughters, sons and their families and relatives occupy the homestead. The area is occupied by people who descended from a common ancestor. Loose communities of kinsmen form a village under a headman. Several villages form a chiefdom under an independent chief. This organisational technology ensures kinship and community security, with Ubuntu as a buffer to protect the community against intruders. Ubuntu refers to a web of relationships which exist among Africans; these relationships are anchored on the spirit of interdependence and mutual trust (reliance on each other daily; Mbaya, 2011).

Currently, corrugated iron and steel windows supplement certain designs. However, these supplementary materials are expensive as they may be available in outlying areas only. Building with earth has stood the test of time. Judged in urban terms, however, mud construction is often associated with poverty. Urban residents would rather build with cement and other materials which are relatively expensive.

The frame of the hut is made of sapling poles placed in a circle, bent inwards and lashed together. The frame is thatched with grass. The floor is made from a mixture of anthill and cow dung. The interior and furnishings include rolled reed as sleeping mats, carved wooden headrests and wooden stools. Everyone is involved in the construction of the homestead with women responsible for wall construction, floors and plastering, while men construct the roof from timber and cover it with thatched grass. The children and elders weave grass ropes and prepare the materials for use. In this manner, children are already trained in design.

The cases described earlier show that indigenous people engage localised technologies and resources. There are advanced designers of some of these technologies. Elders play an important role as, like in the South African case, they teach and train the young ones as they engage in their technological practices.

## Heek's model as a framework for indigenous technology

The technologies described in the above section can be understood through Heek's (2009) model which consists of three core concepts, that is pro-indigenous designs or innovations, para-indigenous designs and per-indigenous designs. Although Heek applies this model in information communication technology (ICT), it can transform design and technology into a culturally appropriate subject (Ladson-Billings, 1995). Pro-indigenous designs are innovations derived outside of the target people and undertaken on behalf of indigenous people. Para-indigenous designs are undertaken alongside indigenous people. Per-indigenous designs are by indigenous people.

I apply the following two versions of Heek's model in design and technology:

1. per-indigenous → para-indigenous → pro-indigenous suited for indigenous contexts
2. pro-indigenous → para-indigenous → per-indigenous suited for non-indigenous contexts

Applying technology according to this proposed order of Heek's model will promote indigenous technology, culture and sustainable development. Considering the Indian bridge design, Indian people understand their local conditions and challenges more than an outsider. They designed the appropriate low-cost bridge (per-indigenous) in response to the harsh monsoon weather which makes river crossing almost impossible. Imposition of external (pro-indigenous) technologies on the Indian local context is impossible unless Indian people make sense it so that it does not erode local technology. They will guard against superimposing it on the local technology. Rather, they will adapt it to endogenous technology (para-indigenous). Foreign technology should be integrated into the community values and culture rather than accepted as is, as Kutay (2020) argues: 'With the application of appropriate technology in development, it is possible for Indigenous communities to adjust technology to their uses and transfer their accumulated knowledge to the development of infrastructure and mechanisms for production incorporating cultural value'.

It can be noticed that Kutay (2020) attaches technology to cultural values, which suggests that technology is not culturally neutral. Hence, the participation of indigenous people in any technological adventure should not be compromised to make technology appropriate to their culture. The application of Heek's model in design and technology is described in the next section.

## The application of Heek's model in the teaching of Technology

There are three fundamentals that accompany indigenous technological designs, which lead to applying Heek's model to ensure justice in the teaching of design and technology. First, indigenous people engage as a collective (Ubuntu) in design activities as it can be noticed from the South African case described earlier – men, women and children engage in the design and construction of the house. This implies social constructivism in the teaching of technology in which there is co-construction of knowledge and skills. From a South African indigenous community point of view, collective engagement anchors on ubuntu (unity, respect, communal, etc.). This can be employed as a guide in learning technology. In the book *Pedagogical principles in technology education: An indigenous perspective* (Gumbo, 2016), an illustration is given about how Ubuntu can be used in teaching technology. Ubuntu also features in the Zimbabwean case through collective activities undertaken by the role players. The case also shows how to engage external technologies – the maize mill resembles non-indigenous technology, but it is deconstructed and reconstructed to suit local conditions.

Second, teaching and training take place in the house project discussed earlier in the South African case as elders show the young how it is done. It is therefore frustrating for indigenous learners to be confined in the physical classroom for their learning activities. Even techno-labs with non-indigenous machinery might not be indigenous learner-friendly, suggesting an open-class teaching approach. Design activities should be planned such that learners can interact with the community and learn in open spaces when necessary. Instead of abandoning their cultures and technology, learners relate the technology that they learn to their cultural milieus and develop a sense of pride. Therefore, it is crucial for education to be responsive to indigenous epistemologies and cultures to achieve desired outcomes (Lewthwaite, Owen, Doiron, Renaud & McMillan, 2014).

Third, the names of indigenous experts behind innovations and designs matter a great deal. Exposing learners to Western inventors and innovators reify Western technology over indigenous technology. Learners risk emulating Western designs and establishments at the expense of indigenous ones (Jokhu & Kutay, 2020). Being confronted with Western names during my schooling career is partly my reason for being indigenous/decolonial researcher. I experienced discomfort in the underrepresentation of indigenous people's contributions. The #FeesMustFall student uprising in the South African universities in 2015 was coupled with the call to decolonise the curriculum. The students' attempt to destroy statues with Western faces on university campuses was to deal with the psychological effect expressed through the non-representation of Africans.

In the light of these fundamentals and the discussions this far, two modified versions of Heek's model are suggested for teaching technology in indigenous/non-Western contexts (Figure 13.1) and in non-indigenous/Western contexts (Figure 13.2) to ensure responsiveness to indigenous learners, even those who are in diaspora. The first model (Figure 13.1) which is acronymised as MTTIC relates to per-indigenous → para-indigenous → pro-indigenous approach.

The MTTIC requires education authorities and technology teachers to ensure the relevance of the subject to indigenous learners. This should start by recognising and identifying indigenous technology as a basis for learners to learn technology. Indigenous technology (definition, concepts, knowledge, skills, volition, etc.) should be audited and used in curriculum design and pedagogical approaches. The aspects of Heek's model should be followed in the order (1–3) indicated in Figure 13.1. Indigenous technology should be the starting point. Teaching technology should thus be based on

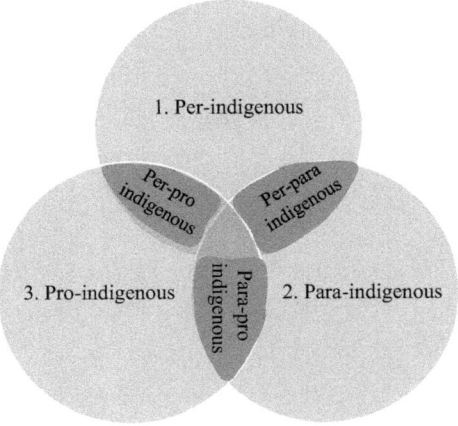

*Figure 13.1* Model for teaching Technology in indigenous contexts.

indigenous designs (per-indigenous) such as the rope bridge design. In the Indian context for example, learners should explore, investigate or analyse existing designs to primarily design for local contexts.

Following the per-indigenous approach, technology teachers should let learners take centre stage to focus their learning on indigenous technology. Indigenous elders and experts should be used to strengthen indigenous technological perspectives (para-indigenous). In this way, para-indigenous approaches will promote indigenous cultural designs indigenous people can identify with. For example, a learner from the Ndebele community in South Africa may be influenced by the function, materials, values, colours and rectangular painting of the Ndebele house design. Per-indigenous and para-indigenous approaches will make sure that exogenous (pro-indigenous) technology is not imposed on the learning of indigenous learners. This approach (per-indigenous → para-indigenous → pro-indigenous) will also expand the understanding of non-indigenous learners as they work on group or team projects in design and technology classes. The weakness of Heek's model is that it was applied in ICT. Technology teachers may be tempted to sway MTTIC towards the dominance of ICT at the expense of indigenous technology.

The MTTNIC illustrated in Figure 13.2 can be applied in non-indigenous (Western) contexts where indigenous people are in diaspora. It follows the pro-indigenous → para-indigenous → per-indigenous logic.

In this version of Heek's model, non-indigenous technology is the starting point in design and technology. However, indigenous technology is recognised and effort is made to integrate it. Non-indigenous learners are given the opportunity to learn indigenous technology alongside non-indigenous technology. Technology teachers should therefore plan learning activities such that non-indigenous learners can make understand technology from an indigenous perspective and collaborate with indigenous learners. MTTNIC

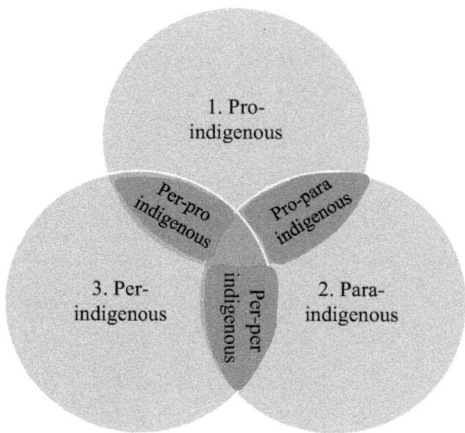

*Figure 13.2* Model for Teaching Technology in Non-Indigenous Contexts.

can help technology teachers to recognise the existence of indigenous people who are part of the society in non-indigenous contexts and their technology. Technology teachers should be wary of the heightened influence of ICT which underlies the conceptualisation of Heeks's model, especially in Western contexts where there is total dominance by ICT. They should not mistake technology education for educational technology or ICT in education. This way, they will be able to deal with the content and pedagogy of technology education. This means, in the context of the issues of indigeneity raised in this chapter, that teachers should critically reflect on the relevance of the subject to indigenous contexts, not only Western contexts.

## Conclusion

Justice should be served in design and technology classrooms. This chapter has argued for teaching technology for justice by recognising indigenous technology. Technology teachers cannot teach indigenous learners who form part of their classes without teaching indigenous technology as well. The discussion in this chapter was based on the exploration of existing designs in indigenous contexts. Heek's model was used to frame the discussion and it was also explained as to how the model can be used to teach indigenous technology. I believe that both indigenous and non-indigenous learners can benefit greatly from learning indigenous technological designs instead of limiting them to learning non-indigenous or Western technological designs only. By its nature, design and technology promotes team and/or group work in learning activities. This presents an opportunity for indigenous and non-indigenous learners to learn the forms of technology that exist in their respective cultural environments. Technology teachers should teach technology as transformation or decolonisation agents. Their practice should allow for critical engagements with the content more so that criticality, creativity and investigation are crucial skills that technology teachers should develop in learners. Learners should therefore be made to learn and think about technology in their cultural contexts. Learners should be allowed space to debate the impact and biases of technology, as well as learn about indigenous technology and culture. Teachers can design tasks which will send their learners on an investigation mission of local technologies. However, teacher education and professional development workshops should empower teachers to integrate indigenous technology in their teaching. Empowering the teachers will ensure that curriculum and pedagogy do not downplay indigenous technology.

## Questions

1 Based on indigenous technology being debated in this chapter, how would you define the term (*indigenous technology*)? How does your definition differ from the modern industry-based definition?
2 Reflect on the issue of technological justice versus technology. Share your reflection with your colleague or friend.
3 Research indigenous technologies from a few contexts. How could you use the per-indigenous approach to integrate them into your lessons?
4 Research answers to the following questions: Does indigenous technology have a place in the Fourth Industrial era? Then consider the question, What impact does your answer have on the fact that indigenous technology contributes toward the sustainable development of indigenous people and culture?

## References

Bang, M., Marin, A., Faber, L. & Suzukovich III, E.S. (2013). Repatriating indigenous technologies in an urban Indian community. *Urban Education*, 48(5), 705–733.
Bruchac, M. (2014). Indigenous knowledge and traditional knowledge. In C. Smith (Ed.). *Encyclopaedia of global archaeology*, pp. 3814–3824. New York: Springer.
Custer, R.L. (1995). Examining the dimensions of technology. *International Journal of Technology and Design Education*, 5(3), 219–244.
Datta, R. (2018). Decolonizing both researcher and research and its effectiveness in indigenous research. *Research Ethics*, 14(2), 1–24.
CEPAL (2014). *Guaranteeing indigenous people's rights in Latin America: Progress in the past decade and renaming challenges. Summary*. Retrieved from: www.cepal.org/es/publicaciones/37050-pueblos-indigenas-america-latina-avances-ultimo-decenio-retos-pendientes-la. Accessed 11 November 2020.
Chilisa, B. (2012). *Indigenous research methodologies*. Los Angeles, CA: Sage.
Chilisa, B., Major, T.E., Gaotlhobogwe, M. & Mokgolodi, H. (2016). Decolonizing and indigenizing evaluation practice in Africa: Toward African relational evaluation approaches. *Canadian Journal of Program Evaluation*, (Special Issue), 313–328.
Department of Basic Education. (2011). *Curriculum and assessment policy statement grades 7 – 9 technology*. Pretoria: Government Printers.

Eggleston, J. (1992). *Teaching design and technology: Developing science and technology education.* Buckingham: Open University Press.

Fujiyoshi, K.F. (2015). Becoming a social justice educator. *Democracy & Education,* 23(1), 1–6.

Gaotlhobogwe, M. (2017). The role of indigenous knowledge systems in addressing the problem of declining enrolments in D&TE. In M.T. Gumbo & V. Msila (eds.). *African voices on indigenisation of the curriculum: Insights from practice,* pp. 285–305. Wandsbeck: Reach.

Gumbo, M.T. (2016). Pedagogical principles in technology education: An indigenous perspective. In G. Emeagwali & E. Shizha (Eds.). *African indigenous knowledge and the sciences: Journeys into the past and present,* pp. 13–32. Rotterdam, Boston, Taipei: Sense.

Gumbo, M.T. (2017). An indigenous perspective on technology education. In P. Ngulube (ed.). *Handbook of research on Indigenous knowledge systems in developing countries,* pp. 137–160. Hershey: IGI.

Gumbo, M.T. (2018). Addressing the factors responsible for the misunderstanding of technology education with other subject fields. *Perspectives in Education,* 36(1): 128–144.

Gumbo, M.T. (2020). What does decolonizing technology education mean? In M.T. Gumbo (Ed.). *Decolonization of technology education: African indigenous perspectives,* pp. 7–24. New York: Peter Lang.

Haig-Brown, C. (2009). Decolonizing diaspora: Whose traditional land are we on? *Cultural and Pedagogical Inquiry,* 1(1), 4–21.

Jacob, M.M., Sabzalian, L., Jansen, J., Tobin, T.J., Vincent, C.G. & LaChance, K.M. (2018). The gift of education: How indigenous knowledge can transform the future of public education. *international Journal of Multicultural Education,* 20(1), 157–185.

Jones, R.A. (2018). After postmodernism, technologism. *Educational Philosophy and Theory,* 50(14), 1606–1607.

Kwaira, P. & Gumbo, M.T. (2017). Taking design and technology to the community: The case of Makonde Rural District in Zimbabwe. In Gumbo, M.T. & Msila, V. (Eds.). *African voices on indigenisation of the curriculum: Insights from practice,* pp. 1–44. Wandsbeck: Reach.

Heeks, R. (2009). The ICT4D 2.0 Manifesto: Where next for ICTs and international development? Development Informatics Working Paper No. 42, IDPM. Retrieved from www.sed.manchester.ac.uk/idpm/research/publications/wp/di/documents/di_wp42.pdf. Accessed 11 November 2020.

Jokhu, P.D. & Kutay, C. (2020). Observation on appropriate technology application in indigenous community using system dynamics modelling. *Sustainability,* 12, 1–12.

Kutay, C. (2017). *Aboriginal engineering: Technologies for an enduring civilisation.* Retrieved from: https://indigenousengineering.org.au/wp-content/uploads/2017/11/IndigenousTechnologybooklet.pdf

Kutay, C. (2020). Observations on appropriate technology application in indigenous community using system dynamics modelling. *Sustainability,* 12(6). Retrieved from: www.mdpi.com/journal/sustainability

ILO. (2018). Social protection for indigenous peoples. Retrieved from: www.ilo.org/wcmsp5/groups/public/---ed_protect/---protrav/---ilo_aids/documents/publication/wcms_626564.pdf.

Ladson-Billings, G. (1995). Toward a theory of culturally relevant pedagogy. *American Educational Research Journal*, 32(3), 465–491.

Lee, Y.A. (2011). What does teaching for social justice mean to teacher candidates? *The Professional Educator*, 35(2). Available from: https://files.eric.ed.gov/fulltext/EJ988204.pdf

Lewthwaite, B.E., Owen, T., Doiron, A., Renaud, R. & McMillan, B. (2014). Culturally responsive teaching in Yukon First Nations setting: What does it look like and what is its influence? *Canadian Journal of Educational Administration and Policy*, 155, 1–34.

Lutz, E.L. (2005). The many meanings of technology. Cultural Survival Quarterly Magazine. Retrieved from: https://www.culturalsurvival.org/publications/cultural-survival-quarterly/many-meanings-technology

Mapara, J. (2009). Indigenous knowledge systems in Zimbabwe: Juxtaposing postcolonial theory. *The Journal of Pan African Studies*, 3(1), 139–155.

Mbaya, H. (2011). Social capital and the imperatives of the concept and life of Ubuntu in the South Africa context. *Sciptura*, 106(2011), 1–8.

Mlambo, H. (2016). *The impact of impucuko (modernisation) of rural homestead living spaces on the dwellers in selected area of Umbumbulu, south of Durban.* Unpublished Master's dissertation. Durban: Durban University of Technology.

Naidoo, L. (2007). Teaching for social justice: Reflections form a core unit in a teacher education program. *Transnational Curriculum Inquiry*, 4(2), 23–37.

Nhemachena, A., Hlabangane, N. & Matowanyika, J.Z.Z. (Eds.). (2020). *Centuries-old colonial/imperial denialism of African originality: An introduction to decolonising STEM in Africa*. Bamenda: Langaa RPCIG.

Papaioannou, T. (2010). *Technological innovation, global justice and politics of development*. Presented at the Workshop on Innovation and Inequality: New Indicators from Pharma and Beyond. Pisa, Italy.

Prime, G.M. (1993). Values in technology: An approach to learning. *Design and Technology Teaching*, 26, 30–36.

Sarivaara, E., Maatta, K. & Uusiaitti, S. (2013). Who is indigenous? Definitions of indigeneity. *European Scientific Journal*, 1, 369–378.

Scheffler, I. (1968). University scholarship and the education of teachers. *Teachers College Record*, 70(1), 1–12.

Seemann, K.W. (2000). *Technacy education: Towards holistic pedagogy and epistemology in general and indigenous/crosscultural technology education*. Presented at International technology education Research Conference. Gold Coast, Australia.

Senanayake, S.G.J.N. (2006). Indigenous knowledge as a key to sustainable development. *The Journal of Agricultural Sciences*, 2(1), 87–94.

Shizha, E. (2014). The indigenous knowledge systems and the curriculum. In G. Emeagwali & G.J.S. Dei (Eds.). *African indigenous knowledge and the disciplines*, pp. 113–130. Rotterdam: Sense.

Smith, L.T. (1999). *Decolonizing methodologies: Research and indigenous peoples.* Dunedin: Zed Books.

Tripathi, D. (1996). Colonialism and technology choices in India: A historical overview. *The Developing Economies* XXXIV(1), 80–97.

UN. (2014). *Indigenous peoples in the Asian region.* New York: UN Department of Public Information.

UN-DESA. (2017). *World population prospects: The 2017 revision, key findings and advance tables*. Working Paper No. ESA/P/WP/248, 2017.

Watson, J. (2019). Lo-Tek, design by radical indigenism. Retrieved from: www.loot.co.za/product/julian-watson-julia-watson-lo-tek-design-by-radical-i/zhfd-6297-g350. Accessed 11 November 2020.

Williams, P.J. (2000). The only methodology of technology? *Journal of Technology Education*, 11(2), 48–60.

World Bank. (2011). Still among the poorest of the poor. Indigenous peoples country brief. Retrieved from: www.worldbank.org/en/news/feature/2010/04/26/indigenous-peoples-still-among-poorest-in-world. Accessed 11 November 2020.

# 14 Design cognition in design and technology classrooms

*Nicolaas Blom*

## Introduction

It is well known that learning and thinking in design and technology result from the interaction between mind, body, and environment. Yet, current theories of cognition are limited in describing how design thinking emerges because of these interactions. There are two prevalent, but opposing, ideas that affect how cognition is viewed in the classroom: information processing and ecological psychology. On one hand, information processing theories of cognition emphasise the internal world of pupils. These theories highlight the evolution of pupils' mental states but neglect the role of the external environment during designing and making. On the other hand, ecological psychology theories of cognition tend to de-emphasise the role of mental representations and the computational nature of thinking while highlighting pupils' social and material interactions during designing and making. In this chapter, I discuss the issues arising from these two limiting theories and introduce a new theory, Extended Design Cognition.

Designing is essentially a cognitive activity that is concentrated on gaining a great amount of information. It is driven by a designer's ability to define the design task and find suitable solutions to satisfy the client's and end users' requirements (Alexiou et al., 2009; Eastman, 2001; Visser, 2009). This characterisation of design as a particular type of cognitive activity is rooted in the specific type of problem-solving that occurs during a design process, that is ill-structured problem-solving. During ill-structured problem-solving, designers are goal-driven to address specific design requirements, constraints, and the needs or wants of clients and end users (Archer, 1984). The end result of designing is a detailed specification list, plan or representation of an artefact, procedure, system, or device (Archer, 1984; Brown & Chandrasekharan, 1989). The cognitive activity required to produce a detailed specification involves a dynamic process, starting with a vague conceptual idea leading to a detailed plan for making a product (Kimbell & Stables, 2008; Seitamaa-Hakkarainen et al., 2014; Visser, 2009). Moreover, it is the ability to effectively navigate between the intended design and its

DOI: 10.4324/9781003166689-18

physical embodiment that contributes to the quality of a design solution, especially during the early phases of the design process (Goel, 2014).

Design cognition is acknowledged as the spark of innovative solutions (Martin, 2010). So, if we want designers to rise above mediocrity and become innovative thinkers at the forefront of innovation, we should prepare them accordingly in design and technology (D&T). However, current theories intended to help with understanding and describing design cognition in D&T classrooms are limited in their explanations of the reality of how pupils engage in designing activities.

The purpose of this chapter is to present different viewpoints on designing through the lenses of three different cognitive theories. In the first section, I outline the basic assumptions underpinning an information processing view of designing and how this might play out in classrooms. In the second section, I discuss the ecological psychology view of designing and its implications for classroom practices. In the third section, I share an integrated framework for considering designing through the lens of extended design cognition. I end this chapter by recommending classroom activities to support extended design thinking in D&T.

## Information-processing theories of designing

Until recently, the information-processing view of designing has dominated research into design cognition. During the 1960s, researchers aimed to understand aspects of designing by studying its processes, and methodologies (Cross, 2011). The studies were carried out based on the argument that to design new or innovative products, designers needed an objective and repeatable design process. In doing this, researchers were said to 'scientise' designing into a generic process that all designers could use.

Designing based on information processing has led to the belief that the act of designing is solely dependent on a brain-bound, or internal processor of, information located in the designer's mind (Goel, 2014; Newell & Simon, 1972). In this view, there is a distinction between thought and action – a differentiation between form, the design idea that exists prior to its physical embodiment, and matter, the physical materials that are manipulated and processed to realise the pre-existing design idea. Preston (2013) succinctly summarises this idea as originally found in the works of Aristotle:

> Aristotle suggests that this mental design is finished prior to the production proper, the actual construction. So, for Aristotle, there are two clearly demarcated phases in the overall production process—an antecedent design phase and a subsequent construction phase. Moreover, since all of the thinking is relegated to the design phase, the construction phase must be a matter of unintelligent execution of the step-by-step instructions. Thus, for Aristotle, the real interest of production lies in the mental process of design, not the actual construction process.
>
> (Preston, 2013, p. 18)

This distinction implies that a cognitive dualism exists between designing and making, one that is a result of the division of labour between professionals who design and those who follow instructions to make (Lawson, 2005). In this regard, Dorment (1993) explains that this differentiation dates as far back as the 14th century when weavers were paid less than the designers of the same product. Unfortunately, the implication of this belief still permeates current educational policy whereby school subjects that include making activities are perceived as lower in status compared to academic disciplines such as science and mathematics. One of the reasons for this unbalanced view might be that conventional theories of cognition – information-processing theories – are not very useful in understanding how designers exercise intelligent actions in the world.

Information-processing theories of designing typically only highlight the role of prior knowledge, mental representations, and designers' mental states during designing activities. For example, one model of design learning that emerged during the 1970s was Laxton's (1969) hydroelectric plant metaphor of designing, which he used to promote a three-phase model of design education for children. The initial phase is likened to a reservoir in which pupils should first develop sufficient technological knowledge, skills and values to be engaged in designing. When the reservoir is filled up and pupils have developed sufficient prior knowledge and experiences, they can then skilfully engage in idea exploration and generation, likened to a generator. Finally, once pupils are able to generate initial ideas for their projects, Laxton (1969) argued that they should then develop reflective and critical appraisal skills to interpret and develop their generated ideas in new contexts. So, in essence, Laxton's (1969) model of design education is based on the idea that pupils' success in engaging with designing is based on prior knowledge primarily. He also proposed a linear approach to designing in which pupils engage in mental states of first finding and consolidating information, then generating solutions leading to transforming solutions. This model assumes designing relies on two initial positions – (1) input information sources or prior knowledge and (2) a design opportunity – which are then systematically transformed during a design process into an output design specification, led by the pupils' design intentions. Put simply, this is an information-processing activity which leads to an outcome.

For D&T classrooms, this information-processing view of designing has several implications. First is the planning and execution of linear schemes of work. Teachers might develop schemes of work where most of the instructional time is spent on developing a conceptual understanding of technological principles, concepts, and skills, after which pupils apply this new understanding to a design and make activity. For example, in a six-week scheme of work on structures, weeks 1 to 4, pupils are taught about different types of structures, forces acting on structures, structural members and ways to strengthen structures. Then in weeks 5 to 6, pupils engage in a bridge-building competition, applying their new knowledge about structures. Such a planning approach could support pupils in developing the necessary knowledge, skills, and values to engage in the process of design, albeit with limited autonomy.

Second, an information-processing view of designing implies that teachers could provide pupils with a prescribed sequence of steps to be followed in order to 'complete' a design process, in other words, a set recipe. These activities are typically in the form of a portfolio with open boxes in which pupils have one to two periods to fill in the information related to the design brief, constraints, requirements, initial ideas, and a chosen and justified design concept. Once the empty portfolio boxes are completed, pupils can then start the process of creating their envisaged design ideas, often without any reference to their previous portfolio work that has been completed. This linear approach to the design process reinforces the separation between design ideas and their physical embodiment in materials.

Third, the information-processing view of designing might imply minimal support during idea generation and idea selection activities as teachers might assume that all of the thinking occurs inside the pupils' minds. In these cases, the portfolio is only used as a one-directional communication tool in which pupils offload their thinking to progress to the next phase of designing or making. Often, interaction with external information sources and information sources is avoided during the design phase. So, once pupils start with the making phase of their project, new ideas emerge because of their interactions with physical materials, leading them to abandon their initially developed ideas.

Although the information-processing view of designing emphasises the central role and transformation of knowledge and skills, and the designer's systematic mental states during designing, it does not account for or elaborate on the interaction between the designer and the social and material world. This implies that only designers' knowledge, and the representation of this knowledge in the form of sketches and physical models, is valued and fostered. Plus, because the information-processing theories of designing emphasise designers' mental states and representations, these theories rely on the fact that designers deal with representations of the world rather than dealing with the actual world (Groth, 2016). As such, the interaction between the designer and the social and material world is not considered part of the processes of designing.

We know now that this information-processing model of design education only covers part of what is necessary to understand how pupils engage in design and make activities. Information-processing theories fail to explain the intelligent actions involved when designers are materially and socially engaged. It is based on these limitations that cognitive theories of designing have developed from fields such as ecological psychology.

## Ecological psychology theories of designing

In the 1970s, design theorists started arguing that the available information-processing theories on designing were too restricted to study authentic design behaviour. This was due to such theories viewing thinking as solely occurring on the inside of designers' minds. This narrow view neglected the role of the social and material world in supporting and enhancing thinking processes during designing. As a result, the need for an alternative approach to study designing was continuously emphasised in studies undertaken at the time (Dorst & Dijkhuis, 1995; Schön & Wiggens, 1992; Visser, 2009). Emphasising designers' interactions within their social and material environments, researchers started focusing on theoretical frameworks from an ecological psychology perspective (Bucciarelli, 1988; Schön & Wiggens, 1992). Scholars taking the lead in situated design research during this era include Schön (1983), as well as Bucciarelli (1988), with the latter focusing on designing as a social process. More recent design research has focused on the embodied nature of design thinking (Groth, 2016).

Ecological psychology views design thinking as a mostly external activity, in contrast to information-processing theories. In ecological psychology, design activities are seen in terms of designers' interactions with their social and material environments. These interactions might include activities such as holding, moving, manipulating, gesturing, rearranging, drawing, and constructing, among others. This idea is supported by the concept of 'emergence', which holds that the origin of design ideas and emergent material forms develop from designers' interactions with their external environments (Claxton et al., 2010; Groth, 2016; Lahti et al., 2016). In this way, design cognition can be characterised as the physical activities of perceiving functional information from the external environment and acting on this information to address any identified design opportunities.

According to ecological psychology, our thought processes are embodied, and our sense-making abilities are embedded in the physical and social environment as our interactions in these environments determine what we know and how we come to know (Robbins & Aydede, 2009). In this view, pupils are viewed as intentionally driven information 'detectors' rather than information 'processors'. As information 'detectors', pupils are seen as being able to detect and act on a wide range of useful information sources (Young, 2004). Gibson (1986) explains that information exists in the external environment that is directly available to pupils and does not need to be recalled or applied from their long-term memory. To emphasise the functional value of information in the environment, Gibson (1986) introduces the concept of affordances to explain how perceiving/obtaining information from the physical and social environment provides opportunities for action.

In the design and technology classroom, ecological psychology holds that design thinking emerges when pupils perceive information specified in the social or material environment, and consequently act on this perceived information. Alternatively, while interacting with physical materials, such as sketches or three-dimensional (3D) models, pupils become aware of useful information, which provides opportunities for future actions. In this way, design cognition develops through cycles of action and perception within the social and material environment, where these cycles become a form of sense-making. For example, when generating design ideas through the medium of sketching, pupils' mark-making provides opportunities for perception, which leads to future actions, as illustrated in Figure 14.1.

While sketching their design ideas (Figure 14.1), the pupil did not begin with a clear idea for their design of a lifting machine, whilst sketching and talking, they clarified their design concept. It was their interactions between the social and physical environments that mutually shaped each other.

Ecological psychology has a few implications for teaching and learning in D&T. First, how teachers plan for pupils to use tools, materials, and participate in group work will influence pupils' sense-making processes when designing. For example, Lahti et al. (2016) found that university students' interactions with physical materials supported collaborative idea generation, evaluation, and communication processes. Without these planned activities, the students might not have been able to articulate or reason about their technical and aesthetic design decisions.

Second, ecological psychology theories of cognition typically avoid descriptions of mental phenomena such as representations and prior knowledge about the problem and possible solutions (Kirsh, 2009). This means that ecological psychological theories of designing are less interested in describing how designers' representations of their design ideas develop because, according to this view, designers deal with the actual world, not representations of the world (Groth, 2016). The danger of this view for D&T lies in the fact that teachers might not value or support pupils' development of their own design intentions and mental models. For example, when pupils face difficulties in articulating their design intentions and ideas, they might get distracted by peer conversations or adopt ideas from

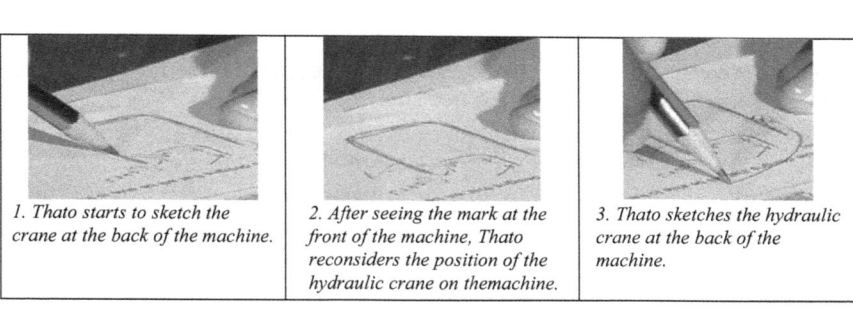

1. Thato starts to sketch the crane at the back of the machine.
2. After seeing the mark at the front of the machine, Thato reconsiders the position of the hydraulic crane on themachine.
3. Thato sketches the hydraulic crane at the back of the machine.

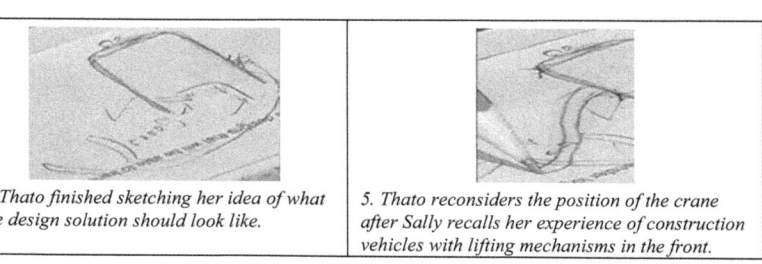

4. Thato finished sketching her idea of what the design solution should look like.
5. Thato reconsiders the position of the crane after Sally recalls her experience of construction vehicles with lifting mechanisms in the front.

*Figure 14.1* Perception and action cycles during sketching.

previous project examples. If teachers do not support or encourage pupils to persist with their design intentions, pupils might lose agency in engaging in designing. The evidence of this loss of agency is often seen during design critiques when pupils engage in evaluating their work at the end of the project when they defend their use of materials, or manufacturing techniques, for example.

Finally, closed-ended projects, where all pupils produce the same outcome (like a Mainly Making activity as described by McLain in Chapter 11), might emphasise interactions in the social and physical environment. However, these projects fail to develop pupils' autonomy in having, growing, and refining their own design ideas. In such projects, it might be valuable for teachers to engage in skill building and affordance recognition, but these projects do not develop pupils' own design ideas. (Read McLain's chapter 'What's so special about D&T?' for a view of when close-ended projects can be useful in D&T.)

Therefore, the issue is these two theories, information processing and ecological psychology, are inadequate to understand pupils' intelligent thought and action during designing activities. Information-processing theory pays specific attention to designers' use of knowledge and mental representations of design ideas but neglects designers' interaction with and use of their material environment. Conversely, ecological psychology theory focuses on the consequences of designers' interactions with, and the influences of, the physical and social environment on design thinking but neglects the role of prior knowledge and mental representations in working on the design opportunity. Because there are deficiencies in these two theories, I think there is a need for a third way – an integrated view of cognition – Extended Design Cognition Theory. There are other frameworks for design cognition: embedded, embodied, enacted, extended, and distributed cognition, with embodied cognition being the most frequently adopted (Robbins & Aydede, 2009) but, in my opinion, these do not satisfactorily explain design cognition, like the two I have already analysed.

## Towards an extended design cognition approach in D&T

Extended Cognition Theory is based on the extended mind thesis (Clark, 2008; Clark & Chalmers, 2010), and developed from situated cognition (Robbins & Aydede, 2009) and distributed cognition theories (Ball & Christensen, 2018; Hutchins, 2014). This theory pays equal attention to the internal and external factors involved in design cognition; in other words, Extended Cognition Theory rejects exclusive internalist or externalist theories of cognition in favour of an integrated model of cognition. Extended Cognition Theory has recently been used in design contexts to study designing activities in professional and school-based contexts (Blom & Bogaers, 2020; Haupt, 2015; Haupt & Webber-Youngman, 2018). When it comes to studying the cognitive activities of designers, Extended Cognition Theory holds that thinking extends beyond designers' minds and bodies into the social and physical environment. As a result of this extension, designers can then perform cognitive acts, such as remembering, ideating, reflecting, or critiquing more efficiently than if they only relied on their minds alone (Heersmink, 2017; Menary & Gillet, 2017; Trybulec, 2015).

Menary (2012) provides a typology of three different types of cognitive actions that require interaction between internal and external factors. First, at a very basic level, is cognitive outsourcing. In terms of designing in schools, this implies that a pupil might get someone or something that does the cognitive act for them, for example asking someone for an answer to a question or using a calculator to calculate the area of a piece of material needed for a project or rotating an object in a CAD (Computer-Aided Design) environment rather than using their own mental rotation faculty.

Second is the process of physically offloading complexity to save on the cost/time of internal information processing. For example, when pupils annotate their design ideas, they offload their descriptions and justifications for their design choices on a piece of paper. Doing so frees up their working memory and avoids cognitive overload, supporting them to look for missing information or to determine future actions. When working memory is freed up, pupils are supported to look at their design ideas from a different perspective.

Third is enculturated cognitive actions, which refers to the way in which the body manipulates external resources, such as artefacts, tools, written words, sketches, 3D models, and number systems. Menary (2012) qualifies that these tools and representational systems are not merely externalisations of internal ideas but that they are active components embedded in historical and current cultural practices. When these representations are used by pupils, their cognitive actions cross from the world into their minds, and it can be said that their cognitive abilities are enculturated. This means that they get to be readers and writers, drawers, and modellers and creators by a process of transforming existing cognitive abilities to perform new, cultural functions. In this way, when exploring design contexts, generating ideas, and developing ideas, pupils' use, and manipulation, of external representations shapes how they process information about their design context and provides opportunities for subsequent design decisions.

Menary and Gillet (2017) further elaborate on the concept of generating and manipulating representations by indicating six types of cognitive practices that can be used during extended cognition: biological coupling; corrective practices; epistemic practices; epistemic tools; representational systems; and blended practices. I contextualise these cognitive practices in terms of D&T classrooms.

*Biological coupling* refers to pupils' direct sensory–motor interactions with the learning environment. These interactions are facilitated by means of perception–action mechanisms where direct perceptual input from the environment reciprocally causes action, which then directly feeds into further perception and more action. For example, during designing, pupils are biologically coupled with external information sources, such as sketches, where each mark made on paper may facilitate further thoughts and action.

*Corrective practices* relate to pupils' abilities to correct their own thinking and doing while working in the environment. Pupils can use any representational means as a corrective tool, and say, for example, "That didn't work, so I'll try this," when using speech as a corrective tool. This supports them to correct their thoughts and actions as they work on the design idea. Alternatively, while pupils are using cardboard to model design ideas, they can dynamically adapt their mental representation of their design idea using the actual physical form in their hands. Corrective practices commonly occur during, and because of, verbal or visual interactions with peers or objects when pupils are busy with a design task.

Next, *epistemic practices* relate to pupils' actions, which could simplify cognitive processing by using the environment. Pupils can, for example, use rulers, calculators, pen-and-paper activities, and computers to support or augment their cognitive processing. Also, pupils could use CAD software to mentally rotate their design idea. Some pupils might have limited spatial abilities to do this on their own and lose information while they are rotating their design idea in their mind's eye. However, through the use of CAD software, they retain information about their design idea as the information is captured in the software.

*Representational systems* relate to the creation, adoption or adaptation of representations during complex cognitive tasks. For example, pupils might use diagrams such as a Gantt chart as part of their planning cycle, which can in turn result in enhanced thinking about the completion of their design task. In D&T, pupils are encouraged to use various representational systems to think, including numerical, digital, verbal, visual, and textual systems. Using these different representational systems allows pupils to dynamically engage with their internal and external worlds during designing.

Finally, *blended practices* involve the combination of different cognitive practices in cycles of information processing. For example, during design tasks, pupils may call on the manipulation of tools in conjunction with the use of representational systems to plan and specify the dimensions of their design idea.

In summary then, extended design cognition accounts for and could be used to describe a pupil's developing interaction with perceived and functional information in the social and material environment. Extended design cognition could also assist in the development of pupils' mental representations and knowledge structures related to their design opportunity.

## An example of an extended design cognition activity

### *Using sticky notes to make sense of research findings*

After pupils have researched a specific user, teachers could encourage them to use sticky notes to capture key observations and insights from their research findings. The pupils could then start their process by writing down or making drawings on sticky notes, offloading their thoughts physically. In this way, the burden of trying to remember all of the key findings is alleviated. Once their thoughts are captured on the sticky notes, the pupils can now read through the individual sticky notes to make sense of the data. When pupils are familiar with their findings, they will be able to identify emergent themes while they physically rearrange the sticky notes according to similarities and differences, creating emergent themes and insights that would allow them to generate user requirements for their design task.

In this way, the pupils are engaged in a complex sequence of iterated interactions with the sticky notes that, in conjunction with their reflective and evaluative thought processes, serve to systematically restructure and refine a preliminary set of initial thoughts about their user into specific user requirements. This example of using sticky notes highlights the importance of external tools in shaping, augmenting and guiding design thinking. As such, this activity supports Extended Design Cognition Theory in that external resources do not only aid in supporting cognition, but they also constitute and form part of the cognitive processes. However, it is also necessary to mention that if we want to foster extended thinking with sticky notes, pupils should be made aware of how these can be returned to and reused through various stages of the design process to support extended thinking. Without this understanding, pupils might only use sticky notes as cognitive offloading devices without realising their potential to help extend their cognition.

## Conclusion

In this chapter, I have discussed current theories for describing design cognition in both professional and school-based design practice. I argued that both theories are limited in their explanatory power when considering how pupils engage in design thinking. Consequently, I have proposed the use of Extended Design Cognition Theory as a suitable alternative to current theories of cognition. For D&T teachers, an understanding of extended design cognition may foster a deeper understanding of our instructional choices in how we support internal and external cognitive processes. If we want pupils to optimally develop how they grow and develop their design ideas, current and future D&T teachers need to design and provide meaningful learning environments in which both internal and external thought processes can be fostered and developed. Failure to provide this support during design tasks could inhibit pupils' development of proficient design skills that are valued and needed to succeed in the world of work.

## Questions

1 How could you incorporate practices that would encourage students to use a balance of internal and external resources to support their design and making activities?
2 In what ways does the curriculum support or prevent the use of extended design cognition?

3 Assessment often dictates how D&T is taught in classrooms. In what ways can Extended Design Cognition Theory positively change the ways in which we assess D&T?
4 How do theories of learning D&T impact the way in which you teach? In what ways could Extended Design Cognition Theory impact on your pedagogy?

## References

Alexiou, K., Zamenopoulos, T., Johnson, J. H., & Gilbert, S. J. (2009). Exploring the neurological basis of design cognition using brain imaging: Some preliminary results. *Design Studies*, 30, 623–647.

Archer, L. B. (1984). Systematic method for designers. In N. Cross (Ed.), *Developments in Design Methodology* (pp. 57–82). John Wiley & Son Ltd.

Ball, L. J., & Christensen, B. T. (2018). Designing in the wild. *Design Studies*, 57, 1–8. doi:10.1016/J.DESTUD.2018.05.001

Blom, N., & Bogaers, A. (2020). Using Linkography to investigate studnets' thinking and information use during a STEM task. *International Journal of Technology and Design Education*, 30, 1–20.

Brown, D. C., & Chandrasekharan, B. (1989). *Design problem solving: Knowledge structures and control strategies*. Morgan Kaufman.

Bucciarelli, L. (1988). An Ethnographic perspective on engineering design. *Design Studies*, 9(3), 159–168.

Clark, A. (2008). *Supersizing the mind: Embodiment, action, and cognitive extension*. Oxford University Press.

Clark, A., & Chalmers, D. (2010). The Extended Mind. In R. Menary (Ed.), *The extended mind* (pp. 27–42). MIT Press.

Claxton, G., Lucas, B., & Webster, R. (2010). *Bodies of knowledge: How the learning sciences could transform practical and vocational education*. Edge Foundation.

Cross, N. (2011). *Design thinking: Understanding how designers think and work*. Berg Publishers.

Dorment, P. (1993). What is a designer? In P. Dormer (Ed.), *Design since 1945* (pp. 9–31). Thames and Hudson.

Dorst, K., & Dijkhuis, J. (1995). Comparing paradigms for describing design activity. *Design Studies*, 16(2), 261–274.

Eastman, C. (2001). New directions in design cognition: Studies of representation and recall. In C. Eastman & M. McCracken (Eds.), *Design knowing and learning: Cognition in design education* (pp. 269–297). Elsevier.

Gibson, J. J. (1986). *The ecological approach to perception*. Lawrence Erlbaum Associates.

Goel, V. (2014). Creative brains: Designing in the real world. *Frontiers in Human Neuroscience*, 8, 1–14. doi:10.3389/fnhum.2014.00241

Groth, C. (2016). Design-and craft thinking analysed as embodied cognition. *Research Journal of Design and Design Education*, 9(1), 1–21. doi:10.7577/formakademisk.1481

Haupt, G. (2015). Learning from experts: Fostering extended thinking in the early phases of the design process. *International Journal of Technology and Design Education*, 25(4), 483–520. doi:10.1007/s10798-014-9295-7

Haupt, G., & Webber-Youngman, R. C. W. (2018). Engineering education: An integrated problem-solving framework for discipline-specific professional development in mining engineering. *Journal of the Southern African Institute of Mining and Metallurgy*, 118(1), 27–37. doi:10.17159/2411-9717/2018/v118n1a4

Heersmink, R. (2017). Distributed selves: Personal identity and extended memory systems. *Synthese*, 194, 3135–3151.

Hutchins, E. (2014). The cultural ecosystem of human cognition. *Philosophical Psychology*, 27(1), 34–49.

Kimbell, R., & Stables, K. (2008). *Researching design learning*. Springer.

Kirsh, D. (2009). Problem solving and situated cognition. In P. Robbins & M. Aydede (Eds.), *The Cambridge handbook of situated cognition* (pp. 264–306). Cambridge University Press.

Lahti, H., Kangas, K., Koponen, V., & Seitamaa-Hakkarainen, P. (2016). Material mediation and embodied actions in collaborative design process. *Techne Series*, 23(1), 15–29.

Lawson, B. (2005). *How designers think: The design process demystified* (4th ed.). Architectural Press.

Laxton, M. (1969). Design education in practice. In K. Baynes (Ed.), *Attitudes in design education* (85–124). Lund Humphries.

Martin, R. (2010). Design thinking: Achieving insights via the knowledge funnel. *Strategy and Leadership*, 38(2), 37–41.

Menary, R. (2012). Cognitive practices and cognitive character. *Philosophical Explorations*, 15(2), 147–164.

Menary, R., & Gillet, A. J. (2017). Embodying culture. In J. Kiverstein (Ed.), *The Routledge handbook of philosophy of the social mind* (pp. 72–87). Routledge.

Newell, A., & Simon, H. (1972). *Human problem solving*. Prentice-Hall.

Preston, B. (2013). *A philosophy of material culture: action, function, and mind*. Routledge.

Robbins, P., & Aydede, M. (2009). A Short primer on situated cognition. In P. Robbins & M. Aydede (Eds.), *The Cambridge handbook of situated cognition* (pp. 3–10). Cambridge University Press.

Schön, D. (1983). *The reflective practitioner*. Temple-Smith.

Schön, D., & Wiggens, A. (1992). Kinds of seeing in designing. *Creativity and Innovation Management*, 1(2), 68–74.

Seitamaa-Hakkarainen, P., Huotilainen, M., Mäkelä, M., Groth, C., & Hakkarainen, K. (2014). The promise of cognitive neuroscience in design studies. In Lim, Y., Niedderer, K., Redström, J., Stolterman, E., & Valtonen, A. (Eds.), *Design's Big Debates - DRS International Conference 2014* (pp. 834–846). 16–19 June, Umeå, Sweden. https://dl.designresearchsociety.org/drs-conference-papers/drs2014/researchpapers/62

Trybulec, B. (2015). Extended cognitive system and epistemic subject. *Studies in Logic Grammar, and Rhetoric*, 40, 111–128.

Visser, W. (2009). Design: one, but in different forms. *Design Studies*, 30(3), 187–223.

Young, M. F. (2004). An ecological psychology of instructional design: Learning and thinking by perceiving-acting systems. In D. H. Jonassen (Ed.), *Handbook of research for educational communications and technology* (pp. 169–177). Lawrence Erlbaum.

# 15 A hybrid design sketching approach that can drive critical thinking in design and technology

*Yaone Rapitsenyane, Richie Moalosi, and Thatayaone Mosepedi*

## Introduction

In any design programme, sketching is a very crucial tool to support critical thinking, communication, creativity and expression of thoughts and ideas. Sketching supports the cognitive modelling activity that allows translation of human creative thinking, supported by certain creative behaviours to achieve the desired needs (Goldschmidt, 2014). Manual design sketching is still widely taught in primary, secondary and design schools (universities) and intensively used in industry because of its flexibility in supporting the creative process and quick visual communication of thoughts. As design sketching technology is being developed to use tools such as Sketchbook Pro and taken up in mainstream education, the future-scape for design sketching should be defined in design and technology education so that advantages of the traditional pen-and-paper approach are not lost. The discussions about the future of design sketching should be centred on whether manual sketching is a thing of the past or it is still necessary for design education and design practice. The processes involved in developing a sketch contribute immensely to enhancing critical thinking skills in students.

The discussions about the future of design sketching should highlight how benefits of manual sketching such as critical thinking will be developed and sustained. Critical thinking is the ability to objectively think clearly and rationally about a process of actively and skillfully conceptualising, applying, analysing, synthesising, and evaluating information gathered from, or generated by, observation, experience, reflection, reasoning, or communication, as a guide to belief and action (Lenin, 2019). It may involve inductive and deductive reasoning, analysis and problem-solving, as well as creative, innovative, and complex approaches to the resolution of challenges (Lenin, 2019). Critical thinking comprises cognitive skills and dispositions. The dispositions can be viewed as attitudes or habits of mind, open and fair-mindedness, inquisitiveness, flexibility, a propensity to seek reason, a desire to be well informed, and a respect for and willingness to entertain diverse viewpoints (Murawski, 2014).

DOI: 10.4324/9781003166689-19

Sketching combines several cognitive processes such as attention, perception, learning, remembering, communicating, problem-solving, reasoning, and thinking at different levels of application. Sketching practices and experiences from students can effectively inform practices for pupils and ensure consistency in academic attainment and motivation after the transition to universities. Problem-based learning approaches to teaching sketching are effective to enhance students sketching skills but require constant practice (Booth et al., 2016). Permanent sketching behaviour change should be effected by regular exercising of complex skills, such as perspective sketching, since perspective sketching can temporarily increase sketching inhibition. Regular exercising reduces inhibition to sketching when breaking down such complex skills. The cognitive demands of sketching require calmness of mind, thus the need for warm-up activities to help reduce inhibition. Art-based warm-up activities are effective in reducing sketch inhibition (Hu, Booth & Reid, 2015). These warm-up activities are aimed at instilling discipline, focus, and skill building, often improving the speed and accuracy of sketching an object. The difficulty levels of the warm-up actitivities vary so that learners' interest and participation are maintained. Examples of such exercises include "The Random Warm-Up", "The Duplication Warm-Up", "The Matching Warm-Up", The Mirror Imaging Warm-Up", and "The Abstract Design Warm-Up" (Brookes, 1996).

Sketching has been the nucleus of ideas conceptualisation for centuries, with its origins detected in the late 15th century (Goldschmidt, 1999). It is a critical way through which design iteration and concept generation are transferred from the cognitive realms to a visual form which is a major part of design pedagogy (Oxman, 2008). According to Oxman (2008), sketches can be described as behavioural responses to visual–mental processes, which can be observed and interpreted. Sketching in this case is viewed as a mental process which is a crucial cognitive process of reasoning between the design problem and its potential solution. In the digital age, the role of the sketch has taken new forms. However, sketches still work as a mediator between people who create new designs. This communication is no longer only paper-based but somewhere in between paper and digital platforms through an intuitive combination of the two. This is called hybrid sketching. Hybrid sketching is the dynamic combination of traditional pen-and-paper and digital sketching that can contribute to new creative processes in interesting fresh ways. It is against this background that this chapter discusses hybrid sketching and its benefits to students, elements of critical thinking, and how they are of benefit to hybrid sketching, the research method used in the study, its findings, discussion, implications for schools, and conclusions. Issues discussed throughout this chapter empahsise defining a future-scape for design sketching as the main debate. The context of this debate is hybrid sketching, as a place for both manual sketching and digital sketching in order to maintain the benefits of the traditional pen-and-paper sketching in an era of digital influence.

Sketching is mostly used at the early stages of the creative process when designs are vague, fluid, and details scarce. It is usually done as preparation, planning, and idea generation, for another subsequent design activity. It helps to make abstract ideas and promising designs more concrete (Cook & Agah, 2009). Sketches can be made rapidly and simply with basic hand tools. Thus, sketches are typically rough in appearance, messy and at times disorganised. This reflects the creative mental process a sketch represents and drives the design thinking process from a vague notion of a developed concept. Cook and Agah (2009) argue that there are three mental components of traditional paper-and-pencil sketching which are the students' principal means of critical thinking:

- Feedback – As a student sketches, they constantly see the results of each stroke of the pencil and reinterpret the visual image on paper, relating it with their mental concept. The student can make improvements to the sketch to bring it closer to their mental image. The student also uses these differences to update their mental image, try new concepts or flesh out areas that were not yet concrete.
- Physical technique of the student (overdrawing/re-sketching) – In this mental process, the student steadily adds new marks over previously drawn images, building up and emphasising some elements of a sketch while de-emphasising others. This overdrawing gives sketches their characteristic sketchy appearance and allows the student to change the drawing just as feedback changes their mental image.
- Incremental refinement – This process can be summed up by the saying "Work from the macroscopic to the microscopic" (Cook & Agah, 2009). As the sketch is gradually being developed the student begins with simple shapes and wide ideas which are then polished through experimentation and exploration into more concrete and detailed descriptions.

The physical activity and mental processes related to sketching form the basis of problem-solving, development, creative, and critical thinking processes. The movement of pen and paper at the same time with forming mental images of what to put down next, is an important combination for problem-solving and development of very strong psychomotor skills needed for a designer career. There is a lack of knowledge about how a sketch can be used as a strategy to increase participation and collaboration in critical thinking and the creative design processes (Berg, 2018). Two or more students can be cooperatively engaged in the learning process through a sketch by analysing its composition and the techniques that were used for profuding the sketch. From building this understanding, the processes and techniques in the sketch can then be repeated and transferred into sketching a different product. This is a very important benefit of hybrid sketching. Hybrid sketches contribute to a shared understanding amongst students and their users.

In the digital age, sketches are still a significant tool for displaying ideas in terms of coordination, cooperation, and collaboration (Lahti, Seitamaa-Hakkarainen & Hakkarainen, 2004). Sketching as an engaging activity stimulates dialogue and feedback from different people meant to consume the sketch. Digitally produced sketches with tools such as Sketchbook Pro can be quickly shared with others to stimulate interactions and actively involve the students in the processes of thinking, reasoning, analysing, and building common understanding. Students use sketches to clarify their ideas as they can be done quickly to show an idea and its visual representation. Evans and Aldoy (2016) argue that digitisation has opened new possibilities to support students' sketching capability by increasing their confidence. Students can be stimulated and excited by computer tools, and this can have a good impact on the conceptualisation phase as well as in the critical thinking and creative thinking processes.

## How hybrid sketching works

Hybrid sketching is an effective approach to making various alternatives to proposed designs with a digital approach, where surfacing (applying any type of artwork such as a pattern or an illustration on a surface to enhance its functionality or visual appearance) quickly gives a more realistic expression, and this can be highly motivating for critical thinking and creative thinking processes (Evans & Aldoy, 2016). In hybrid sketching, a sketch produced from pen and paper is transferred to a digital tool such as Adobe Photoshop or Adobe Illustrator before further development. This is usually done to (a) improve the intent of the sketch where the student is still developing manual sketching skills and (b) to enhance communication of pen-and-paper sketches by giving them a photorealistic look and feel. Adding details that have gone through a critical thinking process to sketches adds life to a sketched idea. The details may emphasise the context of use by showing the surrounding environment or exaggerate interaction sequences that may be easy to miss if the sketch was left in its pen-and-paper form (Berg, 2018). This usually results in the creation of beautiful, powerful, and enlightening hybrid images. Hybrid sketching encourages experimental, experiential, informative sketching and learning as well as helps alleviate students' frustration, fear of failure, and a desire for perfection (Yost, 2015). This is the contention for hybrid sketching in the discussions of this chapter, as the drive towards digitisation becomes inevitable. Students gain confidence, proficiency, willingness, and the desire to experiment.

Hybrid sketching enables students to ideate quickly and freely, particularly in the early stages of the design process, and offer emotive, atmospheric, and temporal qualities which are often difficult to express in a more traditional sketching context (Yost, 2015). It builds on students' existing skill sets of the anatomy of a sketch and a sketch page while challenging them to pursue new representation abilities such as higher-order thinking skills. Yost (2015) advances that hybrid sketching is often simplistic and easily understood, it is a great way to test ideas quickly, challenging for both those with strong graphic skills and for those who are just learning. It bridges the perceived gap between analogue and digital media platforms, and students' internal motivation increases if they are given the freedom and skills to envision, represent, explore, and learn on their own, and switching between the two media is extremely empowering and opens an opportunity for students to express themselves.

## Critical thinking and benefits to hybrid sketching

Preparing students to be critical thinkers is one of the significant goals for any design programme. Educational reforms are often undertaken to incorporate certain competencies into the national curricula. One of the important competencies of the 21st century is critical thinking, which composes of analytical, communication, creative, open-minded and problem-solving skills. In design education, these skills can be supported by various tools – manual and digital sketching, often with a balanced combination of both. Design sketching is one such tool that holistically supports critical thinking and creativity.

The World Economic Forum (2020) identified critical thinking as one of several learning and innovation skills necessary to prepare students for postsecondary education and the workforce. The National Association of Colleges and Employers (NACE; 2018) also indicated that critical thinking/problem-solving skills were ranked amongst the most important skills needed by the 144 surveyed employers in the United States. The three highest levels – analysis, synthesis, and evaluation in Bloom's taxonomy may be viewed to represent critical thinking. Critical thinking is a metacognitive skill – it is a higher-level cognitive skill that involves thinking about thinking (Hitchcock, 2020; Ruggiero, 2012).

Critical thinking occurs when students are analysing, evaluating, interpreting, or synthesising information and applying creative thought to form an argument, solve a problem, or reach an objective conclusion (Lenin, 2019). These processes occur when students conceive a sketch, put it on paper, and further improve their understanding of it by continuous evaluation and creative communication through the use of various tools. Critical thinking aims to promote independent thinking, personal autonomy and reasoned judgement in thought and action. This is an essential contribution during brainstorming sessions as students share ideas and make decisions on how to progress them forward. Therefore, critical thinking should be taught to assist students to try to maintain an 'objective' position or careful goal-directed thinking (Hitchcock, 2020). In design, critical thinking is reduced to the four basic cognitive operations of generation, exploration, comparison and selection, which are applied to the goal and solution spaces in various combinations (Stempfle & Badke-Schaub, 2002). When a person thinks critically, they weigh all sides of an argument and evaluate its strengths and weaknesses to reach an objective decision.

## Elements of critical thinking in sketching

The key elements of critical thinking involved in the following skills (Lai, 2011; Lenin, 2019):

- Analytical thinking – the ability to analyse information is the most significant aspect of critical thinking. It entails not only gathering information and interpreting it but also critically evaluating the data. The sketching process begins with looking for inspiration and exhausting how to translate it into something new.
- Good communication – is essential to convince others that the conclusions reached are correct. This is dependent on the quality of the resultant sketch with non-ambiguous attention to detail.
- Creative thinking – the ability to discover certain patterns of information and make abstract connections between seemingly unrelated data improves one's critical thinking. Creativity and critical thinking are aspects of good, purposeful thinking (Lai, 2011). Creativity is the heart of every design work, often resulting in innovative ideas.
- Open-mindedness – one's previous education and life experiences influence one's ability to objectively evaluate certain situations. Acknowledging any biases enables one to improve critical thinking and the ability to make concrete decisions. In sketching, being open-minded breaks mental blocks and preconceived ideas.
- Ability to solve problems – the ability to correctly analyse a problem, work on alternative solutions and implement a solution is another valuable skill in critical thinking. Hybrid sketching is purposeful since it is usually part of the problem-solving process. It is a critical part of the communication of the thinking process to users.
- Self-evaluation and reflection – evaluating one's contribution or thought process when making certain decisions assists in discovering new ways of solving a problem and improves one's performance. Critical thinking provides the tools for the process of self-evaluation which can be applied effectively as the sketch evolves.

## Components that improve critical thinking

Critical thinking can be improved in students through theory, practice, and attitude:

- Theory – background knowledge is essential if students are to demonstrate their critical thinking skills (Lai, 2011). For one to think properly, the correct rules of reasoning have to be followed. Knowledge of theory includes knowledge of rules involved in sketching, interpreting a sketch, types of sketches, and levels of detailing in a sketch. Questioning is the cornerstone of critical thinking which in turn is the source of knowledge

formation and as such should be taught as a framework for all learning (Lenin, 2019). These are the essential values of critical thinking to be applied during sketching.
- Practice – knowing the principles that distinguish good and bad reasoning is not enough. There is a need to apply theoretical knowledge through constant practice. For one to be good at critical thinking skills, it is essential to adopt theoretical principles so that they can be applied in daily life. This is how hybrid sketching develops – through constant and continuous practice until the skill can be done unconsciously. One needs to do a lot of good-quality exercises of sketching tutorials, designing, discussion, and debates with other students. Furthermore, one has to make connections between related and unrelated ideas.
- Attitudes – apart from knowledge and practice, good critical thinking skills require persistent practice because it can bring about improvements only if one has the right motivation and attitude. The right attitude towards hybrid sketching will support the acquisition of the skill and the competency thereof. One should engage in debates, break away from old habits, and abstract concepts to the reality of learning how to sketch dynamically.

In constructing assessments of critical thinking, educators should use open-ended tasks, real-world or authentic problem contexts, and ill-structured problems that require students to go beyond recalling or restating previously learned information (Lai, 2011). The problem-based learning approach to education, facilitate acquiring critical thinking skills. A real-life scenario of a product that needs to be redesigned can be given to students. In the conceptualisation phase, students will need to bring in their knowledge of how the approach they need for such a product (reasoning and questioning), demonstrate their level of practising the skill and competency demonstrated by the quality of the work (attitude supporting the acquisition of the skill).

Finally, creativity requires the ability to critically evaluate intellectual products, and critical thinking requires the open-mindedness and flexibility that are characteristic of creative thinking. If educators are to be successful in encouraging the development of critical thinking skills through sketching, explicit instruction in critical thinking needs to be included in the sketching curriculum, through infusion into subject-matter content, for example through hybrid sketching. Solving any problem creatively, offering unique insights for potential solutions, demands the ability to be able to think critically, and it also requires that students have confidence in their ability to do so (Changwong, Sukkamart & Sisan, 2018). In-class sketching exercises should then be supported by real-life problem-solving engagements putting emphasis on the exploration of ideas so that creativity and related critical thinking skills such as reasoning and questioning, practice and attitude towards the sketching skill are developed.

## Hybrid sketching teaching strategies

The commonly used approach to teaching design sketching is the design studio. The studio approach enhances learning by integrating theory and practise through active learning (Wrenn & Wrenn, 2009). Active learning involves organising teaching and learning activities in a manner in which students are doing some tasks and thinking about what they are doing. In a studio, the theory is implemented and the instruction is critical analysis focused, demanding a 'Learning-by-Doing' approach. This is a complex undertaking of considering the simultaneous effects of cognitive, affective, motivational, and developmental factors in students' learning experience (Shuell, 2010). The overall sketching experience involves practising principles and the anatomy of a sketch, different approaches to sketching various products from simple to complex and basic to organic forms. In the same way that these skills are practised with pen and paper, various tools are explored to do the same digitally so that the intended communication is not distorted. This often involves transitioning from sketching with pen and paper, scanning the drawing, transferring them onto a digital platform, preparing the canvas, and exploring with various tools in the software used to achieve various sketch effects. A very popular image editing software such as Adobe Photoshop is exploited to demonstrate its intuitiveness in design sketching.

## Integrating hybrid sketching into a design course

The Department of Industrial Design and Technology at the University of Botswana, Botswana has recently revised its two undergraduate programmes – Bachelor of Industrial Design and Bachelor and Design and Technology Education to meet the needs of various stakeholders. The revised programmes have been designed in such a way that they reflect the quality demonstrated at an exceptionally high standard in terms of transformation, fitness for purpose, value for money, and evaluated against customer satisfaction. Given that the design industry is still at its infancy in Botswana, it is important to build sound design practice skills such as sketching. To this regard, there are courses in the programmes which specifically address sketching and related skills. One of the courses, called Product Styling, comes after the manual sketching (pen-and-paper) and digital rendering (Adobe Photoshop) courses. This section shares, as a case study, experiences from the course, demonstrating how hybrid sketching enhanced creatvitiy and critical thinking in design students.

The course was structured to include integrated theory techniques in a problem-based learning design studio environment (Nilson, 2010; Wrenn & Wrenn, 2009). During the introduction of the course, the project aims and objectives and a design task were launched to enlighten students on what was expected of them. In the first four weeks of the course, creative sketching techniques such as mashed-up aesthetics were taught and practised with the students. *Mashed-up* is a term used to describe the method of using software that manipulates images such as Adobe Photoshop, to create combinations of characters for film or television and media celebrities. The process was also used to create visual predictions of new automobile models. In design, mashed-up aesthetics is a trend for reusing and reinterpreting existing designs from different eras, groups, and disciplines by putting them together to create novel design directions. This was followed by digital rendering techniques of the sketches from the mashed aesthetics sketching studio exercises. With a prerequisite knowledge about sketching and rendering for product styling, the students were able to undertake the semester-long project. To kick start the ideation process, students started the creative process by forcing together unrelated two-dimensional images to create a form of the product to style (Figures 15.1a and b). The design brief wanted students to design and style a communication device for a target user group of their choice.

This was the beginning of the idea generation for the development of the product form. It was this mashed-up image that idea generation started. After several iterations of sketching and foam modelling, the final designs were scanned in an A3 scanner and processed digitally in Adobe Photoshop. The deliverables were a design folio demonstrating iterations of the design in manual sketches and a digitally processed photorealistic image of the final design in Adobe Photoshop.

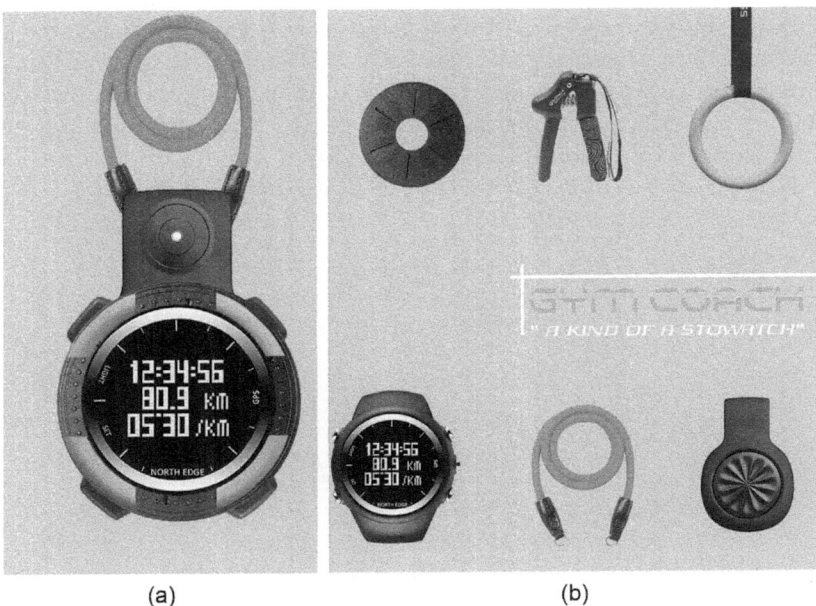

*Figure 15.1* (a) Mashed-up aesthetics. (b) Unrelated images used in the mashed-up form.

## A hybrid sketching model

The results of the case study shared in this chapter show that although digital platforms continue to make design sketching sophisticated and adaptable to the 21st-century digital learner, key cognitive development of critical thinking still benefits from the coordination of the mind and hand from the pen-and-paper approach. This benefit is further enhanced by carefully using both manual and digital sketching approaches, implying that a hybrid model of sketching is the future. The study established that an interplay between the art-based warm-up exercises, manual sketching and digital manipulation of manually produced sketches should be established as demonstrated in Figure 15.2.

Figure 15.2 suggests that art-based exercises can be used as and when needed between the sketching activities and digitisation of manually developed sketches. Using these exercises together will build confidence in both manual sketching and digital sketching tasks and introduce related tools and methods. Working across manual sketching and digitisation of manually drawn sketches should also be kept fluid to allow the development of critical thinking skills to improve the design in the process of digitisation.

### *The ability to create a form*

Following the demonstrations and exercises on mash-up aesthetics, students were able to create their inspirations to drive their form development. Generally, most students were able to define the overall form of the products and positions of key features. However, the level of detail in the mash-ups was low. This was expected as the students were doing the exercise for the first time. Very diverse ideas resulted from this approach as there was no restriction as to what to mash up and how to do it. Students followed their intuition and critical thinking skills to address the design brief and progressively developed the form (Figure 15.3).

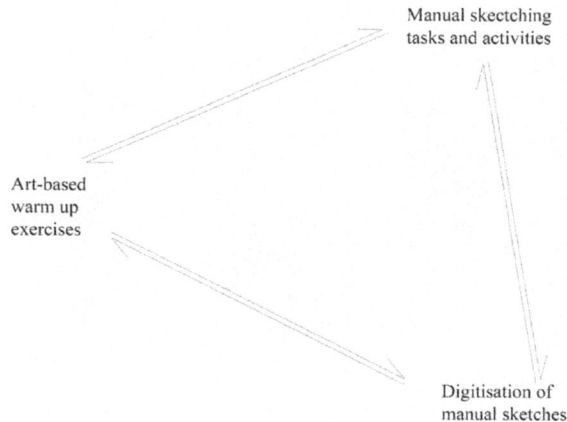

*Figure 15.2* A proposed hybrid sketching model.

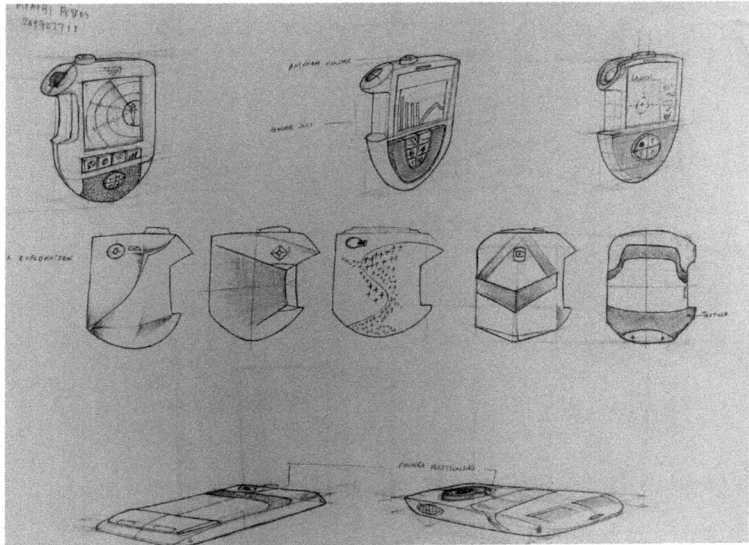

*Figure 15.3* Form development of a communication device for a ranger.

## The ability to visualise form development

This mash-up concept adequately stimulated critical thinking for the students as they displayed some highly creative forms. The subsequent sketches resembled the hallmarks of the mashed-up form, these coincided with what was reiterated by Yang (2009): that the quality of a sketch is dependent on the tool used to generate the idea. Students displayed visual design creativity and brilliance at varying levels as they were able to explore the mash-up form. They, however, showed a wobbly but profound visual creativity as they were able to harness the visual language of the product of their choice without losing the initial inspiration of form triggered by the mash-up technique (Figure 15.4). Most students displayed an average to very good command of the application of sketching techniques and critical thinking skills when sketching organic or complex forms, use of different line weights, setting up and the choice of the right perspective, and the use of sketching enhancements.

## The ability to communicate the created form

The ability to communicate the created form depended on the degree of the level of detail and the level of development that can be put on the sketches. The level of details displayed on the workpieces which, in most cases, was used to measure the quality of a workpiece and its semantics demonstrated a sense of appreciation of the styling language in communicating the created form. The level of detail of their work, which can be thought of as an input to the aforementioned elements showed that they have grasped how to communicate the visual language of the brands they were styling for. However,

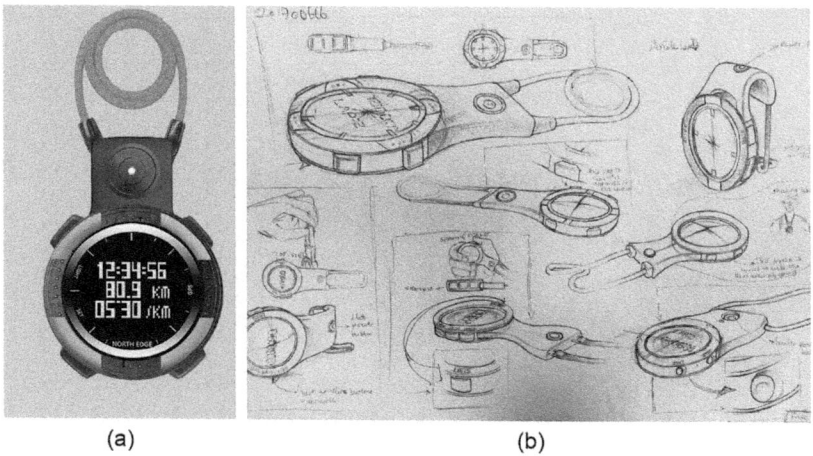

(a)  (b)

*Figure 15.4* (a) Mash-up. (b) Visual creativity inspired by the mash-up.

the work still requires more practice for them to be able to adequately demonstrate the flow of thoughts which is not limited by learning how to express themselves.

### *The ability to enhance the created form and pronounce diversity*

Students explored and manipulated the use of Adobe Photoshop to enhance their work and give it a photorealistic impression. This enabled students to better visualise and communicate their work. Sketching was used as a designing tool while rendering (adding detail such as colour, contours, and the behaviour of the product under lighting) was used as a communication tool. The learners displayed an insightful aptitude to digitally enhance their sketches as the majority of them presented work with a good balance of rendering considerations for digital manipulation of bitmap images (Figure 15.5). However, almost half of them did not display a good intuition in using Adobe Photoshop tools to develop their renderings. Most of the renderings still appeared primitive and unpolished, which suggests that they had not yet reached a good level of proficiency with the use of tools in the digital platform. However, digital rendering showed an advantage in some poorly developed manual sketches (Figure 15.5c). This gave students a second chance to correct some aspects of their sketches, such as the accuracy of ellipses, the accuracy of the perspective and the level of detail in defining product features. The result was good quality renderings (Figure 15.5) which, in some cases, were very much divorced from the manual sketch.

A summary of the thought process was then captured in four presentation boards for display in Figure 15.6. In Figure 15.6, the sequence of the images shows the thought process from top left with the mash-up to top right (sketches), bottom left (the hybrid), and bottom right (evidence of the influence of the mash-up on the final design).

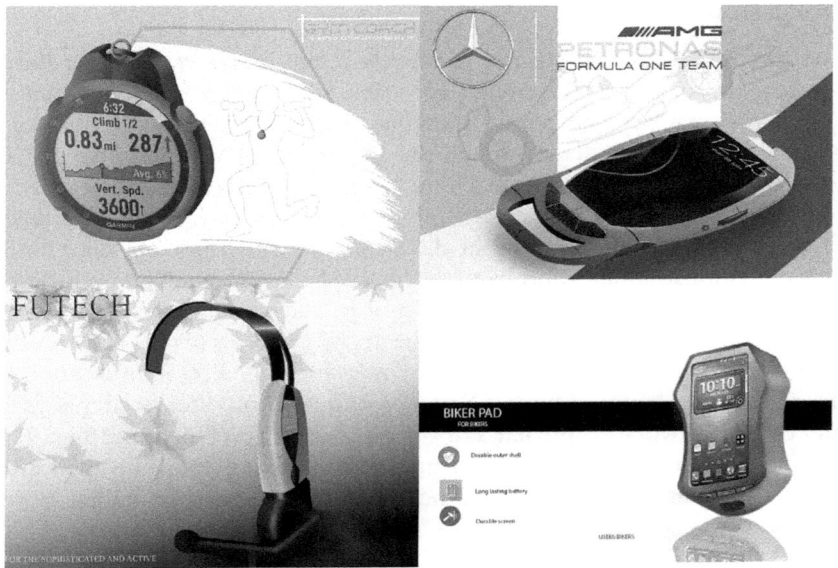

*Figure 15.5* From top left to bottom left (a) semi-polished but highly detailed, (b) unpolished but communicating, (c) flawed sketch corrected digitally, and (d) highly polished and detailed sketch.

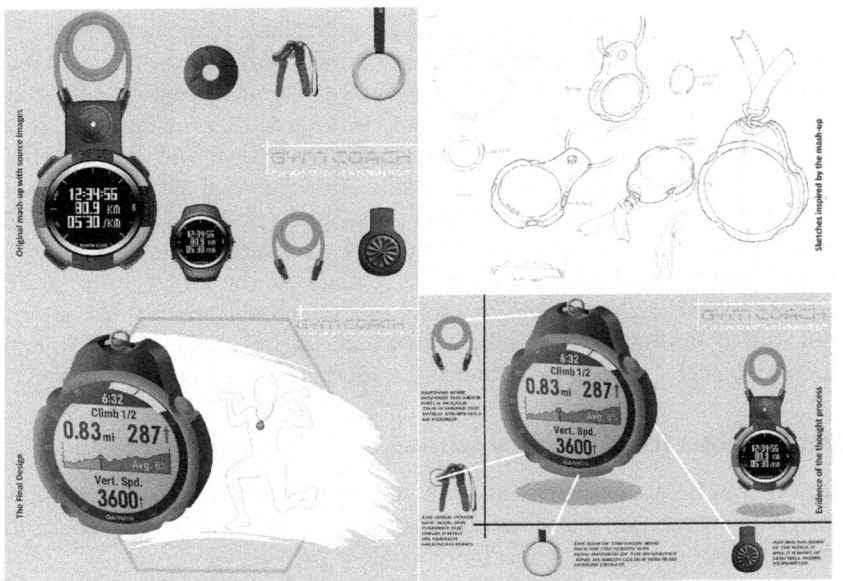

*Figure 15.6* Thought processes for student A.

## Discussion

The aim of this research was not to provide a step-by-step manual for learning how to sketch but the overall approach to sketching pedagogy and its impact on creativity and critical thinking in design students. The use of a practice-based course demonstrated the attainment of critical thinking skills that can contribute to hybrid sketching techniques when applied to a creative course. The analytical and creative aspects of critical thinking have been demonstrated through arriving at different solutions from the same brief, further demonstrating the problem-solving aspect of design. Communication has been key in the visualisation of the process and its outcomes. The visualisation allows analysis and feedback on the iterative process of problem-solving. A good balance between manual sketching and digital communication of sketches should be maintained. Digital communication offers students a second chance to work on the flaws of their manually developed sketches. This can be the case when digital sketching and rendering tools are used after manual sketching so that they do not hinder their creativity earlier in the process as was the case in this study.

This chapter has demonstrated the importance and impact of manual design sketching during the early design stages and its intuitiveness to the flexibility of generating novel ideas (Visser, 2006). It can be verified that the artistic start of mash-up to the sketching process also contributes to the required cognitive confidence to embark on the sketching process. Art-based activities have also been proven to be working especially for female students, as good warm-up exercises (Hu et al., 2015). Better visualisation and communication of form could also be a result of the sequencing of sketching-related courses in the revised programme, building towards the perfection of both manual and digital manipulation of sketches. Considering the cognitive bearing of manual sketching on the creative process, it could be argued that the designer of the future will still need manual sketching skills to inform and improve their design cognition and critical thinking skills. Although digital manipulation of sketches is also a key design communication aspect, this should be carefully brought into the teaching and learning space to ensure that it does not stifle creativity and critical thinking at the early stages of the design process. The digitisation of sketching could be useful as a refinement tool for already created and communicated sketches. However, digital processes of forming inspiration such as mash-up aesthetics are useful early in the design process.

## Implications for secondary schools

Lessons can be drawn from this study for secondary schools as these supply universities with entry-level students in design and technology education and industrial design programmes.

- Design and technology curriculum should integrate sketching topics with related topics in art to demonstrate the benefits that design and technology can reap from art.

- Teaching sketching at high schools should start with art-related drawing skills. These are less technical and could build confidence in students who are less confident in visual communication.
- Teachers with a background in art should be utilised to introduce sketching classes to build confidence and the right attitude in students as they attain or complete artistic sketches.
- Peer review of sketches should begin with the art-based sketches to stimulate open-mindedness as students give each other feedback on less technically demanding sketching.
- Digital sketches are more stimulating, especially with the use of colour and other detailed effects. Building the capacity to produce a digital sketch at high school should be encouraged to excite the students and draw them to create a positive attitude towards design and technology.

## Conclusion

We conclude the debate with a note that a hybrid model should be adopted when teaching and learning design sketching in the future. This is useful in preparing students for future careers in design and technology, product design, industrial design, and other design-related disciplines. Although we acknowledge that a learner of the 21st century should be well conversant with digital platforms of working, the cognitive advantage of manual sketching cannot be ignored. Designers also need art-based exercises as a way of warming up to the technically inclined and psychologically demanding design sketching engagements. Design schools should consider having an art professional in their establishments to support confidence-building activities in novice design students. These artistic activities could be helpful in both manual and digital platforms before challenging design tasks.

In teaching sketching, design educators should strive to improve the following: theory, practice, and attitudes as these factors are important in improving students' critical thinking skills. Students need to be taught background information of sketching as this will act as a good foundation for the course. Integrating this theory with practical activities will demonstrate the value of theory in guiding practice. However, students need to persistently practise or be given exercises to develop their sketching skills. Practice leads to perfection. Moreover, design educators also need to develop the right motivation and positive attitudes in students. In most cases, this can be achieved if the design educators use the problem-based learning approach to teaching. Problem-based learning demands that the design educator gives students complex real-world, open-ended problems to promote student-centred learning of sketching concepts and principles as opposed to direct presentation of facts and concepts. The problem to be solved is what drives motivation and development of a positive attitude and learning critical thinking skills.

## Questions

1 Looking at the trends in the design sketching landscape, how do you see this evolution in the Fourth Industrial Revolution?
2 What do you envision as an important change for the design and technology sketching curricula globally?
3 As digitisation and the internet of things continue to colonise the world, what pedagogies can be developed and best be used for sketching?
4 Does hybrid sketching add any value to learners' creative potential?
5 What will be the creative skills required of the next generation of design and technology teachers for them to cope with future sketching demands?

## Acknowledgements

The authors would like to thank all students whose work has been used in this study.

## References

Berg, A. (2018). Participation in hybrid sketching. *FormAkademisk - Research Journal of Design and Design Education*, 11(3). doi:10.7577/formakademisk.2676.
Booth, J. W., Taborda, E. A., Ramani, K., & Reid, T. (2016). Interventions for teaching sketching skills and reducing inhibition for novice engineering designers. *Design Studies*, 43, 1–23.
Brookes, M. (1996). *Drawing with children: A creative method for adult beginners, too.* New York, NY: Putnam.
Changwong, K., Sukkamart, A. & Sisan, B. (2018). Critical thinking skill development: Analysis of a new learning management model for Thai high schools. *Journal of International Studies*, 11(2), 37–48. doi:10.14254/2071-8330.2018/11-2/3.
Cook, M. T. & Agah, A. (2009). A survey of sketch-based 3-D modelling techniques. *Interacting with Computers*, 21(3), 201–211.
Evans, M., & Aldoy, N. (2016). Digital design sketching using the tablet PC. *Design Journal*, 19(5), 763–787. doi:10.1080/14606925.2016.1196091.
Goldschmidt, G. (1999). The backtalk of self-generated sketches. In Gero, J.S. & Tversky, B. (Eds.), *Visual and spatial reasoning in design. key center of design computing and cognition.* Sydney: University of Sydney, 163–184.
Goldschmidt, G. (2014). Modeling the role of sketching in design idea generation. In Chakrabarti, A., & Blessing, L. (eds), *An anthology of theories and models of design.* London: Springer. doi:10.1007/978-1-4471-6338-1_21.
Hitchcock, D. (2020). *Critical thinking, The Stanford Encyclopedia of Philosophy* (Fall 2020 Edition), Edward N. Zalta (ed.), Retrieved from https://plato.stanford.edu/archives/fall2020/entries/critical-thinking/
Hu, W. L., Booth, J., & Reid, T. (2015, August). Reducing sketch inhibition during concept generation: psychophysiological evidence of the effect of interventions. In *ASME 2015 International Design Engineering Technical Conferences and Computers and Information in Engineering Conference* (pp. V007T06A010-V007T06A010). American Society of Mechanical Engineers.

Lahti, H., Seitamaa-Hakkarainen, P., & Hakkarainen, K. (2004). Collaboration patterns in computer-supported collaborative designing. *Design Studies*, 25(4), 351–371.

Lai, E. R. (2011). *Critical thinking: A literature review*. Retrieved from https://images.pearsonassessments.com/images/tmrs/CriticalThinkingReviewFINAL.pdf

Lenin, I. (2019). Critical thinking and it's importance in education. In *Proceeding of the Cognitive, Psychological and Behavioural Perspectives in Education Conference*. Alagappa University, Karaikudi, India.

Murawski, L. M. (2014). Critical thinking in the classroom … and beyond. *Journal of Learning in Higher Education*, 10(1), 25–30.

National Association of Colleges and Employers [NACE]. (2018). *The key attributes employers seek on students' resumes*. Retrieved from https://www.naceweb.org/about-us/press/2017/the-key-attributes-employers-seek-on-students-resumes/

Nilson, L. B. (2010). *Teaching at its best: A research-based resource for college instructors* (2nd ed.). San Francisco, CA: Jossey-Bass.

Oxman, R. (2008). Digital architecture as a challenge for design pedagogy: Theory, knowledge, models and medium. *Design Studies*, 29(2), 99–120.

Ruggiero, V. R. (2012). *The art of thinking: A guide to critical and creative thought* (10th ed.). New York, NY: Longman.

Shuell, T. J. (2010). Phases of meaningful learning. *Review of Educational Research*, 60(4), 531–547.

Stempfle, J., & Badke-Schaub, P. (2002). Thinking in design teams-an analysis of team communication. *Design studies*, 23(5), 473–496.

Visser, W. (2006). *The cognitive artifacts of designing*. London: Eds Lawrence Erlbaum.

World Economic Forum (2020), The future of jobs report 2020, World Economic Forum, Geneva, viewed 24 Aug 2022, https://www.weforum.org/reports/the-future-of-jobs-report-2020

Wrenn, J., & Wrenn, B. (2009). Enhancing learning by integrating theory and practice. *International Journal of Teaching and Learning in Higher Education*, 21(2), 258–265.

Yang, M. C. (2009). Observations on concept generation and sketching in engineering design. *Research in Engineering Design*, 20(1), 1–11.

Yost, B. L. (2015). Exploring hybrid drawing techniques presentation. *Foundations in Art: Theory and Education Journal*. doi: 10.13140/RG.2.1.2129.0328.

# 16 Exploring the potential of feedback within the creative processes of a design and technology classroom

*Alice Schut*

## Introduction

Design feedback has the potential to greatly benefit pupils' creative design processes and the output they produce. When implemented effectively, critical comments and questions can support pupils' creative thinking processes by encouraging both generative and reflective thinking capabilities. In short, the use of design feedback within a classroom generally starts with a presentation of the design by the pupil designers after which those listening – peers, teachers, clients, and/or other stakeholders – voice their opinions and concerns (i.e. their feedback). Design feedback overlaps with the notion of 'critiquing', which in recent years is gaining more and more in design and technology education (Williams & Stables, 2017). Keirl (2021, p. 156) describes critiquing as follows: 'critiquing is the practice of questioning, judging and debating the relative merits of any design and/or technological product, process or system'.

Both design feedback and critiquing entail the act of questioning, judging and debating the merit of something. Within the design and technology classroom, this 'something' that is critiqued is generally the pupils' own design creations. When done right, these critiquing moments can lead to a valuable and constructive exchange between the feedback giver and receiver. The goal of such an exchange is to help the designing pupil move their creative design process forward, leading to the development of their design into the 'best defensible compromise'.

Despite the apparent benefits that feedback practices can bring to the creative processes in design and technology classrooms, it is not easy to create these valuable and constructive feedback exchanges. As a result, pupils are often not able to make adequate use of the feedback opportunities that are there, which in turn can hamper them in the creative development of their design (Schut, van Mechelen, Klapwijk, Gielen, & de Vries, 2020). Difficulties have been observed with feedback givers as well as receivers. For feedback givers forming relevant feedback can be challenging, while for the receivers, handling and utilising feedback is easier said than done. Whilst we can assume that design feedback is necessary, we cannot assume that pupils know how to make the most of this feedback. The issue, therefore, is not if we should use

DOI: 10.4324/9781003166689-20

feedback in the design and technology classroom, but instead, it is about the how and the why of design feedback and the unintended consequences of poor design feedback practices.

In the next section, I describe the nature of design feedback and then present the challenges and issues related to pupils giving and receiving feedback. The chapter concludes with a description of a recent study where we implemented a design feedback activity in two schools. The aim here is to not only raise issues around design feedback but also provide inspiration for teachers wishing to implement, or improve, the use of design feedback within their pupils' design projects.

## The nature of feedback in creative design processes

The use of design feedback has a longstanding tradition within design disciplines at art academies and universities. The feedback moments within those contexts are generally known as design critiques (crits) or design reviews (Anthony, 1991). They are considered to be one of the backbones to design education and practice (Gray, 2013). It is argued that through these critiquing moments novice designers are socialised into the discipline, thereby preparing them for the 'real world'. It is also recognised as a crucial means by which they obtain expertise from their teachers and other stakeholders in order to improve their design skills and abilities. In the end, the main goal of such feedback exchanges in an educational as well as in a real-world setting is to help move the designer's creative processes forward to improve the design and hand.

Designing is undeniably a creative process, as it confronts pupils with so-called wicked problems for which no single 'right' answer or way of solving exists (Dorst, 2003). Therefore, they need to utilise their creative thinking abilities to explore the problem and generate and develop solutions (Lewis, 2009). It is commonly accepted that creative thinking can be divided into divergent thoughts (DTs) and convergent thoughts (CTs; Goldschmidt, 2014). DT is generative in nature and entails the creation of new thoughts and ideas. A CT is evaluative in nature and entails reflection and evaluation of thoughts and ideas. According to the dual-process theories of creative cognition a continuous shifting between both modes of thinking is needed when working towards a creative solution (Finke, Ward, & Smith, 1992).

Engaging in creative thinking is not an easy task, especially not for pupils who are new to the discipline. Difficulties can be caused by not only external factors, such as the learning environment, teacher beliefs and examination requirements, but also internal factors such as pupils' personality, mindset and cognitive abilities. A rather well-known obstacle for creative thinking is the occurrence of design fixation, which can be described as sort of a mental block. In particular, concept fixation – a type of design fixation which leaves designers stuck in a certain train of thought, adhering to the current possibly unfavourable state of their design – has been observed to impede pupils' convergent and divergent thinking processes, thereby hindering continuous iterations in order to end up with the best defendable compromise (Schut, Klapwijk, Gielen, van Doorn, & de Vries, 2019b). Design feedback can help stimulate and direct these creative thinking processes and mitigate obstacles like fixation, thereby supporting pupils' creative design processes.

As discussed, design feedback is generally focused on the improvement and development of the design at hand. The set-up of these feedback moments is rather universal. It generally starts with some form of presentation by the student on their process and the status of their design to update their teachers, peers and other stakeholders (such as clients and/or potential users). Afterwards, this audience voices their opinions and concerns, often through a verbal dialogue, which allows the student to collect feedback (Oh, Ishizaki, Gross, & Yi-Luen Do, 2013). Ideally, this design feedback supports novice designers (pupils) with the critical reflection and evaluation of their design to help identify various shortcomings and sub-problems within the designs and, in turn, support the generation of new additions and alterations.

Unfortunately, this desired effect is not always accomplished. There are several studies at different educational levels that present how design feedback is not always shared in a constructive manner within the creative process (e.g. Cardoso, Eris, Badke-Schaub, & Aurisicchio, 2014; Yilmaz & Daly, 2016). Additionally, pupils have also been observed to show resistance to the feedback they received, thereby rejecting or ignoring it. On occasion, even a state of defensiveness was observed as they tried to protect the current state of their design (Schut, Klapwijk, Gielen, & De Vries, 2019a; Schut, Klapwijk, Gielen, van Doorn, et al., 2019b). These studies are within the context of the current educational norm, which is that of unguided design feedback practices, meaning that, commonly, the feedback giver and the receiver have been given little help in navigating the delicate and complex process of design feedback. Additionally, the learning environment they are in does not always cater to the actual utilisation of this feedback by the pupils. There are several challenges that can be outlined with giving design feedback as well as receiving feedback, which are outlined in the two following sections.

## Challenges with giving feedback

As described, design feedback can help push pupils towards divergent or convergent directions in their creative process. To have this effect, the feedback shared needs to be valuable and constructive, meaning that it should be appropriate to the task at hand and formulated in a way that encourages openness from the receiver. Yet this is easier said than done. Obstacles in formulating design feedback have been observed on several educational levels. Issues that result from poor feedback formulation are, for example, interpretative challenges and the non-stimulation of generative and evaluative thinking. Interpretive challenges on the design at hand and/or the feedback are problematic, as they can lead to a lack of shared understanding between the giver and receiver (Sadler, 2010). This lack of understanding can have consequences on the value of the design feedback. On one hand, misconceptions about the design at hand can lead to the construction of non-valuable feedback. After all, if the feedback giver does not fully understand the design, there the feedback will likely not be relevant to the receiver. This mismatch can heighten the resistance from the receiver towards the questions and comments that are shared. On the other hand, a misinterpretation of the feedback by the receiver, or the inability to decode it, can lead to a rejection of feedback that could have otherwise been valuable.

As described in the previous section, design feedback can encourage and stimulate pupils' generative and evaluative thinking, thereby pushing them towards divergent or convergent directions within their creative design processes. The design feedback itself can also be classified as divergent or convergent. This means that the questions and comments the feedback consists of can be generative or evaluative in nature. Examples of divergent questions are, *'What if the design could be used outside?'* and *'How can we make the design even more appealing?'* Examples of convergent questions are, *'What material is this part supposed to be made of?'* and *'What if people would pull this handle instead of push it?'* Although it could then be assumed that divergent feedback will push pupils towards generation and convergent feedback will push towards evaluation, this has been found to not be the case (Schut, Klapwijk, Gielen, & De Vries, 2019a). Rather, as a feedback giver, it is important to be aware of the intended direction to push towards and consciously alternate divergent and convergent feedback until this goal is reached.

Both divergent and convergent feedback are considered essential and especially the combination of both types is found to be needed when intending to stimulate creative thinking processes (Schut, Klapwijk, Gielen, & De Vries, 2019a). However, studies show that feedback givers – teachers, clients or peers – naturally have a strong focus on feedback pushing in convergent directions (Cardoso et al., 2014), even though this often does not evoke the expected moments of critical reflection and evaluation. Instead, too much focus on convergence can lead novice designers to continuously try to prove the relevance of their design and even become defensive. This links back to the occurrence of concept fixation, which entails a designer's (unconscious) adherence to the current possibly unfavourable state of their design. Berger (2010, p. 58) labels a design that only the designer loves as 'a dinosaur baby', a 'quirky and idiosyncratic design creation that is destined to be loved by only its designer'. Additionally, this excessive focus on convergence creates a lack of divergent feedback and thereby the prospective orientation – for example the feedforward component. Divergence can be seen as the driving force behind exploratory thinking and risk-taking, which are essential in creative design (Yilmaz & Daly, 2016).

Being aware of this discrepancy between convergent and divergent feedback and striving to pose more feedback that elicits divergent thought processes are therefore essential. In stimulating DTs, openness can be brought back into the feedback exchange.

## Challenges with receiving feedback

In the previous section, I outlined the challenges of giving feedback and some suggestions for how this could be mitigated. Nonetheless, it is not solely the responsibility of those giving feedback to make the exchanges meaningful. After all, in the real world, a designer will be repeatedly confronted with people who have little experience in giving constructive and valuable feedback. It is part of a designer's skill set to handle all kinds of feedback and know how to use it to benefit themselves and the design they are working. For that reason, measures that help pupils process and make sense of feedback are equally important. Novice designers need to have the opportunity to learn how to construct as well as how to receive feedback from an early age and practise this within the safe environment of the classroom. In terms of learning how to receive and process feedback, this brings us to the notion of feedback uptake and feedback literacy.

As described, a crucial goal behind design feedback exchanges is the utilisation of this feedback by novice designers to evaluate, adjust and improve their design. In the context of non-design-oriented higher education, the utilisation of feedback by the learner is known as feedback uptake. This concept goes beyond passive informing by the feedback giver and emphasises the active role learners need to take in order to progress – for more details see Carless and Boud (2018). To become active receivers, pupils need to acquire certain competencies and dispositions, which is known as the notion of feedback literacy. Carless and Boud (2018) describe a set of four key capacities and dispositions feedback literate learners need to have: appreciating feedback, managing affect, making judgements and taking action. Building on their work, Schut et al. (2022) modified these concepts for the context of design education into a process-oriented model of design feedback uptake.

In short, design feedback uptake can be defined as novice designers taking an active role in utilising feedback to inform their future design moves, ultimately leading to the development and improvement of their design. The process of design feedback uptake can be described as a chain of events, in which there is an overlap with the capacities and dispositions attributed to feedback literate learners. In Figure 16.1, a process model of design feedback uptake is showcased.

When design feedback is given, pupils initially have to balance their emotions. This can be viewed as the ability to balance between staying open to the possibility of being misdirected in your creative process while also holding on to that which you believe still holds (creative) value in the face of criticism. This balance interacts with the ability to make evaluative judgements, which entails the sense-making of the feedback and deciding on the relevance and value it has for the creative design process. The result of a genuine and well-considered evaluative process is either the acceptance or the rejection of the feedback in question. If the feedback is taken on board, this decision is followed by the pupils taking action, for example starting a redesign activity through the stimulation of their divergent and convergent thinking processes. Finally, there is the element of 'appreciating feedback',

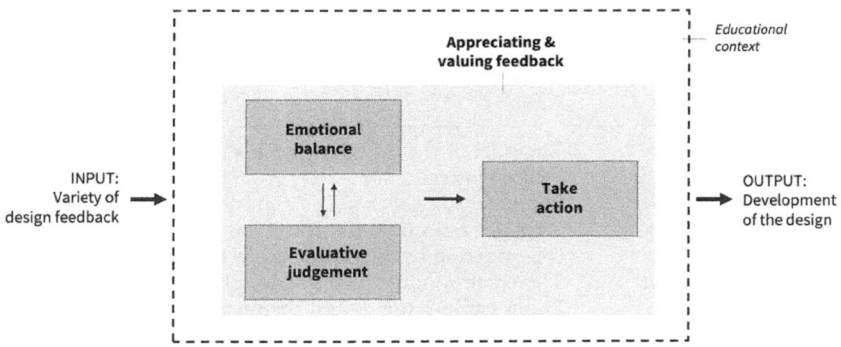

*Figure 16.1* Process model of design feedback uptake, the (active) role of the receiver (Schut et al., 2021).

which we propose has a more overarching position. While the other elements of the model can be viewed on a process level and are more directly influenced by the quality of feedback that is given, we argue that a pupil's appreciation of design feedback and their understanding of its value is, generally speaking, not directly affected by a singular piece of 'bad' feedback.

As shown through the previous discussion, pupils are not able to just take an active role within the design feedback processes. Creating this change in handling design feedback requires attention, the right conditions and a lot of practice. Primary school pupils need to receive guidance when engaging in design feedback processes.

## Implementing design feedback practices in the classroom

So how could design feedback, especially peer feedback, actually be implemented in the design classroom? In this section an example is given of the results of a peer feedback intervention that was developed as part of the research project Co-Design with Kids: Early Mastering of 21st Century Skills, which was implemented in two case studies at two primary schools in The Netherlands. Two classes of pupils (9–12 years old) from each school participated in a design project in which they solved a real-life design challenge presented to them by real clients during the span of six design sessions. Details of where the resources can be found online are at the end of this chapter. The peer feedback intervention entailed an elaborate procedure which was interwoven through several design sessions. Table 16.1 gives an overview of all design sessions and highlights key moments of the peer feedback intervention. It combined the principles described in the previous sections to create a learning environment that would encourage pupils to take an active role in the design feedback process, thereby enabling their feedback uptake. So how was this done? Next is a description of the main components of the intervention – for more detailed information and academic grounding see Schut et al. (2020, 2022).

*Table 16.1* Overview of the design sessions and key moments in the peer feedback intervention

| Design Session | Content |
|---|---|
| Session 0<br>Introduction & Sensitising | The start of the design project is announced with a short introduction.<br>Pupils receive sensitising assignments to do at home to trigger reflection about the design theme. |
| Session 1<br>Exploring the design theme | Introduction to the design cycle and key design skills.<br>The client(s) introduce the design theme.<br>Pupils explore the design theme through stories. |
| Session 2<br>Defining a point of view | Introduction to problem defining.<br>Pupils define a design scope with design question and design criteria. |
| Session 3<br>Ideation, selection & detailing | Pupils ideate guided by brainstorming tools.<br>Pupils select ideas guided by selection tools.<br>Pupils detail selected idea with an elaboration tool. |
| Session 4<br>Feedback design ideas<br>Design critiques | Pupils present their design idea and receive oral and written feedback from the client(s) and their peers.<br>Pupils participate in peer feedback exchanges. |
| Session 5<br>Concept development & elaboration | Pupils are prompted to discuss, evaluate and utilise the written feedback from the client(s) and their peers to improve and develop their design idea.<br>Pupils build models or prototypes to represent and develop the design idea. |
| Session 6<br>Feedback prototypes<br>Design critiques | Pupils present their prototype and receive oral feedback from the client(s) and their peers.<br>Pupils participate in peer feedback exchanges. |

## *Key guiding principles for design feedback*

Our project was based on three key design principles that could help teachers in creating a setting within their design and technology classroom that encourages pupils to actively take part in the process of design feedback uptake, including providing support for both those who give *and* receive the feedback.

*Principle 1: design a learning environment which caters to and asks for active design feedback utilisation*

By creating a learning environment that allows for and caters to feedback utilisation, you can enable pupils to respond more positively to their design feedback. After all, feedback does not occur in a vacuum, and it likely does not initiate further action on its own. This can for example be done by making active feedback utilisation an intrinsic part of a learning assignment. By planning multiple feedback moments in regular intervals, conditions can be created in which feedback utilisation becomes expected. For pupils, this increases the need to take action and make their changes visible through the adjusted and improved design.

*Principle 2: implement high-quality peer feedback practices*

Second, the implementation of high-quality peer feedback is a promising way to improve feedback uptake. By learning how to give appropriate feedback, pupils increase their abilities in receiving feedback. When giving feedback to their peers, pupils will have to apply existing or self-created design criteria, diagnose problems in the designs and suggest creative solutions. It helps pupils' evaluative judgement by developing a sense of quality through comparisons with the work of others and reflecting on their own work. Furthermore, by learning how to construct appropriate feedback, that is valuable and constructive feedback, it will be of higher quality and thus easier to handle when received, thereby improving pupils' emotional balance.

*Principle 3: provide explicit guidance while enabling autonomy*

Finally, the use of explicit guidance is there to ensure that pupils are supported during all steps of the feedback process. Its use will lead the feedback receivers through the process of feedback uptake, from initially receiving feedback, making sense of the content and deciding with which to continue, to actively using to spark their creative thinking and improve the design. Types of guidance are, for example, the implementation of meta-dialogues on the value of design feedback to spark understanding and appreciation, the use of written feedback to help capture the key information and create a delay in receiving to support openness, and the use of verbal prompts to signal each step of the feedback process and make it explicit while ensuring calmness. Creating distinct decision moments signals the importance of feedback utilisation. Additionally, making clear that not all feedback has to be used and that feedback can be rejected creates choice and autonomy. Maintaining some form of autonomy while keeping the guidance explicit supports pupils' motivation.

*Applying these principles to our project*

First, the design of the learning environment was created in such a way that giving, receiving, and utilising design feedback had a central position throughout the design project. This structure intentionally created a learning environment that catered to, and actively asked for, pupils to use the feedback they had received. Second, an important component of the intervention was the implementation of high-quality peer feedback in design sessions 4 (intermediate design critiques) and 6 (final design critiques). Table 16.2 gives an overview of the peer feedback component of the intervention and the guidance that was given.

Figure 16.2 shows the template of the feedback form that was used as a scaffolding tool for written feedback. This template contained the guiding sentences that were used when teaching the pupils how to construct design feedback for their peers.

*Table 16.2* Overview of the peer feedback component of the design feedback intervention

| | |
|---|---|
| Preparation | Meta-dialogue, analysing examples and modelling exercises to teach the intention and the procedure to pupils. This was done mainly at the start of the intermediate design critiques in session 4, but pupils were also reminded at the start of the final design critiques. |

The next steps are followed with each presentation during the design critiques.

| | |
|---|---|
| Step 1 Guiding towards a shared understanding | Pupil(s) present their design idea.<br>Peers and clients receive verbal prompts to pose clarification questions to work towards a shared understanding of the design.<br>*'What do you not yet understand about the design?'* |

In the next steps, the peers and clients receive scaffolding guidance by feedback forms (during intermediate design critiques) to construct written feedback OR verbal prompts (during final design critiques) to construct oral feedback.

| | |
|---|---|
| Step 2 Emphasise positive aspects | Peers and clients are guided to construct specific compliments.<br>*'What do you think is already good about the design?'* |
| Step 3 Stimulating critical reflection and evaluation | Peers and clients are guided to construct convergent feedback.<br>*'We think this could be better about the design . . . because . . .'* |
| Step 4 Providing a way forward | Peers and clients are guided to construct a divergent how-question.<br>*'How can you . . .'*<br>Peers and clients are guided to construct possible solutions to the uncovered shortcoming(s) (answering the how-question).<br>*'We think this could maybe be a solution . . .'* |

Third, the pupils received explicit guidance in design session 5 to help them with the process of receiving, discussing, selecting, and utilising the feedback forms they considered valuable for their creative design process.

## *Highlights from the project*

Our analysis of the two case studies demonstrated that different types of guidance can support pupils to engage in constructive and valuable peer feedback exchanges and encourage their feedback uptake. We found that generally, all pupils were able to use at least some of the received feedback to spark their creative thinking and consequently develop and improve their designs. Several successes were uncovered during the analysis, of which we will highlight a few next.

### *Stimulating cognitive modelling*

First, the peer feedback intervention stimulates pupils' cognitive modelling. When giving feedback to their peers, the pupils repeatedly showcased their cognitive modelling abilities by posing certain convergent feedback questions and comments. Through these types of questions and comments,

*Exploring the potential of feedback* 247

**FEEDBACK REPORT**

Idea title:
-----------------------------

Feedback is for team:                    Feedback is from team:
-----------------------------            ----------------------

We think this is good about the idea!

We think this could be better.

Because ...

Our how-question.

How can you

We think this might be a solution!
(Write/draw the solution on the back of the paper!)

Worksheet forward with feedback    www.tudelft.nl/codesignkids

*Figure 16.2* Template of the feedback form.

the pupils imagined how the design of their peers would be used throughout time and constructed mental models of the design mechanisms and user interactions. A question could for example ask information about a future possible state of use. Cognitive modelling is seen as a key component of designerly thinking, and the peer feedback intervention supports pupils in expressing and practising this.

### Developing evaluative abilities

Second, the peer feedback intervention contributed to the pupil's evaluative abilities, specifically the use of self-made evaluation criteria and the development of a sense of quality. As stated previously, the intervention did not give any specific guidance on how to evaluate and select the received feedback. Several of the pupils' self-made evaluation criteria can be linked back to the structure of the feedback forms. They, for example, do not include the importance of convergent feedback for uncovering shortcomings in their design and divergent feedback to help them move forward. Additional criteria in evaluating the feedback were completeness, clarity, objectivity and a balance between compliments and critical feedback. Altogether, these evaluation criteria, from an extensive list, show how pupils are able to create a good understanding of what compromises quality.

### Taking an active role

Third, the peer feedback intervention encouraged the pupils to take an active role in the feedback process, specifically through the explicit guidance by verbal prompts. Several studies have highlighted the passive and consumerist role pupils often take during unguided feedback processes. The rather strict level of guidance of the peer feedback intervention made it more difficult for pupils to become passive. Nonetheless, active involvement from the pupils was still required for success. Therefore, it could be said that by merely following the guided procedure, a first step in active participation is reached. A next step would be that pupils engage in the following steps of the process of feedback uptake without the need for specific guiding prompts. Here, it is important to note that the agency pupils need in taking such an active role might be more than they possess and should therefore be seen as a shared responsibility with the educators.

### Points of concern

Although the peer feedback intervention initiated many successes, there are some things teachers need to be aware of when implementing something similar in their design and technology classroom. First, it is important to note that for the pupils receiving feedback it appears to matter who actually gives it. During the two case studies, pupils showed more openness towards feedback from the clients than from their peers. This is for example because pupils can see their peers as less knowledgeable and put less value on their feedback because of that. Additionally, the peers generally construct feedback of lesser quality than the clients due to them still learning how to do so (see also next point). Second, the quality of the feedback influences pupils' emotional balance and thereby their openness to the feedback. High-quality feedback, meaning constructive and valuable feedback, creates less resistance than lower-quality feedback and is easier to handle for the pupils. Therefore, it can be useful to put certain quality checks in place when implementing peer feedback practices.

Although there are points of concern, this does not mean that peer feedback practices should not be implemented in the design and technology classrooms. Results from the research project demonstrated that pupils actually appear to get better at receiving feedback when learning how to construct it, as they develop an understanding of feedback quality through the peer feedback process. Evidence of this was an extensive list of self-constructed evaluation criteria. An example of a prominent evaluation criterion used by the pupils was that feedback should uncover relevant and well-explained shortcomings in their design while also providing a 'way forward' through well-constructed how-questions and proposals. We presume that learning how to give divergent feedback enhanced pupils' understanding of how this feedback is meant to help a designer within their creative process, thereby picking up on the underlying intention of 'moving forward'. This is not necessarily a surprising outcome, but a treasured one, as it points towards the value peer feedback can have for the development of young novice designers' evaluative judgement.

## Conclusion

To conclude, guiding design feedback processes in the design and technology classroom can bring many benefits to pupils and support them in showcasing openness, developing a feel for quality, spark their creative thinking to develop their design into the 'best defensible compromise', taking an active role in the feedback processes and many more. Short term, this helps enable pupils' design feedback uptake, and long term, it initiates the development of their design feedback literacy. The interplay of the key guidelines within the peer feedback intervention supports the pupils in achieving this and are solid first steps towards valuable and constructive design feedback processes. Future endeavours to refine and expand these principles can provide valuable improvements to feedback processes in design education and are therefore encouraged.

## Questions

1 What role do you think design feedback (or critiquing) should have within the design and technology classroom?
2 What type of design feedback is dominant within your classroom, and what effect do you think this has on pupils' learning and progression?
3 How do you view the value of peer feedback within design and technology?
4 What other interventions could be done within the classroom to stimulate pupils' creativity while designing?

## Co-design with kids: Early mastering of 21st-century skills

The tools used in the design sessions can be found on the following websites:

- www.tudelft.nl/codesignkids (English version)
- www.tudelft.nl/yourturn (Dutch version)
- Template of the feedback form (shown in Figure 16.1) is available to download from www.tudelft.nl/codesignkids tool 'Forward with feedback'

## References

Anthony, K. H. (1991). *Design Juries on Trial: The Renaissance of the Design Studio*. New York: Van Nostrand Reinhold.

Berger, Warren. (2010). CAD Monkeys, Dinosaur Babies, and T-Shaped People: Inside the World of Design Thinking and How It Can Spark Creativity and Innovation. New York: Penguin.

Cardoso, C., Eris, O., Badke-Schaub, P., & Aurisicchio, M. (2014). Question asking in design reviews: How does inquiry facilitate the learning interaction? In *Design Thinking Research Symposium*.

Carless, D., & Boud, D. (2018). The development of student feedback literacy: Enabling uptake of feedback. *Assessment and Evaluation in Higher Education*, 43(8), 1315–1325.

Dorst, K. (2003). *Understanding Design*. Amsterdam: BIS Publishers.

Finke, R. A., Ward, T. B., & Smith, S. M. (1992). *Creative Cognition: Theory, Research and Application*. Cambridge: MIT Press.

Goldschmidt, G. (2014). *Linkography: Unfolding the Design Process*. Cambridge: MIT Press.

Gray, C. M. (2013). Factors that shape design thinking. *Design and Technology Education: An International Journal*, 18(3), 8–20.

Keirl, S. (2021). The role of critiquing in design and technology. In A. Hardy (Ed.), *Learning to Teach Design and Technology in the Secondary School* (4 ed.). Abingdon, UK: Routledge.

Lewis, T. (2009). Creativity in technology education: Providing children with glimpses of their inventive potential. *International Journal of Technology and Design Education*, 19(3), 255–268.

Oh, Y., Ishizaki, S., Gross, M. D., & Yi-Luen Do, E. (2013). A theoretical framework of design critiquing in architecture studios. *Design Studies*, 34(3), 302–325.

Sadler, D. R. (2010). Beyond feedback: Developing student capability in complex appraisal. *Assessment and Evaluation in Higher Education*, 35(5), 535–550.

Schut, A. (2022) "But, it's just a really good idea!" Investigating the guidance of design feedback processes to mitigate pupils' fixation and stimulate their creative thinking (Unpublished thesis). Delft University of Technology, Delft, The Netherlands.

Schut, A., Klapwijk, R., Gielen, M., & De Vries, M. J. (2019a). Children's responses to divergent and convergent design feedback. *Design and Technology Education: An International Journal*, 24(2), 67–89.

Schut, A., Klapwijk, R., Gielen, M., van Doorn, F., & de Vries, M. (2019b). Uncovering early indicators of fixation during the concept development stage of children's design processes. *International Journal of Technology and Design Education, 30,* 951–972.

Schut, A., van Mechelen, M., Klapwijk, R. M., Gielen, M., & de Vries, M. J. (2020). Towards constructive design feedback dialogues: Guiding peer and client feedback to stimulate children's creative thinking. *International Journal of Technology and Design Education, 32,* 99–127. doi: 10.1007/s10798-020-09612-y

Williams, P. J., & Stables, K. (Eds.). (2017). *Critique in Design and Technology Education* (1st ed.). Singapore: Springer Singapore.

Yilmaz, S., & Daly, S. R. (2016). Feedback in concept development: Comparing design disciplines. *Design Studies, 45,* 137–158. doi:10.1016/j.destud.2015.12.008

# Endpiece

*Alison Hardy*

The chapters in this book have debated a range of issues relevant to the teaching and learning of design and technology (D&T), from its introduction into the school curriculum and its growth around the globe to contemporary issues about its content and its contribution to pupils' education. It is hoped that some of these debates will have resonated with you and will encourage you on to further reading and research.

As Daniel Wakefield and I noted in Chapter 1, D&T as a school subject has had a mildly turbulent history, which other chapters show still impacts today. As changes in the economy affect societies around the world and social changes and technological developments impact education, there is a need for the D&T community to continually monitor what is being taught, and how, to ensure that it provides pupils with a relevant and worthwhile education. When it was first conceived, D&T was intended to be a radical innovation on the school curriculum with a purpose 'to prepare pupils to meet the needs of the twenty-first century; to stimulate originality, enterprise, practical capability in designing and making and the adaptability needed to cope with a rapidly changing society' (DfES/WO, 1988). Where the subject is taught well it meets this brief. Teachers who are prepared to innovate and take risks can provide pupils with challenging and engaging activities that develop a wide range of knowledge and skills, as well as personal qualities. It is this teaching of D&T that needs to be championed and developed. As I have found in my research (Hardy, 2016), there is little agreement about the purpose of D&T, which affects a consensus on what 'good' D&T looks like.

A new, and old, debate to be had relates to the purpose of D&T – how do we define knowledge in D&T. This was one of the reasons why D&T was almost removed from the National Curriculum in England (as Spendlove discusses in Chapter 4 and I explore in Hardy, 2017). In 2021, Ofsted (2022) began publishing research reviews for each school subject that 'consider(s) what the evidence tells us [Ofsted] about a high-quality education in each subject'; at the time of writing, there is no research review for D&T. The evidence eventually presented by Ofsted about D&T will need to be debated by the community, and I expect, as with my research, that there will not necessarily be consensus. But this is what keeps D&T, in fact all school subjects, healthy and fit for purpose – the debate within the subject's community and with others from outside the subject.

The curriculum debates in England have focused on what a knowledge-rich curriculum looks like for each subject (e.g. Bath et al., 2020, Music; Uhlenwinkel et al., 2017, Geography). In D&T, design thinking, capability and creativity are recognised as core curriculum conceptions, and on the surface, these do not meet the criteria for a knowledge-rich curriculum, fitting more with a skills-based curriculum, than a knowledge one (Young & Muller, 2010). As with other subjects, this is something that requires further exploration rather than trying to fit D&T into a narrow definition of a knowledge-rich curriculum (Young, 2020).

Another debate which arose whilst we were compiling this book related to the global pandemic, that is teaching a practical, collaborative, and creative subject online. Although we are, hopefully, moving out of a pandemic and learning to live with COVID-19, some of the changes which were forced on teachers during national and local lockdowns will endure, which and why needs to be debated.

I am glad we have created a space for debating how we do race in D&T in this book, but the inclusion and exclusion of other groups in D&T have not been debated here, such as pupils and teachers with special educational needs and pupils excluded from mainstream schools, plus the intersectionality of these groups. Categorising individual pupils and adults into a single group, whether by race, sex, gender, location or need, belies the complexity of humanity. Individuals are the sum of their parts, separating us into categories ignores our multidimensions. Again, I hope these are debates that will happen, regardless of whether they have a chapter in this second edition.

These are complex debates for D&T teachers to continue to grapple with, and they take place within an ever-changing educational landscape.

Education serves several different purposes, for society and for the individual, and D&T can make a valuable contribution to this. However, to do so, it must have a clarity of purpose and a certainty; teachers must know and understand the subject to be able to explain and defend it to others. This knowledge and understanding come partly from books such as this; whether you agree with the authors of these chapters or not, it is hoped that they have expanded your understanding of some aspects of the subject. To demonstrate this, there needs to be more focused research so that we can evidence clearly what pupils learn in the D&T classroom, and if this book has spurred you on to conduct research into aspects of the subject, that is all to the good.

There is a need for research to provide evidence for the valuable learning that takes place in D&T. We need not only to undertake research into the teaching and learning of D&T but also to ensure that the results of such research are widely reported. What the D&T community needs to ensure is that in all schools, D&T is understood and taught well, and it is hoped that this book has contributed to making that happen.

## References

Bath, N., Daubney, A., Mackrill, D., & Spruce, G. (2020). The declining place of music education in schools in England. *Children & Society*, *34*(5), 443–457.

Department for Education and Science/Welsh Office (DfES/WO) (1988) *National Curriculum Design and Technology Working Group Interim Report*, London: HMSO.

Hardy, A. L. (2016). An assortment box of views: Different perceptions of D&T's purpose and structure. Paper presented at the *PATT2016 - Technology Education for 21st Century Skills Conference*, Utrecht.

Hardy, A. L. (2017). How did the expert panel conclude that D&T should be moved to a basic curriculum? In E. W. L. Norman, & K. Baynes (Eds.), *Design epistemology and curriculum planning*. Loughborough: Loughborough Design Press.

Ofsted. (2022). *Curriculum research reviews*. https://www.gov.uk/government/collections/curriculum-research-reviews

Uhlenwinkel, A., Béneker, T., Bladh, G., Tani, S., & Lambert, D. (2017). GeoCapabilities and curriculum leadership: Balancing the priorities of aim-based and knowledge-led curriculum thinking in schools. *International Research in Geographical and Environmental Education*, *26*(4), 327–341.

Young, M. (2020). From powerful knowledge to the powers of knowledge. In *The researched guide to the curriculum: An evidence-informed guide for teachers* (pp. 19–30). Woodbridge: John Catt.

Young, M., & Muller, J. (2010). Three educational scenarios for the future: Lessons from the sociology of knowledge. *European Journal of Education*, *45*(1), 11–27. doi:10.1111/j.1465-3435.2009.01413.x

# Index

Note: Page numbers in **Bold** indicate tables, page numbers in *Italics* indicate figures and page numbers followed by n indicate notes.

Adobe Photoshop 229, 232
Agah, A. 223
Aldoy, N. 224
Amonoo-Kuofi, E. F. 92
analytical thinking 226
Ankiewicz, P. 34, 123
anti-racist actions 56–57
Anti-Racist Art Education Checklists 57
Archer, B. 1
Aristotle 210
*Aspects of National Curriculum design & technology* 16
assessments 189–190
Aston, S. 183
Atkinson, Stephanie 20
attitudes 227
attrition 165
Australia: indigenous technology 199; technology education in 28–29, 80

Baker, Kenneth 12
Ball, S. J. 150
Bang, M. 197, 198
Barber, M. 173
Barlex, D. 84, 100, 182
Benson, C. 179
Berry, Mary 102
Biden, Joe 29
Bignall, T. 47
*Black Teacher* (Gilroy) 46
Blakemore, E. 49
Borriello, G. 178
Botswana, entrepreneurship in technology education 127–128
Boud, D. 242
Braithwaite, E. R 46
Bramble Cay melomys 65

bridging units 186–187
British Nutrition Foundation (BNF) 99–101
Bucciarelli, L. 213
Buchmann, M. 166
Bury, M. 47

CAD (computer-aided design) 216, 217
Callaghan, James 12
Caribbean Artist Movement (CAM) 46
Caribbean, entrepreneurship in technology education 128
Carless, D. 242
CDT (craft, design and technology) 13
Centre for Studies of Climate Change Denialism 136
CfE *see* Curriculum for Excellence (CfE)
checklist 57
children's attitude towards technology 137
China, technology education in 29–30
Choulerton, Diana 150
coercion 153, 158
cognition 5, 209; *see also* design cognition
cognitive modelling 246, 247
Conservative Education Reform Act (1988) 70
content knowledge (CK) 166; *see also* pedagogical content knowledge (PCK)
continuing professional development (CPD) 184–186
convergent feedback 241
convergent thinking 239
convergent thoughts (CTs) 239
Cook, M. T. 223

corrective practices 217
COVID-19 pandemic 26–27, 42, 101–103, 107, 149
CPD *see* continuing professional development (CPD)
creative thinking 226, 239–240
critical race theory (CRT) 46
critical thinking 221; assessments of 227; benefits to hybrid sketching 225; components that improve 226–227; elements of 226; skills 122
CTs *see* convergent thoughts (CTs)
Curriculum and Assessment Policy Statement (CAPS) 195, 196
curriculum change: case studies 153–160; in D&T 149–161; enabling responses 152–153; Gidden's theory 152; natural events 149–150; policy reforms 150; restrictive responses 153; teachers dealing with 151–160; voluntary reasons 150–151
Curriculum for Excellence (CfE) 39
Curriculum for Wales (2022) 40
curriculum reform 67–68

Dagan, O. 31, 32
Dakers, J. 179, 180, 189
DATA/D&TA *see* Design and Technology Association (DATA/D&TA)
Davies, S. 84, 151
Dearing Report 18
decolonising D&T curriculum 45–48
Department for Education and Employment (DfEE) 70
Department of Basic Education (DBE) 33
Department of Education and Science (DES) 12, 13, 70
design 114–115
design and/or technology 2.0 73–75
design and technology (D&T) 1–6, 252–253; across the world 26–42; changing context 26–27; curriculum change in 149–161; decolonisation and diversity 45–48; failure of 65–76; food education 3, 21, 98–107; four-fold pedagogical model 84–89; future of 91–92; global curricula 80; metaphor 65; purpose of 20–21; race in *see* race and racism; reframing subject knowledge 79–81; role of making in 3, 111–118; signature pedagogy 3, 89–91; speciality of 77–93; teachers of colour 50–55; technological justice for indigenous designs 194–205; in United Kingdom 2, 9–23
Design and Technology Association (DATA/D&TA) 71–72, 101, 189
design cognition 5, 209–210; *see also* extended design cognition approach; ecological psychology view of designing 212–215; information-processing view of designing 210–212
design feedback 5, 238; in creative thinking processes 239–240; and critiquing 238; giving 240–241; implementing 243–249; receiving 242–243; template of feedback form 247; uptake 242, 243
design fixation 88, 239
designing and making (DM) 84
Designing our Tomorrows project 152
design thinking 74
Dimbleby, H. 102
disciplinary knowledge 20
divergent feedback 241, 248, 249
divergent thinking 88, 239
divergent thoughts (DTs) 239
diverse D&T curriculum 47
diversity 45, 48, 52-53, 57
Dorment, P. 211
Dow, W. 179, 180, 189
Doyle, A. 153
D&T National Curriculum 22
DTs *see* divergent thoughts (DTs)
D&T Working Group 12–13, 17

Eboka, O. 124
ecological psychology view of designing 212–215
Education Act (1944) 10
Educational Reform Act (1988) 9, 13
efficacy, of teachers 167, 171–172
Ekeke, O. 51
enabling responses 152–153
England, technology education in 38, 80
English Baccalaureate (EBacc) 38, 68, 100
entrepreneurship 120–121
entrepreneurship education 121
entrepreneurship, in technology education 120–130; in Botswana 127–128; in Caribbean 128; changing context 123; education *about, for,* and *through*

entrepreneurship 125–127; in Estonia 128–129; in Jordan 129; knowledge and skills development 123–124; in Malawi 128; in Malta 129; preparing pupils with skills 122–125; self-employment 124–125; in Sweden 129
epistemic practices 217
epistemology 93n2
Estonia, entrepreneurship in technology education 128–129
ethnicity 49
ethnic minorities 49
Eurocentric curriculum 46, 47, 58
Evans, D. 178
Evans, M. 224
expansive-restrictive continuum 89
exploring technology and society (ETS) 85, 88–89
extended design cognition approach: biological coupling 216; blended practices 217; corrective practices 217; in D&T 215–217; epistemic practices 217; example of 217–218; representational systems 217

Faber, L. 197
Facial recognition technology 50
failure of D&T 65–76
FareShare 102
Faulkner, Wendy 144
feedback practices 5, 223; *see also* design feedback
Feenberg, Andrew 112
Field, A. 178
Fine, G. 99
Floyd, George, killing of 56
focused practical tasks (FPTs) 85, 86
food education: employment in food-related sectors 104–106; health and well-being 101–103; post-16, 106–107; within D&T curriculum 3, 21, 98–107
food product development 100
Food Teachers Centre 101
four-fold pedagogical model 84–89
Fox-Turnbull, W. 123
Fujita, S. 29, 36
Fullan, Michael 149–151
Fuller, A. 89
Future of Education and Skills project (2030) 92

Galton, M. 191
Gaotlhobogwe, M. 197

Gates, Bill 42
gender: concept of 135, 139; inclusiveness 144; individual 142; neutrality 135; stereotypes 139; structural 140–142; studies 140–142; symbolic 140
gender-conscious pedagogy 135, 144
gender contract theory 135, 143–144
gender gap: implications for design and technology 144–145; researching stereotypes 139; socially constructed 137–144; in STEM education 134–136, 138; in Sweden 138
General Certificate of Secondary Education (GCSE) 68, 83; Design and Realisation 112; Food Preparation and Nutrition 104–106; removal of food from 151; Subject Level Conditions and Requirements 105
Germany: secondary schools in 30; technology education in 30–31
Gibb, Nick 68
Gibson, J. J. 213
Giddens, Anthony 152
Gillborn, D. 46
Gillet, A. J. 216
Gilroy, Beryl 46
Given, N. 182
global D&T curricula 80
global inclusion 49–50
Gove, Michael 20, 22, 67
governance 70–73
Grafham, V. 105
grammar schools 10
Groot, W. 188
Gudmundsdottir, S. 166
Gu, J. 29
Gumbo, M. T. 196, 199

Haelermans, C. 188
Halfon, Robert 42
Hallström, J. 129, 137
Harding, Sandra 140, 142
Hardy, A. 20, 21, 47, 84, 112, 153
Healthy Schools initiative 100
Heek's model 5, 194, 200–204
higher education institution (HEIs) 70
Hirachand, Walchnd 197
Hirsch, E. D. 68
Hlabangane, N. 196
Holly, J. 51
Holmegaard, H. 139
Hong Kong, technology education in 80

## 258  Index

hybrid sketching 5, 222; *see also* critical thinking; implications for secondary schools 234–235; integrating 228–229; mashed-up aesthetics 229, *229*; model 230–233; teaching strategies 228, 234–235; working of 224–225

identity drift 167
incremental refinement 223
India, indigenous technology 197–199
indigenous people 196
indigenous technology 197; Australia 199; Heek's model for 200–201; India 197–199; South Africa 200; Zimbabwe 199
individual gender 142
Industrial Revolution 9
information communication technology (ICT) 200, 204
information-processing view of designing 210–212
information technology (IT) 37
intelligence 78, 140
artificial 50
international perspectives on technology education 2, 26, 80; Australia 28–29; China 29–30; England 38; Germany 30–31; Israel 31–32; Northern Ireland 38–39; Scotland 39–40; South Africa 32–34; Sweden 34–36; Taiwan 36–37; UK 37–40; US 41–42; Wales 40
investigate disassemble and evaluate activities (IDEA) 85, 86
Israel: ORT 32; technology education in 31–32
ISTEAM 32
Ivinson, G. 141

Jackson, D. 183
Jamie's School Dinners 100
Jindal-Snape, D. 191
Johnson, Boris 102
joint CPD 184–186
Jordan, entrepreneurship in technology education 129
Joseph-Salisbury, R. 47
Joynes, C. 92

Keirl, S. 238
Kimbell, R. 19, 179
Kirloskar, Laxmanrao 197
knowledge 19-20, 21, 45, 46-47, 76-78, 81-82, 114, 144, 226-227, 253; and skills 101, 105, 111, 115, 120-121, 123, 126, 151, 201, 251; and understanding 18-19, 40, 53, 105; apply 78, 89, 91, 126; body of 78, 81, 82, 83; content 165-166; develop 19, 39-40, 129; functional 30; local 52; measure 135; new 211; pedagogical content 81, 165; prior 88, 211, 214; procedural 85, 89; rich 67, 253; subject 38, 79-81, 165-168; tacit 180; technical 21, 22, 84, 145; validated 29
knowledge-centred model 150
Kodak photography company 49
Kutay, C. 199, 201
Kwaira, P. 199

Lahti, H. 214
Latimer, Lewis 51
Lawson, S. 98
Laxton, M. 211
Layton, David 113
learning environments 181–183, 190–191
Lee, L. S. 36
Leith, Prue 102
Leonardo, Z. 58
Let's Get Cooking Campaign 100
liaison 186–189
living technology (LT) 36–37
logic reasoning 134
Lury, Celia 112

mainly designing (MD) 84, 88
mainly making (MM) 85, 87–88
*Make the Future Work* 118
making, role of: and designing 114–115; and knowledge 114; and skills 113; and well being 115–116; as human activity 112; curriculum 116; in practice 116–118
Malawi, entrepreneurship in technology education 128
Malik, S. 49
Malta, entrepreneurship in technology education 129
Mapara, J. 199
Margolin, Victor 52
Marin, A. 197
Marr, L. 47
Marton, F. 173
mash-up aesthetics 229, *229*, 231, *232*
Matowanyika, J. Z. Z. 196
Mbanefo, M. C. 124
McFarland, J. 51

McKinsey, C. 68
McKinsey, M. M. 68
McLellan, D. 191
McNish, Althea 53
Menary, R. 216
Mlambo, H. 197
Model for Teaching Technology in Indigenous Contexts (MTTIC) 203–204
Model for Teaching Technology in Non-Indigenous Contexts (MTTNIC) 203–204
Morrison-Love, D. 93n4
Mourshed, M. 173
Mulberg, C. 15
Murphy, P. 141

National Curriculum 2, 9, 98; design and technology in 19–22; developments 16–18; developments beyond 2000 18–20; NCC and 13–17; purpose of D&T 20–21; review of 18, 19; timeline of events 11–12
National Curriculum Council (NCC) 13–17
National Society for Education in Art and Design (NSEAD) 56, 57
natural events 149–150
NCC *see* National Curriculum Council (NCC)
*The New Meaning of Educational Change* (Fullan) 149
new teachers, supply and development 68–69
New Zealand, technology education in 80
Nhemachena, A. 196
Nicholl, B. 152
non-examined assessments (NEA) 105
Northern Ireland, technology education in 38–39

Obshchestvo Remeslenava Truda (ORT) 32
Offices for Standards in Education (Ofsted) 18, 72–73, 151, 178, 252
Oliver, Jamie 102
ontology 93n3
open-mindedness 226, 227
Organisation for Economic Co-operation and Development (OECD) 92, 141
outcomes-based learning (OBL) 33

Owen-Jackson, G. 100, 103
Oxman, R. 222

Paechter, C. 77, 153, 158
Papaioannou, T. 195
para-indigenous designs 201, 203
Pavlova, M. 112
pedagogical content knowledge (PCK) 81, 165–167
pedagogical knowledge (PK) 166
*Pedagogical principles in technology education: An indigenous perspective* (Gumbo) 202
performance targets 35
per-indigenous designs 201, 203
PISA *see* Programme for International Student Assessment (PISA)
Pitt, J. 112
policy reforms 150
Porter, R. K. 58
practice 227
Preston, B. 210
primary schools: characteristics 181, 183; culture 180; curriculum 181, 182; learning environment 182
Prime, G. M. 196
Product Styling 228
professional attributes 92
Programme for International Student Assessment (PISA) 135
pro-indigenous designs 201
project-based learning 91, 92
Pyhältö, K. 172

Qualifications Curriculum Development Authority (QCDA) 70
quasi-autonomous non-governmental organisation 70–71
questioning 226

race and racism 3, 45–46, 57; anti-racist actions 56–57; critical race theory 46; definition of 49; examples 49–50; killing of Floyd 56; systemic racism 56; teachers of colour 50–55
Racist Soap Dispenser 49
Rashford, Marcus 102
Relevance of Science Education (ROSE) 136
representational systems 217
restrictive responses 153
Rockland, R. 173
role of making, in D&T 3, 111–118; curriculum 116; design 114–115; as human activity 112; knowledge 114;

# 260  Index

in practice 116–118; skills 113; well being 115–116
Rollock, N. 46
Rossignoli, S. 92
Royal Academy of Engineering (RAE) 51
Rutland, M. 15, 100, 103, 151

Säljö, R. 173
Sarivaara, E. 196
Scheffler, I. 194
Schönborn, K. 129
Schön, D. 213
School Food Plan 100
Schreiner, C. 136
Schut, A. 242
Scotland: Curriculum for Excellence 39; technology education in 39–40
Seabrook, R. 105
secondary schools: characteristics 181, 183; culture 182; curriculum 182–183; learning environment 183
Seemann, K. W. 196
self-employment 124–125
self-sabotaging behaviour 167
Shaw, A. 122
Sherrington, T. 47
Shulman, L. 81, 82, 89, 165–167
signature pedagogies 3; deep structure 82, 83; defined 81; in D&T 89–91; features 83; implicit structure 82; surface structure 82, 89
Sjøberg, S. 136
Sketchbook Pro 224
sketching 214; *see also* hybrid sketching; cognitive processes in 222; future of 221; manual 221; mental components 223; tools 221; warm-up activities 222
skills 113, 122–125
skills development 123
Smith, L. T. 52
socially constructed gender gap 137–144
South Africa: indigenous technology 200; technology education in 32–34, 80
Spens Report (1938) 10
Steeg, T. 182
STEM (science, technology, engineering, mathematics) 26, 30, 41; gender-STEM gap 134–136, 138
Sternberg, R. J. 78
sticky notes 217–218
structural gender 140–142

structural reform of schools 67
Sultan, U. 142
surface approach 170, 173
surfacing 224
Sustainable Development Goals (SDGs) 136
Suzukovich III, E. S. 197
Svärd, J. 129
Sweden: entrepreneurship in technology education 129; gender gap 138; technology education in 34–36, 80
symbolic gender 140

Taiwan, technology education in 36–37
Tangwena people 199
Tata, J. N. 197
teacher(s): anxiety 167, 169, 172, 174; attrition 165; being gender conscious 144; of colour 50–55; confidence 171–173; continuing professional development 184–186; curriculum/curriculum delivery 168–171; dealing with curriculum change 151–160; efficacy 167, 171–172; identity drift 167, 172; pedagogical content knowledge 165–167; self-sabotaging behaviour 167; subject knowledge perceptions 117, 165–175; supply and development 68–69; surface approaches 170, 173
teaching technology, in indigenous contexts 5, 201–204
technical schools: repositioning of 33; in UK 10
technical solutions 35
technological justice 5; *see also* indigenous technology; conceptualisation of 194–196; Heek's model 194, 200–204; for indigenous designs 194–205
technological syndrome 198
technology education 121; entrepreneurship in 120–130; knowledge and skills development 123–124
technology education, international perspectives on 2, 26, 80; Australia 28–29; China 29–30; England 38; Germany 30–31; Israel 31–32; Northern Ireland 38–39; Scotland 39–40; South Africa 32–34; Sweden 34–36; Taiwan 36–37; UK 37–40; US 41–42; Wales 40
*Technosystem* (Feenberg) 112

theory 226–227
three-dimensional (3D) printing technology 114, 115
*To Sir with Love* 46
Training and Development Agency (TDA) 70
transition between primary and secondary school 178–191; bridging units 186–187; collaboration 187; context of 178–179; effective and meaningful liaison 186–189; English school stratification 179; joint CPD 184–186; planning and assessment 189–190; primary and secondary characteristics 180–183; strategies for smooth transition 184–190
Trebell, D. 84
Tripathi, D. 198
Truss, Liz 22
Tunstall, E. 52
21st-century skills 78, 123

Ubuntu 200, 202
Unaipon, David 199
United Kingdom; *see also* National Curriculum; D&T in 2, 9–23; Educational Reform Act 9, 13; hospitality sector 104; Industrial Revolution in 9; Spens Report (1938) 10; technology education in 37–40; tripartite system of education 10
United States: decentralised educational system 41; STEM 41; technology education in 41–42
Unwin, L. 89

van Rens, M. 186, 188
Vincent J. 102

Wales: Curriculum for Wales (2022) 40; technology education in 40
Wang, J. 29
Watson, J. 197
well-being: food education, health and 101–103; role of making 115–116
White, J. 1
wicked problems 86, 93n6
Williams, R. 1
Willmot, Eric 199
Wilshaw, Michael 72
Winn, D. 189

Yang, M. C. 231
Yost, B. L. 224

Zimbabwe, indigenous technology 199

Ingram Content Group UK Ltd.
Milton Keynes UK
UKHW022317140723
425179UK00010B/58